In
Search of
Honour

THE WAR DIARY OF

DR REGINALD HANNAY FOTHERGILL

Thanks Steve.

Best wishes

WITH INTRODUCTION AND NOTES

BY DAVID DUNN

Dave

Published by Honeybee Books
www.honeybeebooks.co.uk

Printed in the UK using paper from sustainable sources

ISBN: 978-1-913675-42-4

Sources of research

Every effort has been made to name the sources of the research that appears in the diary, where this has not been possible, I do apologise.
I have contextualised where possible from The 7th battalion East Surrey Regiment official war diaries, the 134th Field Ambulance official war diary, Commonwealth War Graves Commission and other sources.

Passages from 7th Battalion East Surrey Regiments war diaries can be found at The Queen's Royal Surrey Regiment website:
www.queensroyalsurreys.org.uk

Dave Dunn

MANY THANKS

To Nick Churchill,
for all his input and efforts to help me publish the diary.

To my daughter, Nikki Hart,

for all her input and encouragement.

And to my lovely wife Jane, for putting up with me,
and for taking the time to read it xx.

FOREWORD

Detailed first hand accounts such as Reginald Fothergills from the first world war present a rare opportunity to read the personal thoughts and feelings of those who were closest to the horrors of that appalling conflict.

As a battalion medical officer Reginald repeatedly saw the immediate impact of the war at its most visceral, and is therefore a more powerful account for that reason.

I found '*In Search Of Honour*' a compelling read. The book is much more than a military history book. I commend the book to all.

To regain his self esteem, and in search of honour 'The Doctor' volunteered to enlist as an acting lieutenant in the Royal Army Medical Corp. He found little of what he sought in the field ambulance behind the front line. He longed to become a Medical Officer to an infantry battalion at the front.

When he finally achieved this he found war in the trenches was everything that the paradox of conflict is; long periods of boredom, soldiers becoming ill because of the unsanitary filthy trenches, which he, as a M.O of the battalion tried to mitigate.

Then moments of intense activity, the outcome of which for Reginald were men with horrific wounds he had to treat in the most basic of facilities. He found compassion with the men he served with, and the wounded he treated.

'Honour' was perhaps something Reginald felt he never achieved. Over 100 years later I believe he most certainly did.

Allan Wood
Military Historian and Battlefield Guide

"Little did he realise that his personal diary entries during the great war would enable future readers to share his experiences. I felt at times that I was by his side. It is a truly remarkable book."

Major Ronnie Whiteside MBE

INTRODUCTION

Growing up in the 1960s, to us grandchildren, he was always 'The Doctor' – a kindly old man, a little distant perhaps. Quietly spoken, he was always well dressed in shirt and tie, slacks and cotton jacket, even when pottering around his beloved garden and greenhouse - where he had the most amazing grapevine. Still now, the warm aroma of compost and bone meal takes me right back to those days.

Dr Reginald Hannay Fothergill, Regie to his close family, was my step-grandfather and in the time I knew him, he lived with my grandmother Henrietta in their bungalow at Pauntley Road, Mudeford, Hampshire (now Dorset), just a short walk from the sea. He adored his small, three-tiered garden, each tier separated by a beech hedge, and spent much of his time tending to his plants and sitting in the sun. I believe that he was treated for skin cancer on his leg on at least one occasion. If you showed any interest in things, he would always take the time to explain, even if it was as simple as cutting out individual grapes from a bunch to encourage the others to grow bigger. Twice a day the blackbirds, thrushes and robins would collect on the windowsills waiting to be fed. They would come into the kitchen and feed from his and my grandmother's hands– and if I was lucky, one might even feed from my hand, but that was rare.

My memories of The Doctor start from around the age of eight until my mid-teens and are incredibly vivid, even now. I can remember waking up, along with my brother and sister, to the smell of wholemeal bread baked by my grandmother, and the taste of that warm bread with butter and honey stays with me still. If we were really lucky, there'd be Manx kippers posted from the Isle of Man. After breakfast, I would disappear down to Mudeford Quay to crab fish and watch the netting of salmon, returning for lunch, then head off again to Stanpit Marsh for the afternoon to catch sticklebacks in the briny pools or attempt to catch sea trout from Black Bridge, an old Bailey bridge.

I remember the sounds of the grandfather clock ticking and gently chiming in the hall throughout the night, caravan holidays in Mudeford, stays in the beach huts on Hengistbury Head, and the ferryboat to the sand spit. One day, my sister and I saw a basking shark swim up the quay.

The Doctor was a calm, benevolent presence in our lives, although woe betide us if we ever let slip that we'd suffered a cut or graze. He only had one answer – iodine – and did it sting! If we ever had a boil or a stye, he would concoct some strange poultice for that as well.

Although he would raise his voice if we talked over the early evening news, the only time I recall The Doctor losing his temper was when I talked my younger brother into topping up one of his water butts with earth!

In those days, I never gave any thought to The Doctor's past; to where he had come from, his family, or how he came to be married to my grand-mother. I knew that he had a brother who was an 'archaeologist', and the house was filled with artefacts that used to absolutely fascinate me. One day, I must have been about nine, my grandmother found me looking at a small monkey skull (netsuke) made from bone or ivory. She said to me, "When I think you are old enough to look after it properly, I will let you have it." I had obviously forgotten about this, until lo and behold, in my mid-forties, she handed me the skull… along with The Doctor's diaries.

This was quite a revelation. I was desperate to know what was in them. I would be the first person in a century, most possibly ever, to read them, but try as I might, I just could not decipher his handwriting. I had a number of attempts over the years but his tiny writing, much of it written by candlelight with age-faded ink, or in ship's quarters, littered with medical abbreviations (most probably of his own invention) proved almost impossible to transcribe and ensured his most personal thoughts and feelings remained closely guarded secrets.

That was until, prompted by a school project about World War One, my eldest grandson one day asked me if we had any family members who had served in The Great War. I told him about The Doctor's diaries and said I would try to decipher a short piece for him. Having dug them out of safekeeping, I set about the task, squinting away at the pages into the small hours. Incredibly, a few words eventually revealed themselves to me. A few more followed and then a few more, until I was able to read a few passages. Little could I have known at the time, I was hooked, and ahead of me lay hundreds of hours spent peering at these tiny volumes through a magnifying glass, sometimes two, whilst wearing my strongest reading glasses.

The story that unfolded made it all worthwhile. Crammed into those tiny pages, his delicate handwriting annotated family stories that had been passed down through the years. I remember my father telling me The Doctor had burned a lot of personal papers shortly before his death in 1971, but somehow these diaries – one started in 1906 and the other a war diary opening in 1915 – had survived. Why did he choose to spare these from the flames? Some pages from the ship's diary had been ripped out. Who knows why, maybe he could not bring himself to fully destroy this part of his life. He recorded an illness in the ship's diary that greatly concerned him, so much so that he left instructions for his personal papers stored at Allan Bank (his old home in Grasmere, Lake District) be handed to his brother John, and others to be destroyed. Why?

My interest piqued, as well as transcribing those precious diaries, I set about investigating The Doctor's family starting with his brother John Rowland Fothergill (1876-1957) who happened to be a close friend of Oscar Wilde. As I delved deeper into the lives of Regie's nearest and dearest, I discovered a myriad of long-lost stories, connections and confidences.

It soon became clear to me that Regie was somewhat at odds with the social conventions of the day and spent a lifetime struggling with his true feelings, yet he strove to reconcile his natural inclinations with what he knew was expected of him and his position in society. Is it possible that The Doctor would have been better suited to our more tolerant times? Somehow, I doubt it.

Before I read his surviving diaries, he was simply The Doctor, a kindly old man, sensitive and caring, who looked after my grandmother, tended his garden, fed the birds and was selflessly committed to his adopted family but in the pages of these diaries, he leaves us the clues from which we may draw our own conclusions. Time has given us the distance that allows his story to unfold without judgement.

It has been an incredible privilege to be the first person to read these diaries and to get to know The Doctor in a way that few in life could have done. In his diaries he is a seeker, a dedicated and diligent pursuer of the truth, not only about his own humanity, but also that of his fellows. His diaries offer us a beautiful insight into a different world that should not be lost to time. My hope is that in publishing Regie's diaries, we are able to give him a voice once more. So, this is his story, untouched, just as he wrote it all those years ago.

And what of my grandson's school project? Having got my eye in, with some excitement I carefully copied out one of the livelier sections of the diary and proudly presented it to him… only to be told he no longer needed it!

Regie's diaries, transcribed as they were written over 100 years ago. In recording the names of the fallen in the various actions that Regie recounts, I have followed his example, hoping that my footnotes will stand in tribute to their sacrifice and to remind us that behind every war story are real people that time cannot be permitted to forget.

Dave Dunn

A SHORT FAMILY HISTORY

My research into The Doctor's family began with his brother, John Rowland Fothergill (1876-1957). Listed as a 'pioneer early innkeeper' in *Who's Who*, he was a close friend of Oscar Wilde, who called him affectionately '*The Architect of the moon*' in a signed copy of *The Ballad of Reading Gaol*. John spent time with Wilde when he was exiled in France.

John was on the fringe of the famed Slade School of Art alongside the likes of Augustus John, opening the Carfax Gallery in St James, London with artist William Rothenstein and backed by Edward 'Ned' Perry Warren, the wealthy American art collector and author who idealised homosexual relationships as an alternative lifestyle. The pair were instrumental in Warren's commission of *The Kiss* by Auguste Rodin. John, for a time, lived at Lewes House in East Sussex where Warren had established a 'brotherhood' of like-minded young men, likely employing John as his personal assistant.

In search of conventional respectability perhaps, John was twice married, firstly to Elsie Herring in 1910, which ended in a messy divorce and emotional breakdown. After marrying Kate Headley Kirby in 1918, he forged a reputation as a blunt speaking, snobbish and somewhat eccentric (he kept elephants in the stables of the Royal Ascot Hotel) landlord and author. His best-known book *An Innkeeper's Diary* chronicled his time at the *Spread Eagle Hotel* in Thame where Evelyn Waugh was a regular. In the years that followed he gravitated towards the 'Bright Young Things', those most flamboyant of Bohemian aristocrats, for whom the 1920s roared loudest of all. John's ghost is said to haunt the third pub he ran, *The Three Swans* at Market Harborough. Strange things happened after one of his successors removed John's self-portrait that only stopped when the painting was restored to public view, where it has remained ever since.

Further research revealed that John was something of a renegade presence on the Fothergill family tree. So why would Regie, in 1907 and in his mid-twenties, insist on his personal papers being delivered to the outlandish John? What special connection did they have? Why John and not another of the highly respectable and extremely well-connected Fothergills?

The family fortune was made in the ironworks started by Regie's great grandfather Richard (1758-1821) and his brother John (1765-1828) who left the family home at Lowbridge House in Cumbria to establish a building business in Clapham. After marrying Elizabeth Rowland in 1788, he moved to Caerleon and started a successful foundry at Ponthir, becoming a partner with others at Tredegar, Sirhowy, and Penydarren.

Richard and Elizabeth had three sons – Richard (II) Thomas and Rowland. Thomas took over the foundry at Abernant, which he modernised, and before long, his Aberdare Iron Company became one of the major suppliers of wrought iron rails and fixtures for the growing railway industry.

Regie's grandfather Richard (II) had married Charlotte Elderton in London in 1822 and lived at Lowbridge House, which he developed. They had 11 children – seven girls and four boys – including Regie's father George (1833-1915). His eldest son Richard (III) was apprenticed to his uncle Rowland to learn about the iron industry, including the technical and business aspects, and took over the business in 1848 installing his three younger brothers, George, Thomas and Henry at Taff Vale, Llwydcoed and Abernant. Business was further shored up by marriage, with George and Thomas both marrying daughters of Francis Crawshay, scion of the Crawshay 'Iron Kings' from Cyfrarthfa in a double wedding on 4th October 1862. However, within two years, George, Henry and Thomas had sold their holdings in the ironworks to Richard, with Henry using some of his share to travel the world in the customary 'Grand Tour' of the English upper classes. Starting in 1867, he visited Europe, Asia, the Middle East, the Americas and Russia, no doubt recounting his adventures years later to his favourite nephew Regie, (born 1879), and encouraging his adventures as ship's doctor on board SS Ping Suey.

George and Isabel had seven children before her death from Scarlet Fever just two days after the birth of their son John Rowland, leaving George to marry again in 1878 to Ada Joan Hannay. Regie was their first-born, followed by Merrick, Joan and William. They lived in Royal Leamington Spa until 1884 when they moved to Allan Bank at Grasmere, a move overshadowed by baby Merrick's death, possibly from a reaction to a vaccine. Regie, their mother, Joan and her sister were all seriously ill with scarlet fever and barely four years later, Ada died and was buried alongside her infant son at St Oswald's Church in Grasmere. In 1898, George married his third wife, Flora Chambers. They went on to have a further two sons, Eric and Ronald. In all, Regie had 12 brothers and sisters – two full brothers and a sister, and nine half siblings.

Theirs was quite a family, of that there is no doubt. Another of Regie's ancestors, Elizabeth Gaunt, became the last woman to be executed in this country for a political crime when she was burnt at the stake in 1685. She was wrongly convicted of involvement in the Rye House Plot against Charles II.

Regie's diaries contain his most personal thoughts and feelings and having read these, as well as researching his family, it seems likely that Regie was gay, or had at least explored that side of his nature, possibly in much the same way as his half-brother John had. Educated at Repton and Edinburgh University, Regie alludes in his war diary to a relationship at university with a man called Jack Cox that seems to be rekindled when the pair enlist and are posted to the Western Front - where they appear to live in plain sight as a couple. Things had changed in the intervening years and whereas Jack had continued to pursue his louche ways, Regie had studied the teachings of theosophy and read extensively, exploring mystical insights that caused him to question the ways of his youth. Clearly conflicted, he requested a frontline posting and set off *in search of honour.*

If we can believe the stories passed down through the family, Regie's quest to join the Royal Army Medical Corps (RAMC) was instigated by an act of considerable spite and cruelty. Having established himself in general practice in Dalton-In-Furness, Regie was a bachelor in his mid-thirties when war broke out in 1914 and thoughts of active service were no doubt far from his mind. However, the story goes that when the daughter of his practice partner Dr Cross took a fancy to Regie, he rejected her advances and was duly served a white feather of cowardice one morning with his breakfast. Horrified, he was prompted to enlist.

The Doctor's war diary opens in the company of his old university friend Jack Cox on the ship to France, and for the first few weeks they kick their heels behind the lines, playing tennis, going to dinners, sightseeing and walking in the countryside. However, behind the hi-jinks are greater considerations nagging at Regie's conscience. Twice he mentioned the need to prove himself: "Wish I could get out with honour but must stick to it," and "God! I would give something to get out of this with honour."

In the trenches, and in the grip of a very particular loneliness, he transcribed the Urdu poem *Humayun To Zobeida* (by the contemporary Indian civil rights activist and poet Sarojini Naidu). In doing so, I believe Regie comes as close as he ever got to revealing his true feelings in writing –

Yet, when I crave of you, my sweet, one tender moment's grace,

You cry, "I sit behind the veil, I cannot show my face."

Replace 'she' with 'he' and consider the 'veil' as a screen or mask, something that conceals the truth.

Having forced the issue and taking his frontline position, Regie voiced his disgust for his old house mate Jack who, with his battalion in the thick of it at Ypres, used his ailing mother as an excuse and resigned his commission, leaving Regie to grapple with his true feelings and conscience in the forward trenches as the blood and bullets flew all around. That aside, he described daily life in the trenches, from the mundane to the horrific. With an easy style, he recounted life in the trenches- reading his words, I felt like I was in the trenches with him.

The Doctor's diaries present a remarkable picture of men at war, in which the simple joy of spotting a bird, or noting a plant throwing out shoots of life, kindles much-needed, comforting memories of home. Whether dealing with fellow officers or the enlisted ranks, Regie was equally compassionate and considerate, although he clearly regarded some men with much greater affection than others. He always maintained his respect for authority, even while questioning some of its commands, and for the most part, he reported the slaughter dispassionately.

Surrounded by death, it is perhaps only natural that Regie's thoughts should turn frequently to his immediate family. On one period of leave, he recounted a visit to the grave of his father, who had died the year he enlisted. He also mentioned his eldest half-brother George Algernon (1868-1945), who rejected a life in medicine in order to follow his calling as an artist, but who then enlisted as a medical officer and was stationed at Aldershot. George had an eye for amusing incidents, and his sketches and caricatures featured in Vanity Fair magazine. However, he was best known for his paintings of horses and their owners and his work has been exhibited in the National Portrait Gallery. George also enjoyed the patronage of American millionaire Charles Schwartz whose horse, Jack Horner, won the Grand National in 1926 at the price of 25/1 only to be injured shortly after and retired. The horse, Jack Horner survived, but fate was not so kind to his jockey William Watkinson. Handsomely rewarded with a gift of £4,000 to be paid over four years by Schwartz for guiding Jack Horner to victory, Watkinson was killed in a fall at Bogside Racecourse just three weeks later.

Regie's familial concerns are most apparent in his diary entries that refer to his younger brother William Hannay Fothergill (1887-1955). A somewhat enigmatic figure, at least as far as written records are concerned, he was afforded a different education (Giggleswick) to his brothers, going on to agricultural college and emigrating to Argentina where he joined the ex-pat community of some 40,000. Following the outbreak of war, he and 5,000 others returned to Britain at their own cost to enlist into Kitchener's Army. William was posted to active service in the same division as Regie and stationed close by. The diary reveals the great lengths Regie went to in order to meet his brother whenever he could.

After the war, William was discharged and in 1926 emigrated again, this time to Canada, but had returned to the UK (to Mudeford to be near his brother Regie) by the time of his passing in 1955. He suffered from a brain haemorrhage and lung conditions, likely consequences of being gassed in the trenches. William's death certificate records him as a retired farmer, unmarried, living just a few hundred yards from The Doctor in Mudeford – it seems safe to assume the two remained close to the end.

The diary ends with Regie returning to Blighty, but not before he has introduced the reader to his first wife Alice Whyte (b1879). From what he wrote in his diary, there is no doubt that Regie was fond of her. Alice died in a Birkenhead nursing home in 1938, where she had been for some time, leaving Regie with a house to run as well as his practice.

He needed help, and he found that in his housekeeper Henrietta 'Hettie' Dunn, my grandmother.

Hettie was recently widowed with two young children, Teddy and Frances. Hettie and Regie were already known to each other; he had attended the birth of my father in 1932. Hettie worked as Regie's housekeeper, later becoming his wife when they married in 1945. She was more than thirty years his junior. The absolute dedication and affection they had for each other was obvious, even to a young lad like myself. They remained happily married until Regie's death in 1971.

In Search of Honour

Captain Reginald Hannay Fothergill
1879-1971

May 1915

Saturday 29th

Set out from Tweseldown camp with field ambulance at 5:30am arriving Farnborough at 10:30am where we entrained at 11:20am. I went on the first train.

At Southampton we put our men, horses and equipment on board SS City of Lucknow[1] and set sail about 6pm. Escorted by two destroyers we passed along the south of Isle of Wight.

Jack slept in the first officer's bunk and I on the floor of the saloon; the sea was absolutely calm.

A third destroyer joined in the small hours of morning and warned us of a recent minefield on our course; this necessitated a detour of 35 miles. Arrived in Havre at 6am, disembarked without injury to animals. We had to wait until the evening, we were not allowed to go into town. Took advantage of the most excellent café on the station run by some ladies at cost price.

Jack, Bartholomew and self shared one first class carriage. We got all our equipment etc on one long train and steamed away about 8pm.

Had a most excellent night being only disturbed at 2am by some well-meaning people who sent round coffee at some station or other.

Passed through Abbeville, Noyen and Boulogne. Beautiful green fields, so fresh and green.

---

1. *SS City of Lucknow 3,677 tons – torpedoed by U.21 (Otto Hersing) carrying onions from Alexandria to Liverpool. Sank Sunday 30 April 1916 sixty miles east of Malta. The 42-man crew survived and were rescued by HMS Rifleman.*

Sunday 30th.

Detrained St Omer at 4pm marched field ambulance for five miles to Cormette through beautiful cultivated fields. Cormette, a little hamlet nestling among trees with one large farmhouse, 'The Chateau', which was occupied by the CO. Large rooms riddled in rat holes and nearly all furniture removed in case of Germans. Lovely garden, roses, vines, and lilacs.

We are now in the sound of guns, which are continually rumbling in the distance perhaps 15-20 miles away. I have billet in a public house. The bed looked clean but having a wooden frame I decided not to risk bugs so slept on the floor in valise. I had a splendid night. My men – 20 – were comfortable in a barn with clean straw and slept well being only disturbed by rats which gnawed through some of their haversacks to get at rations.

JUNE 1915

Tuesday 1st

Perfect weather and cloudless sky, the brilliant green of the fields and hedges is almost bewildering in the sunshine. We had a free day and the men were well occupied with washing their clothes and bodies after the long journey from England.

Jack is mess president and so far he has managed to spread excellent meals on the table in the old chateau. They also have very fine wine in the chateau: 1.25 franc (blanc) and 1.50 franc (rouge) per bottle.

In the afternoon Jack, Bartholomew and I rode into St Omer to do some shopping and to get some French money. We had to show pass to get past the sentry into the town, which is a small place with no places of entertainment and very few shops. Guns booming very distinctly in the distance, they are the 9.6-inch guns, English guns we are told.

Wednesday 2nd.

We hear that we are to remain at this place a week then I understand that we shall be sent up to the front.

We have been supplied with respirators, a respirator consists simply of a lump of cotton wool which is saturated with a mixture of sodium carbonate and sodium thiosulfate, this is tied round the head with a piece of muslin. They also supply helmets with talc[2] eyepieces.

---

2. *Talc being an early form of plastic.*

The 12th Division is billeted in the neighbourhood among the hamlets and villages within a radius of about 10 miles. Our brigade: the 35th Infantry Brigade has its headquarters at Galmes nearby.

Had a route march in the morning, slack afternoon. Jack and I walked out to a wood about a mile away and sat down and read most of the afternoon.

We have an interpreter; a Frenchman attached to our field ambulance; he is quite a nice man though a little bothersome at times. We therefore call him 'The Interrupter' among ourselves.

Thursday 3rd.

Got up this morning at 5am, shaved and washed in time for 6am. Parade, breakfast 7:15am. A glorious summer morning and everything so fresh and green, blackbirds singing, one might be in England.

Iron rations given out to officers and men consisting of five very hard biscuits and a tin of corned beef, the whole done up in a bag. It is a beastly weight and nuisance to carry about.

After dinner I had a long talk with the nonconformist minister, a very broad-minded man. He knew some theosophy and we discussed its relevance to Christian doctrines. He explained his own philosophy of life, he agreed with me that each great religion had some truth to give to the world and that no one religion gave all the truth. He agreed that the great religions taken together went to make up one great symphony.

He considered the Christian religion to have completed the symphony, all the truth to have been taught when it was formulated and looks for the symphony to be completed only by the teaching of another religion (or perhaps other religions), which shall continue in its teaching of all the main truths and teachings.

Friday 4th.

Slack day. Marched out men in the morning and gave them elementary French lessons. Jack and I read and wrote letters etc in little wood bathed in glorious sunshine. Quiet peaceful evening in the garden of the old chateau after supper. Roses all out and pinks. (Smoking pipe).

Saturday 5th.

Started on our long march to the firing line, up at 3:45am and joined in behind the 35th Brigade. My horse lame on the right hoof owing to the tethering rope having wound round and therefore walked most of the way and really found it less tiring to walk than to ride.

Riding behind a column of marching men is very fatiguing owing to the fact of having to sit in one position for so long and the difficulty of dismounting with so much luggage. I was orderly officer and had to attend to those that fell out, one or two suffering from heat but mostly feet.

We took the wrong turning at Argues and after remedying this we had a halt of three hours for goodness knows what reason. This made us so late that we decided to stay the night at Rennescure instead of Ebblingham. There being no available houses we all marched with men, horses and wagons into a pasture field and bivouacked.

I was very comfortable and glad to have brought my groundsheet on which I spread my valise, took off boots and wrapped puttees round feet, crept into sleeping bag under a hedge with Jack next to me, and slept very well.

Sunday 6th.

Passing through delightful country with some beautiful chateaux covered with wisteria, especially at Champagne.

Reveille at 3:45am. Very hot march which men began to feel very much after coming straight from England. By 11 o'clock they began to fall out with bad feet and heatstroke.

At first we managed but soon our three ambulances became filled with men and equipment. Things began to look bad as men littered the roadside and there was no way of carrying them. The divisional 21st Motor Transport came to the rescue and Jack and I remained behind picking up the cases and sending bad cases into Hazebrouck.

After this Jack and I found a nice farmhouse where we had wine and ate our rations. Arrived Strazeele at 4:45 pm in time for tea. Found field ambulance snugly packed away in a field on a hill from which we could watch the German shells bursting in the distance.

After tea Jack and I walked out into the country and after a delightful stroll along a track through lovely fields of hay grass we purchased eggs and milk at a little farm. The occupants said that the Germans were in possession of their farm last October and they killed the local priest of the village. Slept in a billet and thanks to a pump in the garden managed to enjoy a wash.

Monday 7th.

Reveille at 3am. Marched out to Bailleul, where we arrived about 8:30 am. Halted at outskirts of town opposite aviation field, Jack and I went and saw a biplane piloted by Captain Vaughan[3]. He had been bombing German positions and was struck by high explosives and bullets which had torn holes into the wings and even blown away a portion of one of his bombs.

Their best machines have Renault engines, eight-cylinder and develop 100-hp and travel 85-90 miles per hour. They are such brave and unassuming fellows.

We watched one man go up with his observer to take photos of German gun positions, a peculiar risky business. They soared up to 600 feet and then moved towards enemy lines. Soon we saw timed high explosive shells bursting all around it, each explosion leaving a beautiful ball of white smoke in the blue sky. They came down later quite unscathed.

Arrived Armentieres in the evening. We now have five motor ambulances attached to our field ambulance. Three are Sunbeams and two Ford.

It is now arranged that 36th and 38th Field Ambulance do the work of the division and 37th (prime) acts as a convalescent hospital further down the lines.

Tuesday 8th.

Slack day. Visited our field ambulance station here. The building is a

---

3. *Ralph Montgomery Vaughan. MC. 1890-1976. Royal Inniskilling Fusiliers. In 1912 he began his flight training at the Bristol Flying School, Salisbury Plain. He subsequently joined No 3 Squadron Netheravon and from there to No 5 Squadron on its formation. Appointed to RFC (Royal Flying Corps) Reserve and in December seconded to the RFC as flying officer.*
On 15 August 1914 on a flight to France Vaughan made a forced landing near Boulogne and was arrested by the French and kept for almost a week, not arriving at his new airfield until 22 August.
He was shot and wounded in the leg on 1 November 1914 and on 17 April 1915 while flying reconnaissance in a B.E.2c his observer Lt John Lascelles* RFC and Rifle Brigade had 24 shots with a rifle, hitting a German pilot in the head and forcing his plane to crash. For this action both were mentioned in despatches and awarded the Military Cross.
*John Lascelles was killed in action on 31 July 1915.
On 28 March 1915 Vaughan was made temporary captain and flight commander in the RFC; then from 6 May to 5 July 1915 he was officer commanding No 5 Squadron in France. He survived the war. (Home of the Firebirds - www.56sqnfirebirds.org.uk).

school and is very suitable for our work. Our men are billeted in the upper rooms and the lower rooms will be wards, operating rooms etc.

Colonel Dunn explained the scheme of work, the wards of the hospital being now in the charge of officers while the bearer subdivision will also have its respective personnel of officers. The two subdivisions carrying on week about.

Walked short way into town with Jack. It was shelled severely last October and many of the houses remain with large holes in the walls. Terribly hot and thundery.

Wednesday 9th.

Jack and I had rather an adventure today. We were filled with curiosity to see the trenches and so we walked out to Chapelle Armentieres about three miles away. This place, a small village, was shelled last October. We inspected the church; the top of the tower was blown away and the front walls smashed in so that the organ was exposed and hung out over the road.

We then entered the reserve trenches and walked along to the communication trench which led to the first line of trenches. Here we met Highlanders in occupation and the Germans were only one thousand yards away. There was some firing on our right. We had not proceeded far when a corporal and men came running after us and arrested us as spies!

It was rather unpleasant and then an officer appeared and said he was afraid we must go before the general. It seemed that some casual questions we had asked civilians on the way down had aroused suspicion.

At the headquarters we appeared before the captain who was CO in absence of the general. He was quite decent but said we must in future have passes before visiting trenches etc. They (enemy) throw about six small shells into the town each evening.

Thursday 10th.

Armentieres. Bought French phrase book. In the afternoon I took men to Recquicken[4] about three miles outside town to bathe in the canal, I rode my horse there. The canal was about three yards wide and quite five-feet six deep at its shallowest point so that it was scarcely safe for those who couldn't swim.

---

4. *To give new life to*

Had a nice letter from Cross (practice partner). I had written advising him to invite our locum Doctor Horegood into a three-way partnership with us in order to prevent the practice from suffering in the event of our failing to get another locum when he goes. Cross appears not to favour the idea.

In the afternoon I visited a house in Rue Sadi Canot where Jack and I are going to billet. It is in the best part of the town and is quite a large fine house, well furnished with a jolly rose garden. The same people look after it as in our present house.

The town billeting major lives there and kindly invited us to take one of the rooms which has two beds and overlooks the garden. The house has been shelled lightly on several occasions. There are holes in the garden made by fragments of small shells.

Friday 11th.

I was very pleasantly surprised with the way the trenches were constructed. The ones we visited are paved with wood just like a pier so that officers could bicycle along quite comfortably from one place to another. There are some trenches that have been constructed for a length of time, there is no mud and there is good sleeping accommodation and protection.

I was orderly officer which meant a good deal of hanging about our field hospital doing nothing very much. Our division has not yet gone into action so that our hospital cases are for the present confined to ordinary cases of sickness. Quite a fine Roman Catholic church here at Armentieres, at least it has a very fine exterior but inside the windows are poor.

Saturday 12th.

Nice long letter from Joan[5]. We are very comfortable in our new billet and is evidently a house belonging to well to do people. The bedroom has two beds with beautiful linen and an anteroom with washbasins, taps and mirror. We overlook the garden which is small but gay with roses and flowers. We brought our Primus stove and I wake up at 5:45am and put on the kettle and we enjoy a nice cup of tea about 6:15am.

---

5. *Joan, sister. 1885-1967. Born Allan Bank. Educated I.O.M. Did not marry. (The Fothergills. A first history)*

Went into the village; the shelling was over and saw the havoc. The population had nearly all left months ago, the few remaining live in their cellars.

Sunday 13th.

Jack and I put our lunch in our haversacks and set out for a long walk of exploration. We crossed the canal and crossed the Belgium boundary into Ploegsteert. We then pushed forward for a mile then turned to the left as we were getting too near our front lines and feared lest we should be held up.

We were determined to push on to Neuve-Église but first of all bought a bottle of wine at a little estaminet. We then sat down in a field to enjoy our grub followed by a sleep despite the two British batteries which kept thundering away at intervals.

We then set out through quiet cornfields. We had just begun to ascend the gentle slope leading up to Neuve-Église when we heard a boom from the German lines, followed by the hum of a shell which grew louder and louder passing over our heads with a screech until it fell with great accuracy onto the roof of the church with a terrible explosion, tearing away a great portion of the wall. We watched about six of these fall among the houses of the village.

Further on we came across a small battery of field guns and 18-pound guns. Visited the major and captain in their dugout. Had tea with them and afterwards walked.

Monday 14th.

The ADMS *(Assistant Director Medical Services)* and DMS *(Director Medical Services)* paid a visit to our hospital in the morning and luckily found us all well occupied as we had the men busy making pads for the various splints. They told us to be ready to move at short notice.

At 4:30pm we received definite orders to move away at 8pm on the morrow. I must say Jack and I are not altogether sorry to leave Armentieres because; although we have luxurious billets there is nothing to do or see in the town, thus one's movements are limited very much by the position of the German lines so as to make walks in the area near impossible without going out of bounds.

Both of our expeditions to Chapelle Armentieres and Neuve-Église were made only by breaking bounds, and, had we been caught at the latter place we would have gotten into some trouble. Armentieres is at the apex of a wedge.

Tuesday 15th.

We brought back some rolls to our rooms on Monday. Reveille at 5am. I made tea and with rolls we had breakfast in bed instead of at the mess.

I am billeting officer and started away in front of the field ambulance[6] in a motor ambulance with my billeting party consisting of an interpreter, Sergeant Butcher and six men. I had no name of a place to help me for a destination, I simply had a point given me on a map being about eight or nine miles away.

However, our maps are so splendid and drawn to such a large scale that I had no difficulty in following the narrow country roads, rapidly finding the exact farmhouse just outside Bailleul, then finding quarters for the men.

Composition of 36th field ambulance:

- Mules 18
- Officer's chargers 17
- Heavy draft 27
- RAMC men 181
- Officers 13
- ASC men 40 (Army Service Corps)
- Mechanic transport 15
- Interpreter One
- Motor ambulances Seven
- Horse ambulance and Wagon

Wednesday 16th.

Had a parade at 9am. Read out a list of enemy trenches recognised during active service at the front with the idea of impressing the men.

Had a short ride with Jack into the countryside. It is flat but pretty,

---

6. *A field ambulance was a mobile medical unit to treat the wounded close to the combat zone. It was not a vehicle. It was manned by the RAMC (Royal Army Medical Corps) and normally under the command of a division.*
The capacity of a field ambulance was 150 casualties but dealt with many more during battle. Responsible for setting up the evacuation chain from RAP (Regimental Aid Post) – ADS (Advanced Dressing Station) – MDS (Main Dressing Station) – RDS (Regimental Dressing Station). The field ambulance would normally set one ADS for each brigade and one MDS for each division)

every inch of ground under cultivation and little if no grazing except in the field immediately behind the farm. No hedges or walls separate the fields but only ditches along which willows are sometimes allowed to grow. Farmhouses scattered here and there prevent any monotony of scheme.

Each farm is wholly surrounded by shady trees. They are for the most part whitewashed and the warm red tiles covered with grey lichen give them a homely appearance.

The Germans were one time masters of this part of the country and most of these farms harboured the bad men. They were mostly Bavarians and treated them very well, paying for all they received.

Orders arrived that we must be prepared to move at two hours' notice. The colonel consequently became panic-stricken and has practically berated everyone. We are getting used to these sorts of orders not to take them seriously and I bet Bartholomew five francs that we would still be here in 24 hours.

Official notice handed in at 8pm informing us of German trenches captured all along our line from Ypres to La Bassee. This explains the sound of heavy guns firing.

Thursday 17th.

Still here despite the two hours' order from headquarters. Glorious day, cloudless skies. More respirators were issued. Weekend with Jack to Steinbeck, nothing doing. Very comfortable at the farm. They bring us café-au-lait at 6am and we then have it again after supper, they will not take more than one cent a cup for it.

Friday 18th.

Walked into Bailleul this afternoon. Rather a miserable place with a large church. Rather fine from the outside but tawdry inside with the large pillars painted to represent marble. We have had orders to return to Armentieres tomorrow.

Saturday 19th.

Got up at 4am and it was very cold. Packed our valises, had breakfast at the farm – eggs, rolls, and café-au-lait. I think the old woman and daughter were sorry to lose us. We gave them about twice as much as they asked for our meal.

My horse was lame from a kick on the knee. The Colonel asked me to act as billeting officer. I went forward in motor to Armentieres, and found it impossible to obtain the same house for the colonel and mess. I then drove to our old billet c/o Madame Fauberque, 89 Rue Sadi Carnot where they kindly welcomed Jack and I again.

They referred me to number 90 in the same street. Number 90 is a magnificent house, well furnished with a caretaker in charge and I was able to book it for the colonel and mess. The colonel arrived in due course, grumbled about the distance of the house from our hospital but the billet was too good to refuse and so he decided to take it on. There is a magnificent bath and hot water all day long.

Sunday 20th.

Jack was orderly officer. I went on a country walk, hunted around for wildflowers and thought of old uncle. I always think of him when I pick wildflowers. The flora much resembles that of southern England. It is not as varied as it was at Cormette.

Monday 21st.

I was orderly officer. The duty now is very irksome as I am obliged to remain at the hospital from 10am until 4pm except an hour for a meal and that must be either at hospital or at the old mess where we have a bedroom and take our meals. A terrible dog whined nearly all night at the moon from a kennel just below my window. The mosquitoes' sound is making it impossible to read. However, I managed to get to sleep without being bitten very much. My birthday by the way, 36 today, what a big boy!

Tuesday 22nd.

Received first casualty today from the trenches. A shrapnel wound of head and not serious.

Have written to Liverpool tobacconist for pipe tobacco. He is going to send me two pounds at a time out of bond at six shillings per pound, post free. This is three shillings per pound cheaper than the price I pay for it in England.

Wednesday 23rd.

One or two casualties today, I have now got the medical ward placed in my care. In the afternoon Jack and I set off on horseback to visit 37th

Field Ambulance at Steenwerck some seven miles. My horse being lame I rode another which was very comfortable. We arrived at 5pm and Malone treated us to some excellent red wine at the estaminet.

We lost our way on the road home and had to follow a track through cornfields for a mile or two in order to reach the canal along the way we wanted to ride home. My horse fell off this track into a narrow deep ditch which was hidden by vegetation. I found myself also at the bottom of it, some way behind the horse, unhurt.

Thursday 24th.

Jack orderly officer. I had an excellent bath and after learning up copious phrases appropriate to the occasion I repaired to the hairdressers.

The ADMS arrived at the mess and explained that we are to organise two ADS on the east of Ploegsteert tomorrow and to send up two motor ambulances twice a day at 8am and 8pm to pick up wounded, then carry them to our field ambulance at Armentieres.

The colonel and adjutant went up this evening to find the positions, a shell burst within 200 yards of them. I am to be the first one to go up tomorrow, I must say I am so glad to go as I am getting utterly sick of doing nothing except hang about here

Friday 25th.

Collected wounded or rather went up to collect but found none. We took up two ambulances, I took my own as far as I was able then completed the journey 400 yards on foot as far as the RDS which was a rather less bombarded estaminet at the edge of the east of Bois de Ploegsteert.

Things were very quiet, I passed along an open bit of road with waving corn on either side, among them the parapets of the trenches sticking out. The only risky part of this journey is during the passage through Ploegsteert village, which is periodically shelled; one must pass through the village to reach the dressing station.

The remainder of the day was rather painful as the colonel was terribly irritable, at times quite irresponsible, giving one order one moment and cancelling it a few moments afterwards. One's work in the hospital is very unsatisfactory, I have the medical ward, it is a mere farce. The whole object of the colonel is to get rid of cases as soon as they come in and so they are shot out often undiagnosed and sent either back to Steenwerck, or back to duty.

Saturday 26th.

The Colonel visited my ward this morning, was extremely irritable and fussy over things as well as giving countless orders then cancelling them a few minutes later, most confusing and unsatisfactory.

Malone and Fitzgerald rode over in the afternoon from Steenwerck and then Jack, Bartholomew, myself and the above two went up to a tennis club which we had heard of. It was in the Rue S Carnot and was splendid with three red gravel courts and clubhouse. You pay one franc a day and they supply you with balls, racquet and shoes. We had some great games; the old service came back after an absence of nine years!

Sunday 27th.

Unfortunately, a showery day, Jack took part in a church parade. After lunch we spent a very lazy afternoon sleeping and reading.

At four o'clock I made tea which I always do thanks to our Primus stove and when that fails my methylated spirit stove. We enjoyed excellent tea and ate Ethel's[7] birthday cake.

Jack and I set out for a walk toward Gris Pot, looked up a concealed battery with a major in charge. We continued our walk and shells came past but not near.

Four shells fell into our transport field this afternoon and exploded but owing to a piece of luck none of the horses were in the field and no damage was done. One shell was dug up and proved to be a French shell. So, the Germans are evidently using the shells they have captured instead of wasting their own.

Monday 28th.

The colonel thinks the mess is too far away, so he has found a room nearer the hospital and gave us permission to find billets anywhere we liked nearer the hospital. Jack and I were extremely lucky to drop on a great big house, quite unfurnished but with a fine old garden enclosed by walls so high as to completely cut one off from overlooking windows.

The garden has an octagonal building partly built into the garden wall, you ascend to the floor level from the old garden and a flight of stone steps. There are frescoes on the wall of hunting scenes. The German soldiers have scrawled a good deal over the walls.

7. *Ethel, sister. 1871-1951. Married Cecil Charles Bullmore. (The Fothergills. A first history)*

13

I have developed a nasty sore throat and probably caught it from some of the many bad throats that we are daily admitting. I don't think this a healthy place, too many drains and bad odor. The sanitary arrangements are decidedly crude. I don't suppose there are a dozen baths in the town. There is one in our house. It is placed in all places in a cellar below the octagonal building like they literally might be ashamed of it.

Tuesday 29th.

Throat still sore and I feel wretched, shivering. Made cup of tea in my bedroom for breakfast. Some seven casualties including a man shot through the lower end of the scapula and out just above the base of heart then through the top button of coat which was flattened out curiously. We give antiserum[8] as routine.

Apart from some ordinary cases of sickness and very slight casualties there is really very little use for a field hospital run on the same lines as this one. Indeed, I consider it to do more harm than good seeing as all casualties it evacuates from the trenches are brought to this hospital. If they arrive here in the evening they remain here until the following day at 10am then they are sent to the clearing hospital at Bailleul to be operated on.

Our field ambulance therefore defeats its own object, because instead of using its splendid cars to take wounded with all speed to the clearing hospital it merely acts as a blockhouse where cases are delayed 10-12 hours on their way to a properly equipped hospital. It is very painful to see this sort of thing going on.

Jack was orderly officer in waiting, taking the two cars up to Gunners farm and Headquarters farm. Shells were bursting, and a machine gun was reportedly trained on the road.

Our chaplain buried two men today, the funeral was shelled in the process and they all had to take cover, some of them throwing themselves into the grave which they had dug.

Wednesday 30th.

Jack and I are now in our 'Palace' and it makes a magnificent billet. We hired two large rugs, a dressing table, jug and basins for four francs a week. We have two mattresses filled with clean straw and on this we have our valises and sleeping bags. There also is an easy chair.

---

8. *Tetanus*

The living room we have chosen abuts on the garden; its two outer walls are all glass with large windows. It has a mosaic floor and a most handsome ceiling with a large frieze very well done. The walls are panelled with dark wood. There have been no real tenants in the house for two or three years.

The conservatory in the garden has very old vines in it, each cane quite six inches in diameter from which hang an unthinned tangle of unpruned shoots. It is amazing. Also, the hundreds of bunches of grapes from almost every twig.

A shell fell today in Sadi Canot Square and killed five people.

JULY 1915

Thursday 1st.

Orderly officer today, went up to Headquarters farm to pick up wounded and also to Gunners farm where we took in one gunshot wound sitting up. While there they brought in a supposed civilian spy, he had a gun and revolver and said he was out to shoot hares.

Several civilian sharpshooters are known to be about, he may be one of these. They live in some of the farmhouses and cottages which are scattered about and probably sneak out at night and take up their position in trees from where they can snipe men who would normally be well protected from enemy trenches.

This evening I had a man with an entrance bullet wound R apex and out at left upper lobe then in appendix. Then at 2am a man with an entrance wound to the larynx and out right upper lobe lung, he was breathing with great difficulty mainly through the larynx wound. I got Jack to come around and I enlarged the wound and put in a tracheotomy tube. He breathed better but died at mid-day from internal hemorrhage!

I also had a compound fracture of the lower jaw from a shell and many sick men.

Friday 2nd.

Jack, not so well, has obviously caught my late disability.

Bart, Jones and Walters came into tea in our billet and afterwards we four went to the tennis club and had a few sets. I went back to my house immediately after dinner. Jack always plays cards with the colonel and does not return till 10:30pm, so I can always count on these undisturbed few hours.

Saturday 3rd.

Made a journey in a car to Gunners farm for wounded, a shell burst on our right but otherwise things are quiet. Had some games of tennis in the afternoon with Jack. Still very out of practice, especially on forehand strokes, serve not so bad considering. Chaps look very amusing playing in khaki and funnier still playing in kilts.

Sunday 4th.

Spent a most ridiculously slack day, but it is Sunday and terribly hot. We made our own breakfast of scrambled eggs, rolls, and tea, then we wrote letters in the garden. We had hard boiled eggs and sardines for lunch and a bottle of white wine. In the afternoon we slept on our stretchers in the garden and had tea at 4:30pm.

Monday 5th.

Sent Cross £54.12 being half my pay from April 1st to June 30th (quarter salary).

In the afternoon rode with Jack, and Bartholomew to Steenwerck. We rode by the canal and made a long route. Had excellent tea with ASC officer then rode back by shorter route joining canal nearer Armentieres. It is jolly going along the banks of the canal which is a placid slow-moving canal about 40 yards wide. Jack went up to the trenches.

Tuesday 6th.

All officers including Colonel Dunn turned out for a riding lesson. I had Sergeant Major Down. We all careered around the field. The whole business was rather absurd and to my mind no useful result was reached seeing that no individual instruction was given. We are to have a course of these lessons daily. Very hot, lay on a stretcher in the garden under trees.

After lunch Jack away as orderly officer. Read some theosophies and made tea on Jack's return. Feel rather despondent; as it is obvious I am wasting my time here. There is nothing to do, the hospital work is a mere make-believe, a perfect farce and all the time I feel I might be doing useful work in my practice in Dalton. All the while I am slacking here Cross writes to say he has had 29 confinements in three weeks and done it single handed, the locum having left.

I have just returned from trenches, one of the bits of work one is called upon to do. Had coffee with Doctor Hacket in Gunners farm. While there the Essex opened fire. What a noise.

Wednesday 7th.

Orderly officer. This means being glued to the hospital most of the day and sleeping there at night. A dreary place, the hospital – dark cheerless rooms, not a ray of sunshine, and no garden. Also, I felt extremely ill all day owing to a modest liver attack brought on by boiled ham and beans the night before. Had a few casualties and many sick cases. We had an undisturbed night.

Thursday 8th.

Had our riding school as usual. I tried a fresh horse which Bartholomew thought might be more comfortable than my own which has a very uncomfortable trot. The brute had a playful way of kicking, also stumbled very badly and I was not impressed to find myself completing a somersault through the air, landing without taking any harm. I shall make the best of my own horse.

We enjoyed a bit of German hate this evening when they began to throw shells into this end of the town. I was walking home at the time and when I got in I heard one coming over and it burst fairly close to our home.

Forgan had a narrow shave while taking the ambulance up to Ploegsteert, a shell burst on the road not 20 yards away, stones hit him but otherwise no harm.

Friday 9th.

Not much going on and the number of casualties reduced. Colonel not quite so fussy though bad enough and apt to lay down the law about some of my cases of illness in a way which is extremely annoying.

The old chap is from what I can see extraordinarily deficient in medical knowledge as one might expect seeing that his experience has been confined to the rough and ready treatment of the 'Tommy' for the last 30 years. But one must bow to his military rank which enables him always to have the last word in the discussion of a case and gives him the right to pronounce a final diagnosis without one dissentient voice being raised.

Then again he is old, and I look young. He probably forgets or does not know that I have been in practice for nearly 10 years.

So often the army from a medical standpoint does not appeal to me when red tape confronts one at every turn, when the army rule of shifting your responsibility with all speed onto someone else's shoulders is reflected in one's treatment of medical cases in such a way as to make the whole thing a perfect farce.

Saturday 10th.

Got a nice letter from Cross sending last quarter's receipts which is:

Receipts £486.8.0

Expenses £155.7.6

Profits £331.0.9

Balance in bank from April £70.4.3. Total £401.5.0.

Not so bad considering he has apparently got very indifferent help from locum.

The locum has now become engaged to Miss Cond and I am very glad this nice girl has found a husband as she has loathed her occupation of teaching for years. She will make a nice cheerful wife. Heard from Parker to say he has got me £500 of war loan stock at 4.5 per cent.

This afternoon Jack and I visited Le Corney and had some magnificent tennis, just the three girls and us. Two of the girls play really well, I mean they ought to win at most tournaments and one has a beautiful overhand serve.

Sunday 11th.

Jack and I ordered our horses for 11:30am and taking a feed of corn set off for Neuve Chapelle. I enjoyed the journey there very much. Enjoyed a much more comfortable seat than usual. We rode to Erquinhem and then struck left to Laventie where we examined the magnificent church now absolutely honeycombed with shell holes. Then passing to the right of Henbaix we reached Rouge Croix, we found a nice farmhouse where we watered and fed the horses then enjoyed a good meal ourselves in the orchard. We had a bottle of graves vin, a tin of tunny fish and some cakes. After riding another 1,000 yards we had to dismount leaving horses in a farm, then took to trenches through Sikh camps. Unfortunately, the Germans were just then throwing shells around and we did not feel very comfortable as we moved along some open land towards a farm where a Lieutenant Anderson was said to be stationed. He was not there so we had to retreat, several shells bursting nearby.

We visited an officer in his dugout and several 'whizz bangs'[9] came over. We were glad to get back to safety. There was nothing of Neuve Chapelle to be seen except a few ruined houses, the German trenches beyond. We had a long and tiring ride home, the distance there and back being about twenty miles by the circuitous route we were obliged to take to miss the unhealthy road.

Tuesday 13th.

Had a close shave this morning. Jack and I were sitting in the garden at 12:45pm just after morning hospital, when suddenly we heard a shell screaming towards us. I shouted, 'My god it's coming!' and flung myself on the ground and Jack did the same. It burst with a terrific roar on the road the other side of our garden wall exactly on a line with our seat in the garden.

We at once ran into the house and had scarcely got in when another came screaming over our garden and fell on the top of the house the other side of our street leaving a hole through the roof and through the two floors.

By an extraordinary chance neither of the shells injured anyone, five others completed this piece of 'hate'. We visited the house and brought away the nose of the shell, still almost too hot to hold.

Wednesday 14th.

This has been an eventful day for me. I took the motor ambulance up to the trenches and when passing through Le Bizet a shell burst about 20 yards in front of the car; against the side of a house. A piece of shell penetrated my radiator causing a leak and another piece hit the iron screen above my head. We drove on to Headquarters farm.

Then I had to make another journey to bring in an officer who had been hit in the trenches that afternoon. I took the car as far as it was safe and left it behind half shelled buildings. I then found that the officer was still in the trenches and so taking two RAMC men with me and led by a corporal we entered the trenches.

In the meantime, a terrific fusillade had started between the opposing lines and the bullets swished over our heads and cut through the barley stalks like the sound of a sighing zephyr. At times the parapet was so low

---

9. *German 77mm field gun – you heard the whizz of shell before the bang of gun.*

that we had to advance in a crouching attitude. After 20 minutes of this zigzagging we found ourselves in the second or support trench which was filled with troops.

Here the rattle of musketry and machine guns was tremendous, the whole scene was made weird by the star shells from the German lines. We were now rather to the right of the firing and in a trench which was in progress of being built and so shallow that one had to fairly grovel to keep below the parapet.

Here we found the officer wounded through the lungs, it was well dusk and quite impossible to evacuate him by the trenches. We simply had to leave the trench and start away over the open. The slow progress caused by bearing a man on a stretcher and the stray bullets which passed us made one feel rather uncomfortable.

I was considerably relieved when we eventually reached the farm where we gave the poor officer some hot soup through a catheter. I arrived home about 11:45pm.

Thursday 15th.

The officer died at 9:45am and some of his brother officers were just in time to see him before he lost consciousness.

Today is the French President's birthday and the people celebrated by having a holiday, the Huns by throwing nearly 200 shells into the town. Comparatively little damage was done but the people are very scared and moving out in great numbers.

Friday 16th.

Not much doing today, we hear that we shall be moved away from here very soon. It is a pity as we are now very comfortable and have bought a wooden tub as a bath, cold. I also made an excellent tea table today out of a box and some shelves from the bedroom on the top floor of the house.

The clearing hospital officers invited Jack and I down to dinner this evening and two of them took us down in their car, a Vauxhall.

We went down to Baillent at about 40 miles per hour, then on to their billet, a jolly farm near where we were ourselves billeted a month ago. We had a most excellent dinner with raspberries and cream etc. Jack afterwards played poker for low stakes and I talked to one of the officers.

Saturday 17th.

The Germans successfully shelled the church at Neuve-Église until it took fire and burnt with tremendous flames which were fanned by a strong wind.

The Colonel was in a mighty frenzy today and found fault with everyone and anything, which is usual with him on these occasions. He kept giving orders then counter-ceding them a minute afterwards, accused one of all sorts of minor omissions in one's work and wouldn't wait for an explanation – an irresponsible little man who never compliments anyone or encourages anyone, but is always trying to find something wrong.

Very wet this afternoon, Jack went up to the trenches this evening and the machine gun at Headquarters farm played down the road while he was in the farm, but he got away safely.

Sunday 18th.

I had a real 'spring clean' of our room with Pte Branch. I helped him to beat the carpets in the garden until we nearly choked with dust and I had to go and buy wine as an antidote. Had a glorious bask in the garden this afternoon.

Jack and I usually take out our stretchers which make the most comfortable couches with a pillow at one end. After tea we went to Le Corney for tennis and found three or four other officers there and had some good games. We have great fun with our 'French' and their 'English'.

This evening I had an excellent hot bath thanks to our boiler and the wooden tub that I bought. It takes about two hours to heat up thoroughly and there is ample water for four people.

I have been up to the trenches this evening at Gunners farm. How quirky, thank goodness things are very quiet. Jack has gone to hospital for wounded.

Monday 19th.

Went with Jack in the afternoon to Le Corney and had some good sets with the girls.

Tuesday 20th.

Our batteries around Gunners farm turned their attention to a chimney tower in the enemy's zone. The Huns replied later by plumping 31 shells into and around the farm. Two men had slight head wounds

21

because of this bombardment, one calf was killed and the old lady in the farm died of shock.

Wednesday 21st.

This has been an interesting day. The MO (*medical officer*) of the Suffolks stationed Despear farm (*Despierre*) above Gunners farm was reported ill and I was sent to take his place.

I therefore packed my valise and went up in the motor ambulance. I walked up by the communication trench to Despear farm where I found the MO. He was better and would not hear of leaving, but he volunteered to show me round the trenches, and we set off forthright.

After a good deal of walking we found ourselves in the first line of trenches and at one point we were only 30 yards from the opposing trenches. At 120 yards from the enemy's trenches I looked through a periscope, to which was attached a powerful field binocular and I had the best view through them.

With the aid of these one could see the minutest detail of the opposing lines and I was only disappointed in not observing any of the bad men. I saw our men preparing hand grenades also.

I was disappointed in not being able to take the place of the MO as I would far rather fill such a post than remain in this field ambulance where one is practically useless.

Thursday 22nd.

Gunners farm has now been taken over by the 37th Field Ambulance and so we have to evacuate the wounded mainly from Houplines and Headquarters farm.

We invited three officers to dinner from the Baillent convoy and two from the 38th Field Ambulance. We had quite a good dinner and afterwards played bridge at one table while six of us played poker at the other. The stakes were mild at first but towards the end we had 'ace pots' and things began to move a bit. I won 21 francs and Jack lost 20.

Friday 23rd.

I took the field ambulance for a route march and Jack took out the transport. Jack and I also walked out in the afternoon and afterwards played tennis at Le Corney. They also took us up onto the top of the brasserie from where we had a magnificent view of the countryside.

"There is only one temptation in the world that is worthwhile resisting, which is – spring onions." (Tatler)

Saturday 24th.

Received orders this morning to go and take the place of the MO Lieutenant Logan of the Royal West Kent Regiment temporarily. So, I packed my valise again and went up to Gunners farm but found the regiment had gone down to Oosthove farm for the week, so down I went there.

Lieutenant Logan, being an expert on gas poisoning, had been ordered to headquarters at St Omer. I found the farm had been shelled that morning though only two slight casualties were reported. The lieutenant colonel and officers are very nice. I wish it could develop into a permanent job.

We all expected the shelling to be repeated in the evening and when just after dinner a tremendous bang came outside we all stampeded for shelter. We soon found it was only our 4.7-inch battery opening fire and great amusement resulted.

Sunday 25th.

I saw my sick at 9am and there was practically nothing more to be done.

The flies are in millions in the house, the walls almost black in places. The usual manure water which is present in every French courtyard and this farm is no doubt responsible for these pests. I have now had paraffin sprinkled over all this stagnant water and tried formalin (*formaldehyde*) in the rooms.

Wrote to Nellie[10] this afternoon.

Monday 26th.

Oosthove farm consists of the usual crowd of outhouses, barns etc and on to this is built a large house of three storey's high.

The colonel and some of the senior officers occupied this building. I had my bedroom there. Most of the officers however prefer to sleep in dugouts owing to the possibility of shelling. I however and one or two others thought it better to risk the shells and sleep comfortably in a bedroom.

---

10. Nellie (sister) 1873-1957. Educated Wiesbaden. Married Reverend John Arthur Legh, vicar of Rydal. (The Fothergills. A first history)

Logan turned up from St Omer. They seemed anxious for him to join a committee or board which is going into the question of 'Gas'. In the event of him leaving I hope to be able to take his place as MO to the 6th Royal West Kent Regiment.

So, I returned home about lunchtime to find our CO Colonel Dunn was gone!! Great consternation! I think everyone is considerably relieved to be rid of this dear old hen, always fussing and never satisfied with anyone.

Major Turner has taken his place; he is young and good-looking with an intellectual face. I feel almost sorry to have started to pull strings to get the regimental appointment.

Tuesday 27th.

A time may come when with the advent of an advance the field ambulance may be able to work on the lines upon which it was trained. As it is with trench warfare dominating everything the field ambulance has practically nothing to do, it justifies its existence by meddling quite unnecessarily with cases sent down from the RAP, often delaying their evacuation to the clearing hospitals and so lessening the chances of the wounded.

Frequently, cases sent down here by the motor ambulances in the afternoon are kept until the following morning, whereas as a routine the motor convoy from Baillent arrives. Such cases might just as well have continued the journey from trenches straight to Baillent instead of being delayed by coming here. Speed is everything. Why should the field ambulance be allowed to act as a blockhouse on the way? Major Turner has made me sanitary officer for the camp, which if it doesn't mean much at least gives one an opportunity of escaping from the orderly room in the morning. A great relief.

Wednesday 28th.

Yesterday evening I took a stroll by myself along the banks of the River Lys. It was getting dusk and suddenly hearing a peculiar little noise in the grass I stopped and out ran two little animals toward me. At first I thought they were hedgehogs and then guinea pigs but then the mother jumped onto the road and seeing me, hesitated for a moment then disappeared into the undergrowth. She looked about the size of a rabbit.

I picked up one of the young ones and found it was covered in beautiful soft brown hair. It was quite fierce. On putting it on the ground it made for my feet or appeared to do so by uttering small 'barks'. The other youngster was particularly fierce. I felt the prick of its teeth in my finger when I tried to pick it up. I think they were young stoats. It was a pleasant episode.

Major Turner is a great improvement on old Colonel Dunn, there is no red tape about him like there was with the old hen. I really feel almost sorry that I have put in for the regimental work. But when all is said and done there is no work at present for 36th Field Ambulance, while there is always something to do in a regiment and one is there, right in it. I hope I may get this job.

George Gibson called here yesterday; he is a Captain RAMC Canadians at Ploegsteert. Told us a lot of interesting things about the earlier parts of the war around Ypres.

William[11] has I think sailed today for France.

Thursday 29th.

Went up to Houplines this morning. It was shelled rather badly at 8am. One shell burst on the top of Doctor Thompson's dressing station and the nose of the projectile came through the ceiling onto his floor. He was in bed at the time ill. The MO who was taking his place took me up to the firing trench and I had an excellent view of the German trenches.

Things were hot there last night. The Huns treated us to two goes of 'sausages'. They are a kind of aerial torpedo full of high explosive. We replied by using a 60-pound mortar with great effect.

Some of our trenches come down to the river and the officers bathe regularly every day.

I have made myself a mosquito net out of some muslin and find it most effective, but it is hard work getting under it. Tennis this afternoon at Le Corney, great fun, taught them some English slang viz 'hot stuff'. They were delighted.

---

11. *William Hannay Fothergill (brother), 1887-1955. Trooper 961, A-squadron. 1st King Edwards' Horse (KEH) attached to the 12th Division. Returned from Argentina. Enlisted 1914. Discharged 3 March 1919. Emigrated Canada 20 August 1926.*

Friday 30th.

Jack went to Boulogne for the day, Taylor taking him in his car. Delightful day. I am orderly officer and have a lot of casualties and sick cases, also teeth for extraction but thank goodness Sergeant Martin is a dentist and so he attends to them.

Quiet journeys to trenches, no shells. I forgot to say that a German aeroplane passed over Armentieres yesterday and threw three bombs. Jack and I were on our way to the mess for breakfast, I heard the thing come whistling down but although it didn't sound like a shell I never thought of a bomb until I saw people gazing up. Terrific explosion but no harm done.

Extraordinary the number of shells that burst and never kill anybody – seems almost providential.

Saturday 31st.

A quiet day. Lovely letter from Angy[12] telling me of quiet picnics with John and Charlotte Fletcher among scenery I know so well near Barrule.

How wonderful to think that while all this horrible fighting is going on around me, the little stream is still chattering merrily through the meadows at Grenaby, the delightful green pools and moss-covered stones, beautiful banks crimson with bell heather, so fragrant with honeysuckle that overhangs the stream.

I see it all, I am there now, wandering on the bank with my uncle looking for the 'lesser skullcap' and other flowers. What peace and happiness – action and reaction, pleasure and pain. Undoubtedly, we must suffer one to appreciate the other.

AUGUST 1915

Sunday 1st.

We had a shrapnel shell over our garden yesterday. I was reading in the garden and heard the shell coming, so bolted toward the end of the greenhouse. It burst just over the factory and the bullets peppered our garden but did not find me. I picked up three bullets in our courtyard the size of marbles made of lead. Took the church parade. Major Turner paid

---

12. *Agnes (sister). 1866-1956. Married Harry Percival Hannay of Bagnio House, Isle of Man. Brother of Ada Joan Hannay, Regie's mother. (The Fothergills. A first history)*

us a visit last night, Jack brought him back from the hospital at 11:15pm after doing a Trephine[13]. He sat and talked for over half an hour. He is a very good sort.

Tuesday 3rd.

I have been detailed to examine all stagnant water in our zone of work with the object of finding larvae anopheles. A few cases of malaria[14] have occurred in the British lines. I have been excused from all duty and must hand in my report by Thursday.

The weather is quite unsuitable as it is blowing hard and raining. I took our servant Branch this morning in the car to Houplines and examined water around the officers' mess. Then the colonel gave me a servant to guide us and we proceeded up the trenches to two farms which had moats of stagnant water around them.

One of these farms was in the firing trench and while I was peering into the weedy water for the larvae the German bullets were hitting the sandbags like pistol shots. I thought: 'how inconsiderate'! To be pursuing natural history in the firing line.

Wednesday 4th.

This is the anniversary of the declaration of war on Germany. We expect a dose of hate in the shape of a copious shelling of town. All is however quiet so far, 10am. At 9pm we had no hate.

Major Turner asked me to take him up to see Houplines trench farm which has stagnant water. We went up by car and Jack came too, trenches horribly slippery.

Jack had a shot with a rifle, selecting a farmhouse in the German lines in the absence of a Bosch as a target. The major had tea in our garden. He is a real good sort! What a change after that miserable old colonel!

Thursday 5th.

---

13. Trephine: surgical instrument, cylindrical saw for removing disc of bone, especially for skull.

14. On the Western Front, malaria could theoretically have been present seasonally in the low-lying land. There were outbreaks of malaria in England, France, Belgium, Holland and Germany. There were no epidemics on the Western Front. British soldiers returning from malaria areas introduced the disease to southern England and 500 or so cases were recorded in the civilian population. (The Western Front Association)

Although apparently cheerful and very healthy I loathe my war-like surroundings and long for peace and a return home. If left to myself for any length of time in the quiet garden I find myself retrospecting at once. I throw myself into beautiful Lakeland scenery and so intense is my imagination that I am actually there, wandering about and revelling in the sound of mountain streams and the smell of bracken and sweet-scented ferns.

Jack was orderly today, so I went down to Le Corney and had a rather nasty experience. One of our aeroplanes was circling above when the Germans fired a shrapnel at it. I never thought of any danger until suddenly I heard a shrill whizzing sound and at once realised that the nose of the shell was coming down!

A horrible second or two passed but thank God the thing struck the tennis court about six feet from the pretty Miss L C T. They were all very plucky and wanted to go on, but I thought we had better stop until the aeroplane moved away. How terrible if it had struck one of them!

Two captains[15] died in our hospital today, both hit through the head by snipers. God! What a lot of terrible wounds! What a hopeless state of affairs.

Friday 6th.

A shell burst in the headquarters of a regiment in the town today and did much damage. Among them were two brothers[16]. They were brought to the hospital on stretchers. The one who was more severely injured entreated his brother to look after his wife and children. He died two hours later.

And now this afternoon the remaining brother has followed him. What terrible suffering there must be at home!!

Saturday 7th.

The prospects of continuing to live amicably with Jack are not very bright. The novelty of renewing our acquaintance after a break of eight years has gradually worn off and we must at last rely on intellect and an

---

15. *Captain. Fraser, Hugh Crawford. Age 38. Royal Scots Fusiliers. Le Touret Military Cemetery. Captain. Mills, Teulon Lewis. Age 23. Middlesex Regiment. Cite Bonjean military cemetery.*

16. *1379. Pte Cardy. R. Royal Fusiliers. Cite Bonjean military cemetery, Armentieres. 49. Corp Cardy. M. Age 26. Royal Fusiliers. Cite Bonjean military cemetery, Armentieres.*

interchange of sympathies to keep us together. I fear we have very little in common now, I have never touched on topics of religion with him, nor have I opened up theosophical subjects.

Yesterday however some question of the deeper truth was allowed to. He showed such antipathy to the idea of anyone wishing to question the why and wherefore of life and showed such complete satisfaction in merely desiring to live and not think that I felt almost amazed.

He has really no true feelings of sympathy towards me. He never takes the smallest interest in the embarrassed state of my practice. Never enquires after it, never asks after any of my relations, nearly all of whom he knows, including John *(brother)* something of whose case he knows.

He is entirely wrapped up in himself and I have often thought that he merely uses us for his pleasure. I have always pandered to his wants and done nearly all the running about in connection with our house life. So here we are today not on speaking terms after last night when he railed on me in a most unfriendly way over some trivial misunderstanding with our carpets.

Sunday 8th.

I now hear William is somewhere and I must try and seek him out as he has been attached to our division and cannot be far away.

"Young clothes on an elderly woman are like curry sauce on an elderly egg, they only draw attention to an obvious fact." (Tatler).

Tuesday 10th.

We are more 'friends' but it is all very pathetic. During the nine years of absence from one civilian society Jack has continued to live the same life. He has been merrily seeking pleasure from year to year using his professional position mainly as a means of getting from one set of experiences to another. And I, well God knows, I have nothing to boast of. But still for the last seven years I have at least thought more deeply and thanks to theosophy have placed some ideals, and one has struggled feebly enough towards them. I cannot resume the old loose life of the University days.

Poor old Jack makes no effort and never thinks about religion and his reaction to it, he is content to drift on pleasantly. He complains that I am changed, whereas my silent complaint is that he has not changed. Whether we find ourselves with a sufficiency of things in common to carry us through remains to be seen, I hope we shall.

Wednesday 11th.

Set out at 1:45pm on horseback to find William. I took my large-scale map and with its help had no difficulty in locating Le Crèche where KEH were said to be. I had some trouble in finding the troop but eventually did so.

William was on main guard but an officer had him relieved and so we got away together. He was looking very fit and has been detailed off for machine gun tuition. While with him we witnessed an exchange of shots between a Bosch and one of our aeroplanes. No damage done.

I had tea with his CO Major Russell[17] whom I liked very well, although he told me he was unpopular among the men. However, I talked about William and he said there ought to be no difficulty about his getting a commission later.

Had a nice ride back by the canal. My frightfully fresh horse nearly pulled my arms out going home. Ambulance concert in the evening. Local talent is quite strong, plenty of good fun.

Thursday 12th.

Orderly officer today, bad head case and gunshot wound of thigh. Good news from Dardanelles, have landed troops to the north of Gallipoli!

Two shells just screamed over to the right. The first didn't burst, the second did and must have been near our hospital. I will go and see. Jack and Major went to Le Corney having had tea here in the garden.

Friday 13th.

Strong rumours running that our division goes back to St Omer for a rest. We have now been in the trenches for nearly three months, they say we will get leave.

I am now appointed permanent sanitary officer and am not sorry as it gives one something to do. The RAMC work is a most pathetic farce. To begin with, the whole division could be adequately looked after by two field ambulances. Again, the number of medical men required has been

---

17. *Major George Gray Russell. Awarded DSO for conspicuous gallantry and devotion to duty when in command of two squadrons attached to an infantry brigade during an advance. He frequently moved about in the foremost line directing reconnaissance work under heavy machine-gun fire, when the right flank of the brigade was dangerously exposed he conducted a valuable reconnaissance with great skill and resource and cleared up the situation. Mentioned in despatches three times. (King Edward's Horse – www.kingedwardshorse.net)*

absolutely over estimated – half the work that falls to one lot as officers could be done just as efficiently by non-combatant NCOs (*Non-Commissioned Officer*) or officer.

At first I felt a perfect fraud when I realised that I was getting £1.4.0 daily and doing practically nothing for it, but now my conscience sleeps and I accept it without bothering. And after all, what can one do?

What I have done is to ask the ADMS personally to give me the first vacant MO that goes begging. As MO to a regiment one has plenty to do, often far too much and the risk is proportionately greater.

Saturday 14th.

As anaesthetist for the week I gave chloroform this morning for the Major in an abdominal case. We also gave intravenous saline.

Our pears are beginning to drop from the trees in the garden and we are taking advantage of them. They are as hard as bricks but will ripen in a drawer I dare say.

Sunday 15th.

Jack being orderly I walked out towards Houplines along the left bank of the canal and watched the Bosch shelling some buildings which were separated from me by some fields. I discovered a jolly walk through pleasant fields of corn.

Just returned from Headquarters farm. Very uneventful journey of late, no shells, no nothing. Two splendid cakes from Angy.

"There have been wars begun for transient objects – but this war is none of these. In this war mighty principles are battling for the mastery.

Ideals are locked in deadly combat. The friction of the march of our present civilisation upwards or downwards depends on the issue of the struggle.

Two ideals of world-empire are balanced on the scales of the future. That is what raises this war above all the others known in the brief history of the west, it is the latest of the pivots on which, in successive ages, the immediate future of the world has turned.

Of the two possible world-empires, that of Great Britain, that of Germany, one is already far advanced in the making and shows its quality with Dominions and Colonies, with India at its side.

The other is but an embryo but can be judged by its theories. "The" chosen people of the German "God" stink in the nostrils of troops.

This embryo of empire of the bottomless pit, conceived of hatred and shaped in the womb of ambition, must never come to the birth. It is the antithesis of all that is noble, compassionate, humane."

(Annie Besant, Theosophist)

Tuesday 17th.

Feel low and depressed today. For one thing I had a rotten night at the hospital. I was disturbed four times and had to get up and dress each time to attend to the injuries of the wounded. A bad abdominal case with bowels hanging out and both hands shot through, he died this morning but did not suffer as I gave plenty of morphine.[18] Then a head case, and one or two others less severe.

Busied myself among the incinerators this morning and visited with the Major the vaults of the neighbouring brasserie and decided that in the event of a bombardment of the town the field ambulance should retire there with all speed. There is a rumour of a probable bombardment of the town.

Very cold just now and not a bit like summer. The garden is still very green. It is curious how the spurge is the outstanding weed in the garden, it makes the most beautiful green carpets of the one-time flower beds.

Walked with Jack to the cemetery which is a wonderful place and the sham wreath reigns supreme, quite six feet in circumference. There were some quiet nooks and shady bushes and trees. My God! How fed up everyone is with the war!!

Wednesday 18th.

Made a country walk this afternoon with Jack towards Gris Pot through corn fields, most of them are now cut and the grain stacked. Small boys and old men working in the fields.

A shell passed us toward some of our concealed batteries, so we sheared off home. We saw one or two shells thrown into Houplines and one of them started a fire.

Am now alone and it is 9:15pm and have just finished reading an article by Leadbeater on "Love" (*Charles Webster Leadbeater, Theosophical Society*) and as I read I heard some terrible explosions towards the other end of town caused by an aeroplane throwing down bombs. How inconsiderate!

---

18. *17376 L.Cpl. G DE Beger. Age 30. 5th Bn Northamptonshire Regt. Cite Bonjean military cemetery Armentieres.*

For some reason my mind keeps recalling the eclipse *(Clypse)* reservoir in the Isle of Man. I am there with my dear old uncle. He is fishing one side and I the other of the lake. Such peace reigns, the lovely long grass and the heather in full bloom and the little stream trickling into the upper end of the reservoir. What a picture! Then the thought that he is gone, a terrible feeling of sadness.

Thursday 19th.

Major Turner, Jack and I went to Le Corney for tennis this afternoon after tea in the garden. Had some good men's fours, went back for dinner and there was news.

Jack has been ordered to join as MO to the 2nd Suffolk Regiment 3rd Division! And I am going to the 7th East Surrey Regiment!* had been previously warned about my appointment, the thing was new and unexpected to Jack.

---

*Note

 7th battalion, the East Surrey Regiment was formed at Kingston-upon-Thames, August 1914 part of Kitchener's Army, joining 37th Brigade in 12th Eastern Division. Training was carried out in Purfleet and over wintered in billets at Sandgate. In February 1915 moved to Albuhera barracks in Aldershot for final training. Entered France, 2 June, landing Boulogne. By 6 June it was based in the Meteren-Steenwerck area with headquarters based at Nieppe. Had further training with 48th South Midland Division taking over a section of the front line at Ploegsteert Wood on 23 June.

In action in the Battle of Loos from 30 September taking over a section from Gun trench to Hulluch quarries under heavy artillery fire. On 8 October repelled a heavy German infantry attack and on 13th took

part in the action at Hohenzollern Redoubt taking the Gun trench and south western face of Hulluch quarries.

During the period at Loos, 117 officers and 3,237 men from the 12th Division were dead, wounded or missing. Around 21 October they moved to Fouquieres-les-Bethune for brief rest, returning to the front at Hohenzollern Redoubt until 15 November going into reserve at Lillers. On 9 December the Royal Fusiliers helped in the round up

---

Friday 20th. Le Bizet.

(francs 180 after leaving field ambulance)

Poor old Jack was very depressed at the thought of going to join as MO, we were also very sorry to leave each other as we had hoped to see the war through together. He left at 2:30pm for Bailent and then probably to Ypres. I had not far to go as my regiment was down from the trenches and in billets close to hand. So, I finished my packing and said goodbye to the garden, which had afforded us so many sunny hours of repose and a month of quiet afternoon teas.

I went to report myself at the regiment headquarters but finding Colonel Baldwin out went on to the MO, Lieutenant Rogers whose billet was nearby. I reported to the CO later and found him very pleasant. Our mess at 7:30pm was rather an eye opener! Present was the colonel, Major Wilson, Captain Nicholls (adjutant), Lieutenant Gibson and the interpreter lieutenant. They were all very nice and made me thoroughly at home.

After our frugal fare in the ambulance it came as rather a shock to sit down to a six-course meal – soup, d'oeuvres, joint and vegetables, sweet, savoury, fruit, beer, white wine, and port. Personally, I would much prefer the more frugal fare. It will be rather amusing to see the mess subscriptions. I wonder how they will compare with our field ambulance weekly sub of ten francs with even then too much money accumulating.

Saturday 21st. Surrey farm.

Had news of Jack. He had difficulty in finding his unit at Ypres and I hear his car had to shelter for two hours because of shells, I fear he is going into a warm quarter.

Spent most of my day becoming acquainted with my medical equipment, inspecting billets, and gathering together what belongings I intend to take up to the trenches. At 8am I waylaid our field ambulance with

34

my equipment and accompanied by the colonel and major we were soon up at Surrey farm. I then walked up to my dressing station further up the trenches. It is a battered house, or rather a battered group of small houses, at Le Touquet station. But with the use of sandbags we have made one or two rooms secure against bullets and there is a cellar to get into in case of a bombardment.

I have a most excellent servant or orderly full of enterprise and a perfect maniac for making me comfortable. He rigged me up with a most humorous 'bed' made by fixing wire netting over a wooden frame. He brought me a tub of splendid hot water this morning. Fancy, a hot bath every morning in the trenches!!

Sunday 22nd.

Had quite a good night despite rifle shots which rang out incessantly, while the Bosch bullets broke against the sandbags like pistol shots.

Feel ill owing to the greengage and grapes of yesterday, pains inside etc and sinking feeling. Visited D-coy *(D Company)* trenches with Corporal Poulton. Trenches are most excellent and well foot boarded except in a few places where one appreciated what it must have been like before trench construction was perfected. (Ankle deep in mud after only night's rain).

Went to bed in the afternoon but received a message to go to Lys farm at the extreme right of our trenches, so I got up feeling rotten. Found man doubled with colic and had to stretcher him back along trenches full of traverses, it necessitated lifting stretcher. I carried the stretcher for a time.

Retired early to bed with aspirin and high temperature and good sweat, woke at 1am feeling quite well. Wonderful thing, aspirin! Slept well and had no casualties.

Monday 23rd.

Most interesting morning in B-coy trenches. At Suicide corner trenches are a network of huge sandbag barricades and the Bosch trenches are only 30 feet away.

Here I heard our men talking to the Huns. Looking through a periscope, I saw seven or eight of them with their heads and shoulders above the parapet laughing. They had round blue cloth caps and some had

khaki coloured ditto. They shouted in English we will send you a note
– and sure enough the report of a rifle grenade rang out and into our
trench dropped a note.

As I was the only officer present they brought it to me and I read
in English: "To the opposition, we will send you some newspapers by
non-explosive rifle grenade, is peace in sight? Please answer." There was
also an opportunity for our men to show themselves above the trenches
with the promise that they (the Germans) would not shoot. But nobody
cared to risk the invitation.

Passages from 7th Battalion East Surrey Regiments war diaries.

Friday 20th.

*Armentieres full of troops, all kinds of regiments digging extra lines
behind the firing lines including*

Lifeguards and 10th Hussars.

Saturday 21st.

*We relieved the Queens in the trenches. A draft of 30 arrived from
the base.*

Sunday 22nd.

Enemy very quiet, a few shells sent at Lys farm did no damage.

Monday 23rd.

*Enemy very quiet and is inclined to be very talkative. They sent over
the following message attached to an old harmless rifle grenade: "To
the opposition, we have sent by rifle grenade newspapers over, when
you get it stick up a white flag and we don't shoot, wait a minute
and newspaper comes by non-explosive rifle grenade, is peace in sight,
please answer."*

*The papers came but fell outside of the parapet, we have not yet been
able to retrieve them as they have laid a machine gun on them. Our
men would all like to talk to them, but we must be very strict on that
point and insist on a bullet being the only means of conversation. The
day passed quietly, no casualties, but our snipers got five hits.*

Tuesday 24th. Le Touquet.

Felt quite well again, only one trivial casualty today, a graze of a finger by bullet. The lad said he was 19 but I laughed, and he confessed to being 17 and looked 16. Nice boy and so proud of his wound which, thank God, was a mere scratch.

Did a round through trenches; they were 700 yards from the Bosch line. Wrote letters outside in the afternoon but felt uncomfortable as our shells and those of the Hun were coming over my house, safe but very disconcerting. Our headquarters mess which is further down the trenches consists Colonel Baldwin, Captain Nicholls, Lieutenant Gibson and Major Wilson, quite nice men all of them.

My orderly is a wonderful fellow and looks after me so well. He keeps finding from goodness knows where all sorts of things. Yesterday he produced a gaudy tablecloth and today two handsome candlesticks. We shall soon be quite furnished until the first shell bursts through the flimsy roof.

How extraordinary to think that this day twelve months ago I was at my uncle's bedside in Edinburgh as he lay dying. How it all comes back. I fear poor Angy will be feeling it at Grasmere.

Wednesday 25th.

This is the anniversary of uncle's death. I remember so vividly that last night when he gradually sank away. "I do so wish to die," he said. Then Angy said: "Do you know me?" and he answered: "I should know you in a thousand years." Then as the sun rose crimson above the houses he passed away quickly and left his painful body behind. What a relief it was for all three of us.

Things are quieter than ever. The general told us today that two of our men crawled right into the Hun's trenches and found it empty, as far as they could see! Went into a dugout and came away with a helmet. I believe that they have practically no men except a few on sentry in the front trenches and that they are probably in trenches much further behind.

Perhaps one day the British army may become sufficiently enterprising to make a general address and then they may be surprised when the true state of affairs is disclosed behind these much-dreaded trenches!

Have just been round our extreme right trenches, which terminate at the canal. Had tea with Lieutenant Gibson at Lys farm.

Thursday 26th.

At 3:45 this afternoon the artillery officer who works the howitzer from the observation post came in for something for a headache and he said we were going to open fire at 4pm on a certain position. At 4pm we fairly strafed them with our heavy guns.

In the meantime, I went down to the mess for tea and then the Huns bombarded our lines with trench mortars, sausages, whizz bangs and shells. The colonel told me not to go back to the dressing station until it was over. People were saying that my dressing station was in the middle of it all. As a matter of fact, not a single shell fell on it but only in the field in front of it and there wasn't a single casualty amongst our men. Most extraordinary.

Just had a short note from Jack, he doesn't say much but seems to suggest that things will get warm for him when he returns to the trenches. (His regiment is 'down' at present.) This is our last day 'up', Major Turner came up this morning and I took him round the trenches. He proposes tennis tomorrow afternoon.

Friday 27th.

A most delightful day with glorious sunshine and a cloudless sky. We have had a very nice week in trenches, which have been getting gradually drier and harder. We only had three casualties during the week, which was wonderful, in addition to these I had four or five casualties from working parties among my trenches belonging to the Rifles.

Had an interesting talk with the forward observation officer of an 18-pounder battery in our trenches. He was telling me about the show yesterday, he said he had to allow 400 yards for the sun that afternoon, cordite explodes more frequently in hot sun. Our guns that afternoon got nine direct hits on the Hun's machine gun house which was the objective. The Queens took over our trenches tonight. I have come back by the motor ambulance.

Saturday 28th.

Extraordinary and delightful to sleep in a nice clean soft bed, my billet is quite comfortable and the dressing station is very handy two doors away. Took our interpreter with me this morning to get my field boots stretched, he had two hits of shell through his cap yesterday and was rather upset.

This afternoon I went with Captain Felan; the man who had taken Jack's place in the field ambulance to Le Corney, we had some good games and a little music afterwards. Miss C played Largo on the cello; she is a dear girl.

Paid my first messing bill, messing 14 francs, wine five francs. This doesn't represent the true total because there was some money in hand which went towards paying for the outstanding bills. An airplane bomb fell audibly in the vicinity as we played tennis today, the machine was too high up to be seen.

Sunday 29th.

Had a busy morning seeing my sick and going on sanitary round of latrines and superintending the building of an incinerator which must destroy all the rubbish.

Walked out to the cemetery this afternoon and read for a time sitting on a seat well hidden by shrubs. A wonderful place is this cemetery; with masses of sham wreaths some of them six feet high. It contains several little shrines. In fact, every important family has its vault with a shrine built on the top. Some of these shrines were very simple and beautiful, many of them costing thousands of pounds.

Monday 30th.

I was awakened at 2am this morning by the steady beat of men marching past and as they marched they sang in harmony with this simple and plaintive air. It sounded very solemn and somehow pathetic in the dead of night, rising and falling as it did through the perfect stillness of the night except for dismal rifle fire in the distance. It seemed to voice the sadness which must surround so many homes just now among the poor of Europe.

I wonder what sort of music would faithfully interpret the spirit of this frightful war. I think that on the side of the Allies, sad rather than crashing majestic music would interpret it since there is no real bitterness or at any rate hatred felt by us towards the Germans. And what music must now interpret their feelings?

This morning the colonel, myself, and three or four officers at the invitation of Major Turner drove down by ambulance to Baillue to see an exhibition of sanitary things. It was not very wonderful.

At 4pm I went to Le Corney and was joined by Major Turner and Fernell. There was also a French colonel and a major in such nice uniforms.

We had hardly started playing when a huge shell came along and fell on some disused land short of the tennis court. A minute or two later, with a regular roar we heard another one I thought right on to us and I wasn't far wrong as it actually fell on the roof of Le Corney brasserie whose walls rise up at the side of the court.

Luckily it never burst and it simply by its own weight crashed through the roof and then through a reinforced concrete floor and was lying in large fragments in the basement. The yellow lyddite which surrounded the fuse stained everything around with its yellow colour and filled the rooms with irritating vapour.

In the evening I dined with Forgan at the Officers Convalescent Home – an excellent dinner with port and a plentiful supply of fruit.

Tuesday 31st. Le Touquet-Le Bizet.

Rather busy morning with the sick, a lot of impetigo and septic blisters, a peculiar crop. Curious how some of these men scratch themselves for weeks until they bleed and come to you for treatment and you are first to discover them.

Passages from 7th Battalion East Surrey Regiments war diaries

Tuesday 24th.

At night the Germans became very talkative, they put up dummies and their hands and even heads, when our people fired on them they said: 'Are you Queens? Don't fire. East Surreys, you shoot too well.' This is probably because our snipers have been doing rather well since we have been in these trenches having accounted for 55 Germans and we have only had nine men sniped up to date.

The success of our snipers is mainly due to Major Wilson, who being a big game shot treats the matter scientifically and only allows the snipers to shoot when they are practically certain of the hit. Shooting

---

40

> *at periscopes etc is absolutely forbidden so none of our sniping positions are yet known to the enemy. At four o'clock our howitzers opened fire at a bit of the enemy's parapet, they fired about 10 shots with considerable success.*
>
> ### Friday 27th.
>
> *We were successfully relieved by the Queens at night, the relief taking one hour and 55 minutes, again a record. The snipers got 21 hits during the week which is the best up to date considering the scarcity of targets.*
>
> *Casualties for period: Officers killed, one; wounded two. Other ranks killed, 12, wounded, 60. Sickness, 43.*

SEPTEMBER 1915

Wednesday 1st. Le Bizet.

Found a louse on my vest this morning! Horrible discovery. Tried to ride out to see William but rain came on and prevented me. However, I had a little ride around on my horse and found him exceedingly comfortable, a great relief after my pony with the ambulance.

This evening we had a concert which was very good, some of the turns were exceedingly clever and one of the soldiers had a magnificent voice.

Very cold, wet and miserable. The weather throughout July and August has been very bad as a whole, it has been so cloudy, sunshine has been very scarce. I expected it would be very hot out here during the summer but as a matter of fact it has been much colder than one would expect, resembling a typical summer in the north of England.

Thursday 2nd.

A miserable day again, cold, rainy, and gloomy but it was fine in the morning and I bought a whole lot of absurd pastries and things to take out to William. It rained so badly about 3:30pm that I gave it up.

At 2:30pm the battalion was inspected by General Plumer the CO of the 2nd Army, he looked like an old German and I was not impressed.

Went up to the trenches at 8pm, luckily got a ride up in the ambulance, pitch dark and raining in torrents. Made my way up to the dressing station through trenches which are slippery, loathsome with mud. However,

I noticed that our rifle fire and that of the enemy is quite extinguished by rain, no firing means no casualties. A very satisfactory state of affairs as one does not rejoice to leave one's bed when it is night and raining hard.

How different from civil practice when a loathsome night seems always to be the signal for people to get ill or be confused. We hear that splendid news from the Dardanelles is anticipated as the Turks are getting short of ammunition. Let us hope it is true.

Friday 3rd. Le Touquet.

Wretched day again and how I pity the poor chaps in the trenches! How I dread the prospect of winter spent under these and perhaps worse conditions! Rained practically all day long, rifle and artillery fire silenced.

I am gradually furnishing my dressing station from the uninhabited cottages around, today we brought in a coke stove which is most in vogue in this part of France. Unfortunately, it was rather battered and in consequence the smoke filtered into my room and I was obliged to put it out.

Bitterly cold for the time of year, found another louse[19] in my pyjamas! A dreadful great black one. Think the two blankets they borrowed for me must be the source.

Passages from 7th Battalion East Surrey Regiments war diaries.

Wednesday 1st.

The 12th Divisional concert party gave us a concert in our billet which was a great success, nearly all the artists being professionals, though soldiers serving in the division.

Thursday 2nd.

A quiet day, at 2:30pm General Plumer commanding the 2nd Army inspected the battalion lined up along the road outside our billets in Le Bizet. The line was a perfect one owing to tramlines running the whole way along. In the evening we relieved the Queens in the trenches, very wet.

Friday 3rd.

A frightfully wet day but very quiet. General Wing and General Fowler both expressed their pleasure at the appearance of the troops on parade yesterday.

---

19. *Trench fever' plagued the soldiers of WW1, It infected up to a million soldiers and was spread by body lice that were rife in the trenches.*

Saturday 4th.

A perfectly beautiful morning with glorious sun which must have cheered the poor fellows in the trenches. Went around the trenches in the morning and found them terrible with mud and most difficult to negotiate. Weather broke down again this afternoon, pouring with rain.

During night I had one or two casualties to working parties and at 3am the ceiling of my connecting room gave way and the rain began pouring in, we had to rescue the dressings etc.

Sunday 5th.

At 4:30pm, just when we had finished tea, they began to throw in shrapnel at us. We watched them bursting from orderly room.

Then the colonel and I set off to see some alteration I had in hand at the ADS and we had to crouch in the trenches while two or three went over us but burst really at a safe distance.

After visiting every house in the ADS, it being a row of houses, I found only one room which offered any prospect of keeping out rain, and this was the next house to my own room. I had therefore determined to dig a trench up its garden to bring it in communication with the main trench and the colonel approved and promised me sandbags.

Monday 6th.

Owing to an inspiration I decided to abandon the trench digging scheme and instead I got my men to knock a hole through my house and again through the next garden wall and in this way I have got a ready means of bringing my stretcher cases straight through.

As a result of rummaging in the other houses of this row I have found one or two quite nice additions to my own room. A very nice cooking stove such as they are in Belgium and north of France, a good sideboard and nice oak table.

How nice the colonel, the major and other officers whom I have met are, I am very lucky to have been landed among such gentlemanly chaps.

At 11pm I just had a sergeant of a working party wounded in the head. He ran to my dressing station with stretcher bearers and ambulance men at his heels. He was very hysterical and amusing:' Is it a 'Blighty?' he said. Blighty means England.

Tuesday 7th.

Extraordinarily peaceful here today, a glorious sun shines from a blue sky and hardly a rifle shot this morning.

I watched two spiders make love, a most loathsome affair. The female, a huge speckled monster swung on her web. Opposite her approached very tentatively her very worse half so slender and insignificant was he that you would scarcely recognise him being of the same species.

He approached his love, now advancing a step and now retreating. At last after touching one another he sprang lightly upon her; remained a second and then like a flash darted away.

Once again he approached and once again sprang on his better half, but no sooner was he there she suddenly pinned him down and swept a web around him like a winding sheet, then devoured him. I thought the whole affair was the most cruel and unnatural scene that I had ever witnessed in the insect world.

Wednesday 8th.

Hurrah! We leave the trenches this evening, "what a beautiful day." Anderson, the Queens' MO, came up at teatime to see my improvements and I hope he will carry on with them during the week. Walked back down from the trenches. I arrived at my billet about 9:30pm.

Thursday 9th. Le Bizet, Billet.

There is a general feeling that this place will soon be bombarded by the enemy. The civilians are gradually clearing out. This afternoon I borrowed a bike (my only pair of boots were being mended so I couldn't ride) and rode out to William's camp but found he was at Nieppe, so rode on to the MMP *(Military Mounted Police)* headquarters where he was. Found William very fit and liking his duties. He will come over to me tomorrow.

I had ordered a Thresher[20] trench coat and it arrived today. It consists an outer covering, a sort of Burberry and two inner linings, one oiled silk and another of sheepskin. It has a belt behind. It cost £7.10.0, which is of course a ridiculous price, but if it will only keep one warm and dry it will be worth its price.

20. *Thresher & Glenny outfitters, Strand, London. 'Three-in-one' Campaigning Coat combined the properties of the Greatcoat, British Warm and Raincoat.*

Friday 10th.

Busy with sick; had 30 this morning and general inspection. After lunch came back to my billet and waited for William sitting at my window in the most glorious sun.

William arrived at 4pm and after tea we went on a walk together and I showed him Frelinghien, close to our own trenches. We had some grub at 'Au Boeuf' and I walked back to Nieppe with William. He must try and get a commission. Glad to see him looking so well.

Saturday 11th.

We have now a new brick incinerator which is burning all the excrement. Went on a ride this afternoon along the canal bank but riding is no pleasure as I make use of my horse too seldom. My backside is never hard enough, so that when I do ride it is perfect agony after a few miles of trotting.

Had tea at mess and then walked to the cemetery where I spent a pleasant hour roaming about among the graves which are now so beautiful with roses and other flowers. The place is quite deserted, and it is very pleasant to sit and read there for a quiet hour or so. After dinner I strolled up to the ambulance and watched bridge for some time.

The Germans shelled with 5.9-inch shells this morning in a field close to my billet. They were trying to find a battery of guns but failed. I watched for some time the shells bursting harmlessly in the field.

Sunday 12th.

Went around to Le Corney in the afternoon and had tea with them. Two other officers were there who played rather badly which was a pity as I had brought a dozen balls, a present from Cox (*Jack*) and myself.

Dined with Major Turner at 36th Field Ambulance and enjoyed the evening very much. The major has very decided ideas as to the war and its ideals. His theories are all exceedingly optimistic. He is rather a pleasant person to listen to just now when everyone is rather depressed since the last push at the Dardanelles failed.

Monday 13th.

Awoke with rather a 'cold' this morning, feeling also somewhat irritable and I fear the sick suffered in consequence.

A German aeroplane was said to have been brought down. I heard our anti aerial gun at work this morning but didn't trouble to get out of bed to see.

It transpired that one of our aeroplanes came on the scene and because of a duel the Hun came down. The machine still under control came down near Steenwerck and a captain and sergeant[21] were in her. The story goes that on landing they attempted to repair the damage and turned their machine gun on a body of our own men who were coming up. They were shot.

I rode out in the afternoon and was just in time to see the body of the machine before it was taken away.

Regimental concert in the evening, Major Turner, Adjutant and Captain Felan came to dinner.

Tuesday 14th. Le Touquet.

Walked back to the trenches at 8:30 with the colonel, quite fine but cloudy. My 'cold' is loathsome and I feel rotten. Anderson has made one or two good improvements including a window to our private room which opens and shuts from one's bed by pulling a string.

Wednesday 15th.

Feel slightly better. Went around trenches in the morning, while there our heavies bombarded Hun's trenches with high explosive, tremendous explosions! We expected sausages back, but they didn't come.

Nice photos from Joan and letter. Walked down Lys farm with a nasty headache. Had one man been killed by our own guns, an 18-pounder fell short about a mile.

Thursday 16th.

Had a fatal head case brought in last night, not one of our men though. Had to go through his pockets and make an inventory of items and money. Very pathetic to find a photo of his wife and child, the former young and smiling and to think he was lying before you with his brains blown out while she knew it not. Such things cause the most harrowing reality to rise before one's eyes.

Yesterday one of our men was hit by our own 18-pounder shell which

---

21. *Josef Suwelack. Pilot. Oscar Teichmann. Photographer. Erquinghem-Lys churchyard extension.*

burst short a mile or more behind the trenches. This is the first of such that has come under my notice. Feel most excellently well today, cold absolutely dried up. There is talk of our going into the reserve brigade.

Friday 17th.

Pretty quiet along our own line but large trench mortars were thrown into West Kent lines causing death of signaller* who was blown to pieces in his dugout while two others were injured.

The West Kent's right joins our left wing, a very handy trench runs down at this junction leading to my dressing station. It follows that they evacuate their wounded to me in all cases occurring thereabouts. It is rather rough that I should have to do this work. It really belongs to the MO of the Kent's division.

A deserter came into the 36th Brigade lines last night and among the information imparted by him was the news that these houses, including my dressing station were to be shelled today. We have waited all day for this treat but three of these houses have excellent cellars and I have detailed off my men to the same in case of bombardment.

Leave is now stopped, Boulogne harbour temporarily closed. Very reassuring speech from Kitchener on the war in its various areas. The war costs £3,500,000 a day.

Passages from 7th Battalion East Surrey Regiments war diaries.
Wednesday 15th.

A deserter who went over to the 36th Brigade. We hear that the Saxons have been taken away and sent to Russia as they were not active enough in this post. They were relieved by Landwehr regiments which consisted of 9/10 Landsturm, very old, one battalion being commanded by a major of sixty years old.

Saturday 18th.

We bombarded the brewery heavily with practically no response from the enemy. About 4:30pm we sent over about 50 rifle grenades which at last woke the enemy up, who responded with a great many trench mortars at our trenches at Le Touquet houses. However, they did no damage, and we had no casualties. The Queens had two men killed by rifle grenades. We finished off with 28 trench mortars and said goodnight.

> *Sunday 19th.*
>
> *Very quiet all day. At night the enemy sent over one or two rifle gre-*
> *nades, one of which wounded Captain Martin in the head and arm,*
> *neither wound being serious.*

Saturday 18th.

This was a lucky day for the regiment, at 4:30pm the Huns oppo-site Barkesham farm started on us with trench mortars and rifle grenades. They threw about 50 mortars and we threw during the bombardment about twenty-eight. I watched this from my dress-ing station. I could see the dust and debris rise in our lines at each explosion. I expected many casualties but as a matter of fact the regiment didn't lose a man or have a single casualty.

The only ones who suffered were the working party of Queens' men, two of them were killed by the first rifle grenade fired. It was curious about these men; they were standing side by side and one of them had the whole of his head except the face blown off, while upon the other I could only find two quite small wounds, one on the right arm and the other over the third right rib. I consider that he died entirely from shock.

Sunday 19th.

Feel liverish today and realise that I shall find it a difficult mat-ter to keep well while in the trenches during the coming months. There is practically no exercise to be enjoyed while in the trenches except such as is afforded by walking along the lines. I am going to eat very little in the future when I'm up here. Had tea with Captain Pendrell in the trench.

Monday 20th.

Captain Martin came in at 3:45am with two small wounds from rifle grenade, he will be all right in a week or so. Evidentially the German deserter was correct when he said that the Bavarians had left, and the Prussian Regiment are now facing us. They may be only old men, but their fighting spirit is there judging by the increased amount of 'strafing' that is taking place since they arrived.

A horrible bilious headache came on in the afternoon despite having starved myself. I felt cold and shivery. I was beginning to feel better and warmer when a message came to go to Lys farm. Went by car and found seven men (five of them Queens) wounded by a shell fuse, which, carrying as a souvenir, one of the Queens men dropped. He was one of a party going at the time to the farm. It was dusk when I got there and the men were lying on the ground, multiple wounds all over their bodies though none of them severe. My head was by this time wracking with pain.

Walked back home to my billet. Oh, what a joy to get into bed!

Tuesday 21st.

I must undoubtedly diet myself when up at the trenches where lack of exercise so predisposes me to liver trouble. I can see it is going to be a problem as to how to keep fit in these trenches during the winter months.

I got up to see my sick but felt so miserable that I went to bed afterwards with stone cold feet which resisted all attempts to get them warm for over two hours. Skipped luncheon but at 4pm had tea and biscuits and then feeling griping pains dressed and went on a short stroll. Had boiled egg and toast at 7:30pm then brought an eventful day to a close by retiring to bed. I feel much better now at 11pm.

Culwick, my medical orderly is now a full corporal thanks to me applying on his behalf and the colonel and CO decently giving it. Culwick is a very attentive man, knows his work well and looks after me most carefully. A sign painter by profession and aged about 47, he gave up his business to join the ranks.

My other man is called Leeds. He is officially the chiropodist to the regiment, a position which has its use when on the move but quite useless as things are now. He is a very nice fellow and comes in very handy as a second medical orderly.

Wednesday 22nd.

Lay in bed most of yesterday, feeling better but ridiculously weak, especially when I got up in the afternoon and tried to walk around by the canal. Think there must have been some infection at the bottom of the whole thing, but I had thought that the latter part of the illness was mainly the liver. Today I feel very much better and took a walk of four miles this afternoon.

On Aug 29th the entry about midnight song. I find it is the chorus to rather a feeble sort of popular march. The words are – "keep the home fires burning, while your hearts are yearning, though your lads are far away, they dream of home, there's a silver lining through the dark cloud shining".

Thursday 23rd.

Nothing much to relate. It is the hush before the storm.

Friday 24th.

Very close night and I could not sleep and started reading at 2:30am. At 4am a tremendous bombardment of the German lines developed on the right of the salient and very near. It was very grand to hear rapid and continuous fire from many batteries and see the flashes in the sky. Things are developing!! Had secret orders read today and had consultation with ADMS also with Major Turner and officers. The ambulances evidently intend to come into the limelight and are to be prepared for a rush. Turner has made all sorts of elaborate preparations, meaning well but rather interfering with our own work at the trenches.

Saturday 25th.

Walked up to the trenches at 2:45am, it was drizzling slightly but very warm. This is 'the day', the Dertag, the day of the Huns. And even as they prepared for their day so have we, and today the Allies are going to make a combined effort at 9:45a.m. Glorious news has come in all day by wires from brigade HQ.

I understand the plan was for the main 'push' to be made by the French somewhere south in particular and by the English 2nd Army. No advance was ordered on the Armentieres salient but in the event of favourable opportunity arising it was decided that the small salient in front of our - the Surreys - line should be taken.

The Queens being in the trenches it lay with us - the Surreys - to make the assault. A furious bombardment had been evidently going on toward the south all yesterday and night indeed to mask the programme. We also kept up a tremendous cannonade on this salient and must have done much damage.

Our little 'show' fell through and no attack took place much to the disappointment of the men. The last wire I read says that the French have captured the whole of the first line of trenches and let their cavalry[22] through. The English have been successful everywhere except for one point.

Passages from 7th Battalion East Surrey Regiments war diaries.
Friday 24th.

Received orders that the French and our 1st Army were going to assume a general offensive. The 2nd Army is to hold the enemy in front and at the same time show local activity to deceive the enemy as to the position the main attack is coming off and with a view to this, the battalion is ordered to occupy Le Touquet salient if the enemy vacate it.

Saturday 25th

The battalion moved to their positions at 2:30am and all in position by 4am. At 5am the artillery bombarded the German salient at Le Touquet till 6:30am.

At 5:56am we sent up a smoke screen all along our front with smoke bombs, burning straw etc. The enemy only answered with a few whizz bangs.

---

22. *A Times reporter in Paris wrote on Tuesday 28 September about the fighting on the previous Saturday (25th):*
"The dash displayed was so great that the French Colonial Cavalry got the chance which all good Hussars have been praying for throughout the period of trench warfare. Under the brilliant leadership of Marchand's right hand man in his Colonial conquest, General Baratier, the cavalry really came into action for the first time on the Western Front for many months. They doubtless suffered heavily, but their activities probably explain the great number of prisoners in such a short time on such a short front." (The Times – PRC, The Great War Forum) (It is highly probable that there was no cavalry charge but likely the Hussars were used as reserve infantry)

> *Our bombardment did not sufficiently damage the enemy's wire or make him give up his trenches, so it was decided no attack would be made as from a tactical point of view there was nothing to be gained. Our whole objective being to make sufficient aggression to prevent him moving any troops to other parts.*
>
> *At 1pm we received orders that we could go back to billets, the bombardments and aggression is still to go on from time to time, so the enemy gets no rest. Our men were very disappointed that no attack was made but were consolidated hearing the splendid news which kept coming in.*
>
> *A summary of messages attached. "THE DAY HAS COME" – at last, everybody has been longing for it and no one questions the idea of anything but crushing success all along the line. From reports received it is evident the French and ourselves used 'Gas', which owing to the German breach of faith has become a legal weapon of war. And it is to be hoped that we will make full use of it and avenge the terrific suffering our men have received from the German gas. Everybody realises that the 2nd Army front, roughly from Ypres to Bois Grenier being in advance of the general line will have to hold the enemy until the line straightens and then 'our' day will come.*

Sunday 26th.

Walked out to William this afternoon, got him excused stables so that we had until 8pm together. We strolled into Nieppe, had tea etc, improbably moving.

Got back to Armentieres in time for dinner. A wire came to say that total French prisoners were over 10,000 and English over 2,000. Last wire said Sonchey had fallen to the French, there was no word about the cavalry and altogether I do not feel so optimistic as yesterday.

We received word that we were not to go up to trenches until tomorrow night.

Monday 27th.

News that the French have now taken 18,000 prisoners, 31 guns and 1st and 2nd line of trenches over 21 kilometres. We occupy Loos and have taken nine field guns.

We are going today, where, when, we have no orders and it is 6pm.

A perfect chaos here at headquarters and our regiment not yet away.

At last we are sent to billets in the town near the station and eventually get settled for the night. Slept on the floor but very comfortable and warm.

Tuesday 28th.

News still seems good from the Champagne and Loos area. Fine house this, with a good garden with central pond and vulgar bridge over it, very suburban taste.

We are moving tomorrow. The men and ourselves by train, the transport by road. Probably go to Bethune.

Thank goodness we go south; the winter weather may be better there. Also, we shall be in the big push. Our transport departed early and took our valises.

I asked the interpreter to get me a bed which he did. I was glad of anything as it was very cold and raining in torrents, I felt suspicious of the bed and indeed my misgivings were well founded as it proved after an hour's sleep, waking and discovering bugs and an enormous flea. After that sleep being impossible I lit a candle and read until 4:45am then we got away.

Wednesday 29th.

Left Armentieres about 6:30am and we all marched to Steenwerck station, seven miles.

On the march the more I appreciated my position after field ambulance life. Today for instance I simply walked at the very back of the column very independently.

It began to rain badly as soon as we entrained, some of our men in open trucks looked cold and miserable.

We detrained at Fouquereuil. Here the whole brigade was huddled in a field for two hours and the place was converted into a quagmire before long. The men however, were very cheerful.

Had coffee and biscuits then we all moved on through the rain and over roads which in places were ankle deep in evil smelling semi-liquid mud. My Thresher coat and cavalry cape kept me perfectly warm and dry. Also, we passed through country which was far more attractive than around Armentieres.

Finally, we arrived at Verquin where we found our billets. I have a beautiful clean bed in a butcher's shop. Culwick met me and showed me a tub he had procured for my bath; he is a fine fellow!

No official news but hear of an increase in the number of prisoners.

Thursday 30th.

Very comfortable night and the most excellent hot bath. Have taken all one's meals so far in estaminet. The Brigade – 37th – started at 1pm, this time mounted. Very cold, but sunny. Arrived at our destination Vermelles about 4pm. We had to find billets among shelled houses which lay on the edge of a great flat plain leading up to a low ridge, over which the Huns are entrenched.

The prospect of finding a decent billet and dressing station seemed utterly out of the question. By great luck I met an artillery officer and he offered me a bed in his house on the understanding I evacuated it in the event of his battery officers returning from the lines. He has a lovely hot fire and I am making a dressing station of his front room.

A fleet of 14 English aeroplanes flew over us yesterday while on the march, it was surprising what a noise they made. There is a report that the Dardanelles have been forced!

OCTOBER 1915

Friday 1st.

Sleep was almost impossible partly owing to the bitter cold and mostly due to a fierce artillery bombardment of the Hun's trenches by our batteries, some of which was close beside my house. This is the most bitter cold weather with a strong east wind. I have made a splendid dressing station out of this room; thanks to a fire I am able to keep comfortably warm.

Thompson[23] MO to the Sussex 36th Brigade was killed this morning by a shell at his dressing station and Bell, of my old field ambulance, was seriously injured by shrapnel.

I have just come back from visiting the recent battlefields, their first two lines of trenches which we captured from them. From Vermelles there is a flat plain which gradually slopes up to a ridge, on the summit of this were ours and the Hun's trenches separated by about a 100 yards. There

23. *No record of Thompson, Sussex Regt/RAMC death fitting the dates on CWGC.* *(Commonwealth War Graves Commission)*

was a good deal of shrapnel and high explosive being thrown about, so we had to cover the distance between the two trenches fairly rapidly.

It was a typical battlefield, littered with bodies of our brave Highlanders who led the assault with bombing parties. They still lay stiff with their arms outstretched in the act of throwing the bomb.

We entered the Hun's first line of trenches and saw a good many Bosch lying in and around their dugouts, some of them with ghastly wounds. One German officer lay at the mouth of his dugout with a Femur almost torn in half. Most of the dead wore respirators.

Their dugouts are wonderfully strong and beat ours at Armentieres to bits seeing that they go down often 15 feet and were built with good timber as well. There were hand grenades, rifles and cartridges lying everywhere.

At one place I found myself standing on the body of a Hun who had been trampled beneath the mud of the trench. In some of the dugouts there were loaves of pumpernickel and Dutch cheese.

Behind their second trench you looked down to the village of Loos in the hollow, then beyond Loos rose the hill (*Hill 70*) up which we pushed the enemy and captured the crest, and there we are now.

We returned, me and Monroe-Favre, the way we had come. Two high explosive shells burst uncomfortably near us and we were showered with pebbles and earth.

Saturday 2nd.

They have shelled our batteries all afternoon. Just heard our divisional General Wing[24] has been killed by shell bursting in his battle headquarters, a great loss.

---

24. *In 1913 Major-General Frederick Drummond Vincent Wing. Age 54. CB was in command of the artillery corps of the 3rd Infantry Division and accompanied them to France at the outbreak of WW1. Wing served at all the major battles of 1914. Early in 1915 a German shell exploded directly above his car during a tour of his artillery positions, his chauffeur was injured. On 22 September 1915 General Wing was wounded in the calf by a shrapnel bullet. He returned to duty the next day. Later in 1915 Wing took overall command of the newly raised army 12th (Eastern) Division. In the Battle of Loos, Generals Thesiger and Capper were killed. Less than a week later, on 2 October at 3:45pm a shell exploded in the road outside the 12th Division's forward report centre, Mazingarbe, killing Wing and his aide-de-camp (Lieutenant Christopher Cecil Tower, age 30) instantly. Both are buried in Noeux-Les-Mines communal cemetery. (Wikipedia)*

Passages from 7th Battalion East Surrey Regiments war diaries.

Friday 1st October.

Most of the officers paid visits to the battlefields in front of Loos, it gave one a good impression of what the battle on the 25th and 26th must have been. The German trenches and wire were practically destroyed altogether.

There was a good amount of shelling going on but mostly from our side. The ground right up to the Germans' old trenches is undercover from the front and right and one can only be seen from the left near Hohenzollern Redoubt, and unless many bunch together it is comparatively safe to walk about in the open.

Bomb practice under Lieutenant Marshal went on all day. Great stress is being laid on the absolute importance of having efficient bomb throwers. A lesson learnt from the attack on Saturday 25th was that our men throw the bombs much too hard and wildly whereas the Germans merely place them gently in the trenches, but with much more valuable effect.

---

*Note

The Battle of Loos: 25 September – 15 October 1915.

The first large-scale British offensive action in a supporting role to a large French attack in the third Battle of Artois. The British thought that the ground over which they were being called upon to advance was not suitable. This was rejected. The battle is noted for the first British use of poison gas. Twelve battalions suffered 8,000 casualties out of 10,000 in the first four hours.

Although the 37th Brigade succeeded in their task, this was considered to be just a minor consolation among bigger failures. The British regarded Loos as a disaster.

Between 25 September and 16 October there were 61,000 casualties, 50,000 of these between Loos and Givenchy, the remainder during the subsidiary attacks.

The number of men who died was 7,766.

The objective had not been achieved and the Hohenzollern Redoubt stayed in German possession until near the end of the war.

General Fowler was mentioned in despatches of Field Marshal Sir John French and was awarded the CB, the Most Honourable Order of the Bath.

*

The version of eyewitness Major General Richard Hilton (forward observation officer) differed:

"A great deal of nonsense has been written about Loos. The real tragedy of that battle was its nearness to complete success. Most of us reached the crest of Hill 70 and survived and were firmly convinced that we had broken through on that Sunday, 25 September 1915. There seemed to be nothing ahead of us, but an unoccupied and incomplete trench system. The only two things that prevented our advancing into the suburbs of Lens were, firstly, the exhaustion of the 'Jocks' themselves (for they had undergone a bellyful of marching and fighting that day) and, secondly, the flanking fire of numerous German machine guns, which swept the bare hill from some factory buildings in Cite St Auguste to the south of us. All that we needed was more artillery ammunition to blast those clearly located machine guns, plus some fresh infantry to take over from the weary 'Jocks'. But, alas neither ammunition nor reinforcements were immediately available, and the great opportunity passed." (The Battle of Loos. 1976 Philip Warner. Wordsworth).

Sunday 3rd.

Received orders for our battalion to go up into and occupy the two original first line trenches – the trenches from where the recent advance was made. We went up in the afternoon, the colonel, adjutant and me up last, made our way along the long communication trench which leads to the top of the hill. Meanwhile the enemy threw crumps *(German 5.9-cm shell)* along the hillside which exploded with terrific reports.

I must say I never thought we should get up without casualties, but we did. We found two very strong dugouts for our headquarters; I fear the men suffered much in the trenches as it was a bitterly cold night.

My trench coat is a 'godsend' it keeps my body warm as toast. Indeed, I passed a comfortable night, but our position is bad as we are entirely enfiladed from the left by the guns on the Fosse 8 (*slag heap*) which is still occupied by the Huns and they throw over coalboxes[25] all day and night. We now hold the extreme right of the English line and we can see the French batteries on our right quite close by.

Monday 4th.

My old 36th Field Ambulance had come in for it the day before yesterday, poor Stanley Bell was killed together with a sergeant and some men. Also, one of the ambulances was blown up and the driver killed.

A wonderful night to look round over the land which offers an uninterrupted view in front for a long way, seeing the Hun shells bursting and the shrapnel. God!! I would give something to get out of this with honour.

Jack Cox has not played the game if I hear correctly, he has resigned from MO to the 2nd Suffolks, gone home and got some government job there. No doubt he used his mother as an excuse. I am afraid it was an excuse, one which he never made while he was in the field ambulance.

I went up to the front line of trenches to see a sick man and while there they began to put coal boxes among us. I got into a dugout with the last one which unfortunately exploded in a dugout close-by completely burying three men.

King was inside but got out badly shaken, he came running to tell us and we rushed with spades etc and after half hour digging got out one man who was badly hurt but a sergeant was killed and one of my stretcher bearers was blown to pieces, his head severed completely.

> ### Passages from 7th Battalion East Surrey Regiments war diaries.
> ### Sunday 3rd.
>
> *The battalion and the Queens moved up into the old British trenches with the Queens right on the Lens road and ours left on the Loos road. The Buffs, West Kents and brigade went back to Masingarbe. The Guards divisions came up again and took our billets, they are now in the firing line on the left of the 36th Brigade. The crowd in*

25. German 8-inch howitzer shell on impact sending up columns of greasy black smoke.

> the trenches is terrible, we have only 1,000 yards of front and there are two regiments in the trenches as well as about a thousand cavalry who are burying the dead.
>
> *Monday 4th.*
>
> We were subjected to a great deal of shelling during the day because there were several batteries in our line. We had eight casualties, two killed and six wounded. The difficulty of getting water is somewhat felt, all water must be drawn at night from the water carts which come right up. But as nearly all the men are out on working parties all night it is difficult to manage anything.
>
> Lieutenant King went back to the transport lines as he was in a dug-out on which a large shell obtained a direct hit, though it buried four men it didn't touch him, but the concussion shook him very much.
>
> *Tuesday 5th.*
>
> A battery in D-coy trench got a severe shelling about 8am resulting in several casualties. Lieutenant Hastings was killed, also two men and nine others wounded. About 6pm we heard we had to move and relieve the 3rd Guards Brigade in the trenches, continuing the line to the left occupied by the 36th Brigade.

Tuesday 5th.

This has been a sad morning. The Huns shelled the batteries immediately around the trenches among which our men were billeting with the result that one shell fell on a shelter under which poor Hastings was taking cover, killing him instantly. His head was blown off and his thigh shattered. I liked Hastings very much. He was a beautiful singer. His nerves had recently shown signs of giving way.

It is a terrible strain for anyone highly strung. It scarcely invites confidence in the higher command when you see our battalion placed in reserve trenches which have our own batteries, not only on either side but also among them and in front of them – 30 yards.

Such a position would not be so bad with efficient dugouts but not even one in the two front trenches is strong enough to withstand a six-inch high explosive. We cannot complain if we suffer severely but understandingly.

We are moving out this evening into trenches which are further advanced. Attended to my wounded with utmost difficulty. Trenches too narrow for stretchers: drizzling rain etc. What a life!!

Wednesday 6th-Thursday 7th.

Last night we all left our quarters and started to take up our position in the old German trenches off the Hulluch road. It was a most terrible journey through mud which was in places more than ankle deep and very greasy. I think everyone fell more than once.

The latter part of the journey was along the Hulluch road and here we had one or two shrapnel over us and were subjected to a good supply of stray bullets. We were lucky and the whole battalion got in with only one casualty and without the enemy being aware of our movements.

The MO of the Guards took me to his dressing station. My dressing station was probably built for that purpose by the Germans and is one of the best. It is well below the ground and is roofed with closely applied baulks of timber and supported by the same. Also, a thick iron girder runs along the entire ceiling. It has a depth of earth on it and must easily withstand 6-inch shells. It is 20 feet long and the floor space is taken up by broad bunks. It was in a filthy state but after cleaning up looked very well.

We are in support at present, so I do not look for many casualties. I, Major Wilson, and Monroe-Favre sleep here and we also have our HQ mess because of the stove, which we only light after dark. The HQ dugout is extraordinarily strong, it is far down and approached by a steep awkward flight of stairs.

I had a long journey down the trenches to get a man shot through the chest. It is quite impossible to get him out of the trenches until after dark, so had to make him as comfortable as possible and get back dodging shrapnel[26] along a shallow trench.

Terrible artillery fire going on from both sides and things are only quiet for a few minutes at a time. I fear our troops in the firing line are having a bad time as their trenches are still shallow and the enemy knows it.

The absence of water supply is troublesome and we rely entirely on our water cart which comes up after dark. Washing is out of the question and it is only my spirit lamp which gives one a chance of shaving in the morning.

26. *Shrapnel shells were anti-personnel artillery carrying lead balls which were released near the target area.*

Friday 8th

This has been a quiet day! It had been planned for the West Kents to take a position held by the Huns. This position of 500-yards lay curiously across our front lines, interrupting it. The attack was timed for 4:45pm. At one o'clock the Huns who had discovered by aircraft this morning that we occupied their old trenches began an intense or at any rate a fierce bombardment of our trenches with large shells and shrapnel.

I had to make three separate journeys into the trenches during this bombardment to attend cases and it was an experience, my first real experience of attending wounded under fierce shellfire. The noise of exploding passing shells was so great that I had to shout to my stretcher bearers to make myself heard at only a two paces interval. I went out with my medical orderly and we had to keep diving to the bottom of the shallow trench to avoid bursting shrapnel etc.

When you get into it you don't feel at all scared, you just feel highly strung and somewhat excited and get quite cool.

I had nothing to eat from 8:30am until 6:30pm being busy with wounded nearly all the time.

Well, our bombardment started at 4:45pm and we gave them 10 times more than they gave us and it was tremendous to hear our 8-inch shells going over like many trains. We kept it up, the Huns subsided, then at a given signal the West Kents attacked and I hear they took the position. It remains to be seen whether they can consolidate their position.

Saturday 9th.

Everyone depressed: The West Kents attack failed. One hears all sorts of reasons, the shortage of bombs at the critical moment, the Pioneers not arriving in time as one etc, and other reasons. The West Kents had 100 casualties.

Our battalion was only represented as far as the machine guns went up and poor Gibson was killed, shot through the head and carried very bravely under fire by a West Kent officer alive to the protection of the trench.

Things look bad for our battalion, two officers today, captains, have collapsed and I have had to send them 'down' and then this afternoon others, Captain Dresser and Lieutenant Devenish were both knocked over by a sniper's bullet through the thighs. I had to crawl along a shallow trench to reach them and do the dressings lying flat in order not to expose myself to the same sniper.

So now we are 13 officers short for the battalion! I now begin to see a good many cases of nerves among the men, they are also getting very verminous and I think we ought to be sent down for a wash if not for a rest.

After dark the battalion left its trenches to take over trenches held by the West Kents. My dressing station is very strong but small and dirty.

Passages from 7th Battalion East Surrey Regiments war diaries.

Friday 8th

Lieutenant Gibson and one of our machine guns went up and fired at the Germans from their parapet, doing considerable damage. Lieutenant Gibson and the corporal were killed, and three others seriously wounded. The attack had to be given up, the West Kents having lost over 100 men. The battalion stood down till 1pm. When they were ordered to stand down. We had Lieutenant Gibson and two men killed. Captain Wyatt and 20 men wounded.

Saturday 9th.

Captain Dresser and Lieutenant Devenish were both wounded in the thigh by a sniper while relieving, Captain Penderel went sick. The night passed quietly for this part of the world.

Sunday 10th.

No casualties during night but continually disturbed by parties who had lost their way in moving into combat etc. One whizz bang exploded just outside my dressing station and killed our colonel's servant. We are now in the firing trenches.

Monday 11th.

The French are heavily bombarding enemy lines on our right. William's glasses which he lent me have arrived and they are splendid. I can now recognise the enemy's aircraft with ease and altogether makes it more interesting.

A good many snipers about who occasion one a certain amount of trouble. We had one or two casualties today from our own shells dropping short into our trenches. Rather hard for the men to be exposed to shellfire from both sides. Accidents will happen!

Tuesday 12th.

The East Surreys are called upon to take the trench held by the enemy which the West Kents and before them the Guards had failed to take. Minutest preparation in progress.

Wednesday 13th.

To meet a likely run of wounded a large dugout was erected by the road but owing to lack of time was hardly covered to withstand large shells.

At 11:30am I took up my position in the dugout with my staff and was joined by Captain Milne from the 38th Field Ambulance who brought 20 RAMC men with him.

At midday we started two hours of intense bombardment. The noise was appalling as the Germans replied vigorously. Very soon we had two direct hits on the centre of the dugout which did no harm. Then later two high explosives struck the edge of the roof where it was not so strong and gave way with a terrific and blinding crash, the hole made was not large and being on the opposite side from where we were sitting caused no casualty At 2pm the guns lifted their fire and the Surreys attacked and we could hear the enemy's machine guns playing on the poor chaps as they advanced at the run. A terrible time for us, waiting and doing nothing. At 2:30pm however the first wounded; the walking cases began to come in. And now from 2:30 pm to 5:30 am – 15 hours – I was continually dressing wounded with only occasionally a rest for five minutes. Hard work it was, involving not only dressing of cases but helping to lift wounded on heavy stretchers etc.

Thursday 14th-Friday 15th.

During the action the field ambulance failed to lend much support despite an urgent message for ambulances to be sent up for our 100 wounded whom I had already dressed and waiting to be sent down. Eventually they sent up cars at odd intervals and we got the place nearly cleared by 5:30am and I could get a sit down and something to eat.

After that the worst cases began to come in, and we got busy again for some hours. I should have said that at 3:30am another field ambulance officer came to aid us in the place of Milne who went back to accelerate cars. Then ADMS and Major Turner turned up and congratulated us on our work. Towards evening we heard our battalion would be relieved and this was cheering indeed.

A large percent of the wounds were terrible, especially those caused by bombs, hand grenades etc. Thank God no crumps hit our dugout, although, at one period they were falling all around our place when it was simply packed with wounded.

The relief was not completed until about 2am, then the colonel, adjutant, major and I set out on our four mile walk to Neuvilles by Vermelles which we reached by walking over the exposed road where stray and spent bullets were uncomfortably frequent. However, we got there about 4am, I had a good meal and fell into bed.

Well, the Surreys did very well, at 2pm they left their trench led by a bombing party and were soon in the German trench where they bombed a good many of the enemy and held on very well. They lost very heavily coming over the open and some of our best men went down.

Three officers were hit, one died. Not many Germans were taken prisoner as they retired down their communication trench very quickly. They made or started to make a counterattack, but we raked them as they came on with rifle fire and squashed it.

Unfortunately, the synchronised attack on the Hohenzollern Redoubt and upon the Quarries was a failure. My stretcher bearers worked most heroically throughout the show and I had one casualty among them, a fractured arm.

Saturday 16th

Nothing much to note, revelled in a most good night. A rather picturesque church here, though shelled to pieces. We are surrounded with heavy batteries but the noise they make is preferable to the beastly row of the field guns and whizz bangs.

Passages from 7th Battalion East Surrey Regiments war diaries.
Wednesday 13th-Thursday 14th.
The division was ordered to attack in conjunction with general attack all along the line. The artillery bombardment began and continued until two o'clock. Smoke and gas began at one o'clock and

continued until two o'clock. The attack was made by the 46th, 12th and first Divisions.

Its main object was to straighten our line and if possible to take from the enemy one or two very nasty positions he held which enfiladed our line. The 46th were to take Hohenzollern Redoubt and Fosse no-8. The 12th the Quarries to Gun trench and Gun trench. The first Division to take the line of Lens – La Bassee road.

Result – the 46th took part of Hohenzollern Redoubt but could go no further. The 12th took the Hohenzollern – Windy corner of the Quarries, failed to take trench from Quarries to Gun trench. The East Surreys took and held Gun trench. The first took line of the road but were subsequently shelled out of the northern portion in front of Hulluch.

The 46th and 35th advanced under gas and smoke, the remainder under smoke only. At 2pm exactly, B-company – two platoons – led by Lieutenant Hewitt assaulted the whole of gun trench by a frontal, at the same time bombing parties from A and B attacked both flanks, the frontal attack got in at once, the Germans running as soon as we got close.

The night passed quietly except for bombing. At about 4:30am we started to organise our front line which had become somewhat muddled with different regiments and companies. At 6am the line was organised. The enemy made a counterattack on our left side at 5:30am which we easily repulsed with rifle fire. During the rest of the day things were quiet and the time was spent in consolidating the position won.

A-coy under Captain Tomkins with two platoons followed up at 50-yard interval but kept too much to the north and were badly cut up by machine gun fire in the open, and did not get in from the front, the flank bombing attacks both made ground.

A-Coy's attack, having failed frontally, followed up from the flank. The northern bombing attack was led most gallantly by Sergeant Martin. Behind A-coy came Lieutenant Findlay and Coy's bombers, whose duty was to clear and block for 100 yards the German communication trench running back to Cite St Elie, which they did. As *soon as this was done C-coy advanced from their position in second support to the front line and gradually reinforced the captured trench mostly on the right.*

Reinforcements were soon called for again, D-coy was sent up from the third support trench and one-coy under Captain Dawson of the West Kents were sent for, these went straight up into the new trench. Later a coy of the Queens under Major Roberts went up, half to our old first support line and half to our third support line. The two platoons in the first support line were subsequently in reserve.

There was a great deal of bombing on both sides. Our men suffered rather heavily from enfilade fire from the Quarries on our left and the dump, also the trenches were shelled somewhat heavily with high explosive. However, the result was exactly what we had set out to do, we won the trench, held it, and blocked the communication trench for 100 yards.

The Buffs on our left were unable to take their trench owing to very heavy machine gun fire so we had to block the end of the trench.

Later at about 10:30pm two coys of the 8th Fusiliers came up and occupied the old German trenches in reserve in case they might be needed.

The men fought splendidly all through and attacked with great dash, this was especially creditable as they had been in the trenches for four months without a rest and the last five days had undergone a continual and heavy bombardment.

The casualties were heavy. Captain Tomkins, Lieutenant Brasnett were killed. Lieutenants Knight and Marshal wounded. 56 other ranks were killed, 160 wounded and 33 missing (7th Batt) which many hope will subsequently be brought in wounded.

We took about 16 prisoners, one machine gun and three trench mortars with a lot of ammunition. In the evening we were relieved by the 11th Middlesex and went into billets at Noyelles Des Vermelles.

Sunday 17th.

Walked over to Bethune with Robinson, a very nice fellow. Great treat to be among nice shops and see women and children walking about, the place full of troops of course. Very picturesque market square and old town hall.

Had omelette and coffee at 'the Red Lion' and drinks at the 'Globe' which is a mess for English officers. Everyone drinking champagne and cocktails – a franc at a time. Got a ride part way on a limber, very good if you want an abortion or shake up your liver!

Monday 18th.

By means of a letter from William and our arranged code I made my way to Labourse where I found him without much difficulty, we had coffee at an estaminet. Very glad to find him so well. We walked back together to Noyelles Des Vermelles.

Tuesday 19th.

Paid groom 30-francs.

Tremendous amount of firing during the night. We hear unofficially that the Essex repulsed a violent German attack and the Germans were mown down by their three machine guns.

I have had quite a comfortable night in the colonel's room. I had some clean straw put down and my valise on top making a most comfortable bed. The men also had plenty of clean straw and were quite happy and warm. The colonel is seedy, and I am keeping him in bed, he has piles, bronchitis, and septic in-growing toenail!

Letter from Cross, he is evidently keeping practice well together with the help of an elderly locum. He shows for the quarter ending Sept 30th

Receipts £414.0.11 - Expenses £47.4.5 - Balance £1.5.0 - Total £368.1.6. Which is very good.

Wednesday 20th. Vaudricourt.

This is a very picturesque village with plenty of trees and little woods dotted about. The country around is also pleasantly undulating and in the absence of troops it would be quite an attractive spot.

This afternoon Nicholls, interpreter; Mons Dutrec and self, rode into Bethune. It is two and a half miles away and did some shopping, had tea and drinks at the Globe but failed to get either haircut or bath owing to fearful crush and number of troops. There were plenty of French officers about and their brilliant uniforms looked very gay. The shops are quite good. It is a relief to walk about among shops away from the sound of guns.

Thursday 21st.

Battalion inspected by divisional General Scott[27] this morning. Scott has taken General Wing's place. He made a speech and backed the men up by congratulating them on the trench they had taken.

I went on such a jolly walk afterwards through woods and fields and not a shred of khaki to be seen nearly all the way. In the afternoon I rode to Labourse to see ADMS ref disinfection of men's clothes, they are all very lousy.

Saw William and we had tea and walked, chatted together. He moves to Forchieres tomorrow.

Friday 22nd.

Still at Vaudricourt. The colonel who has been very seedy is much better and I and Major Wilson at present share his room which is in an estaminet. The estaminet, owing to them abusing their position (selling liquor to troops) are only allowed to carry on business from 12-1pm and from 6-8pm. So, the English are rather unpopular in this village! Busy all morning going around billets lecturing my 16 reserve stretcher bearers. A visit from 'Messer Johnson'. Colonel gone on leave.

Saturday 23rd.

A quiet day in the village, a dear old church here, dated 1635 with a curious tower, six sided. But the peace of the country was destroyed by khaki.

Sunday 24th.

My medical orderly went on leave. Have made 16 conditional or reserve stretcher bearers – four to a coy. My 16 stretchers (canvas and pole) made especially short and narrow have arrived and will be very useful indeed. As mess president I am rather dissatisfied with the amount of money

---

27. *Sir Arthur Binny Scott b.1862 in Scotland. At the start of WW2 Scott and his wife moved out of London to escape the blitz and moved to Red Lodge.(now Red Leys) Chesham Bois. The home received a direct hit during a bombing raid and Scott was killed, his wife Lady Scott was rescued from the wreckage and escaped serious injury.*

required to keep this mess going, I am determined to investigate this matter.

Walked into Verquin and visited Malone of the 37th Field Ambulance. Rode into Bethune with Nicholls in the afternoon and had a bath and changed into clean clothes. suppose we shall muddle through this wretched war sometime. But all we do seems so amateurish compared with the Germans' method, but we are learning no doubt.

Bombing is the most prominent method of attack at present. We used to consider it quite sufficient for a few brave fellows to throw bombs promiscuously into the trenches. Point is, we have since discerned that the Germans organise and train their bombers most carefully, bombing a trench is a science.

Monday 25th.

Paid Corporal Turner for mess 112-Francs – 20.60 each.

Rain and mud. I am sharing the colonel's room with Major Wilson and we have in it a stove that was here, it is delightfully warm. Was called out to a civilian patient, a girl whom I interviewed with the interpreter, who had some menstrual pain, a rather difficult case with an interpreter as medium.

This is our last night here and tomorrow we face the Hohenzollern Redoubt.

Tuesday 26th.

Started early, saw my sick at 7:30am, and the battalion moved away at 9am. I walked as it was rather cold but delightful sunshine. Made a long halt at 11am and everyone had lunch. I brought up the rear and we entered the trenches about 4pm, and after floundering through terrible mud found my dressing station. It was an agreeable surprise. A small low dugout about eight-foot-long but with a fireplace and a stretcher fixed on one side for a bed.

'Oh joy,' an easy chair!! Most comfortable. Immediately outside is another dugout which will hold three of my men. Leeds will sleep here with me. We hold the line opposite the Hohenzollern Redoubt, the lines are so near to one another that there is not much shelling, only bombing etc.

Wednesday 27th.

Things extraordinarily quiet – a certain amount of shelling toward our support trenches, but no casualties. Lines about 40 yards apart, too far for bomb throwing although both sides attempted it. All drop short.

Slight rain and mist. I am too far from headquarters to mess with them so I have my own food here and Leeds cooks very well and looks after me very well too.

Thursday 28th.

Raining and misty. Mud in trenches past description, either liquid and over a man's boots or thick and sticky and almost pulling off one's boots, so glad I brought my gum boots.

Lieutenant Owen sent us four pheasants and I am enjoying one now. So sorry for the men in trenches, many of them have no dugouts and are cold and miserable. Two gunshot wounds of hands today, perhaps self-inflicted!

Mons Dutrec came up and spent the night with me.

Letter from Jack. Got a job in England, made his mother his excuse. Have written and told him he has not played the game. Wish I could get out of it with honour but must stick to it.

Friday 29th-Saturday 30th.

Never imagined mud could be so bad. In places it is halfway to the knees, in others it is as sticky as glue and not so deep and almost pulls one's boots off walking.

Germans shelled our support trenches this afternoon, only one crump did damage and caused three casualties. I went around trenches and was glad to find men quite cheerful despite the rain and cold yesterday.

I am ridiculously comfortable in my dugout, one feels a brute being so cosy, but I merely took over the place as I found it. I am now sitting at 6:30pm in a very delicious armchair before a bright fire of wood and coal. My candle is sufficient to light up the little place with a soft light.

All is quiet except for sniper's bullets which smack against the trench outside and a few of the enemy's whizz bangs whistle over towards the Hulluch road.

I have theosophical literature at hand and the sketch of Tatler for lighter moments. How different may be my next dressing station?

A great source of amusement is an iron girder which runs across the ceiling and projects from it. We all spent the first day knocking ourselves silly against it.

I practically lost consciousness after an unusually cruel blow. My medical orderly Leeds whose movements are normally very quick has suffered severely and only this morning he recoiled from the obstruction gibbering incoherently – a most ludicrous sight. However, we are learning from the bitter experience of concussion! Had a few cases today because of German crumping our trenches.

Sunday 31st.

Quiet day. Visit from ADMS, he was very nice and cheerful as usual, talking twenty to the dozen. Colonel arrived back from leave and Corporal Culwick back from leave. I have asked Holt to pay half my pay into Cross's banking account, they paid July 1st – Sept 30th £51.1.3. Started to smoke the first ounce tin of half pound of Players navy cut.

Passages from 7th Battalion East Surrey Regiments war diaries.
Tuesday 26th.

The battalion marched to Vermelles and took over the trenches at Hohenzollern Redoubt from the 4th Grenadiers, we began relieving at 2pm and had finished by 5:30pm. The 12th Division is now holding the corps front. The 35th Brigade on the right between the Hohenzollern Redoubt and the Quarries, the 37th brigade the Hohenzollern Redoubt and north of it. The battalion holds the Kaiserin trench, a new trench continuing to the west face of the Redoubt in a southeast direction. One coy in the Kaiserin trench, two Coys in the old British line behind the west face and one coy behind them in reserve.

Battalion headquarters in the old British first support trench. The transport is at Sailly Labourse about four miles back. The water supply is as usual rather difficult but being nearer Vermelles it is possible to get some water in the daytime.

Wednesday 27th.

A quiet day, about twelve crumps fell near battalion HQ between four and six pm, no casualties but a certain amount of damage was done to the support trenches. Our snipers hit four Germans in the morning. At night the whole battalion were out on working parties principally making a new communication trench.

Thursday 28th.

Quiet all day but very wet, in many places the parapet has fallen in both trench and support lines. Our snipers seem to have quite silenced the enemy's snipers as there is practically none now, whereas they were rather troublesome. We hit three Germans. At night we fired the whole front of the Kaiserin trench.

Friday 29th.

A fairly quiet day, the enemy shelled our lines somewhat heavily in the afternoon with 5.9-inch, causing a good deal of damage to our parapets. Our men were at work all night repairing them. Three men were buried with a shell, one killed, one died on his way to the ambulance, the other one slightly wounded and considerably shaken.

Saturday 30th.

The enemy shelled our lines all over the place from midday to dark, principally with 5.9-inch, I think merely to annoy us, they did a certain amount of damage to our parapets but beyond that practically no other damage. One man was killed and one wounded.

Sunday 31st.

The day passed fairly quietly except for promiscuous shelling of the whole of our trenches with 5.9-inch which however seemed to be

silenced by ten salvos of 18-pounders. We called them up four times during the last 24 hours, on each occasion the hostile shelling ceased. This finishes a very strenuous month for the division but a successful one especially as far as this battalion is concerned. We have taken part in one attack and took and maintained all we have been asked to do.

The casualties during the month are: Killed: Officers four, OR 68. Wounded: Officers two, OR 260. Sick: (England): Officers one, OR 17. Missing: Officers one, OR 33. Total casualties from battalion: Officers 11, OR 332. (OR = Other Ranks) Strength 31 October Officers 23. OR 883.

NOVEMBER 1915.

Monday 1st

Last night Germans sent over crumps but a very large majority of them never exploded. We have noticed this lately and it is a good sign.

Ethel writes to say Cecil is joining RAMC, very sporting! We 'go out' today, it has been a very comfortable six days of trenches. Leeds has been so attentive and such a good and tactful companion. I have also had the dugout to myself instead of being crowded out as hitherto by all sorts of people.

Thus, I have for the first time in the trenches been able to do some good reading of theosophical books. A good fire also has made reading possible. How impossible it is to do any reading when one's feet and body are cold.

Tuesday 2nd

Yesterday afternoon I was relieved by the MO of 8th Fusiliers at 4:45pm. It had been raining all day and Leeds and I had a terrible journey down the trench through appalling mud and holes full of water.

It was dark when we reached the bottom. We started over the flat open country, stumbling in and out of shell holes full of water and slippery mud thick and deep. I fell once and I was absolutely covered in mud, and the rain, it was pouring down adding more discomfiture.

An officer directed us wrong and in consequence we walked for unnecessary miles, perhaps six before we reached Sailly Labourse. However, thanks to my trench coat, good boots, and cavalry cape I arrived perfectly dry.

The comfortable night to which I was looking forward to was spoiled by finding that my sleeping bag was wringing wet. So, I had to sleep in my breeches once again.

Raining hard today and rivers of water running down the streets. Poor devils in the trenches.

Culwick borrowed a huge washing tub and boiled plenty of water. I enjoyed a lovely bath and changed into clean clothes: Oh! Joy.

Wednesday 3rd. Sailly Labourse.

The men have been served out with waterproof capes and I am agitating for a more liberal supply of boots and socks. We are now moved into i.e. our division, the first corps; we were in the 11th.

Turned out of our billet so the major and I found a very comfortable place, two rooms of a farmhouse communicating by a door. In the major's room is a good coke stove so that once again I have the satisfaction of being able to read and write in comfort.

The Adjutant Captain Nicholls told me privately that my name had been sent up to divisional headquarters among those of our battalion (three in number) recommended for some mark of distinction.

I believe in my case it was for attending wounded in the trenches under shellfire. I don't really feel I deserve any special mark of distinction as so many others did more than me. In any case, I do not expect I shall hear anymore about it.

Corporal Culwick, my medical orderly and servant, told me something of his history. He was a professional boxer and acted as second to Pedlar Palmer[28] who got five years for killing a man in a railway carriage.

Passages from 7th Battalion East Surrey Regiments war diaries.
Wednesday 3rd.

Battalion practiced the assault on 'Little Willie' (trench). Trenches were dug to represent our Sticky trench and the German Little Willie so that the men could see on the ground what they could face if they were called upon to carry out such an attack. This is the idea now before carrying out an attack on a hostile trench. The trenches are of course dug from an aeroplane photograph. General Scott was present.

Saturday 6th.

Practice attacking Little Willie again.

Sergeant Evans was presented with the Croix de Guerre by the first army commander – General Sir Douglas Haig – for bravery on 13

---

28. *Pedlar Palmer, born Thomas Palmer. Held world bantamweight championship from 1895-1899. Palmer was a heavy drinker. In April 1907 he killed Robert Croat/Choate on a train returning from Epsom Races. Convicted of manslaughter and served five years. For the last twenty years of his life he was a bookmaker in Brighton. Died 13 February 1949 aged 72. (Wikipedia)*

> *October. He continued bombing at a sap head from 2pm until mid-night when he was relieved being quite exhausted. He soon regained his strength and continued to do splendid work bombing and organising bombing parties throughout the following day. This is the first honour conferred on this battalion up to date.*

Thursday 4th.

Theosophy and social problems.

"The duty of the state of organised society is to serve to every one of its members at least the minimum of welfare – of food, clothing, shelter, education, leisure – of which will enable each to develop to the full faculties which he brought into the world."

"Government should be in the hands of the elders i.e. the wisest, the most experienced of the morally best, that the possession of ability of power imposes the duty of service, the freedom brings happiness only to the educated and self-controlled."

"That co-operation and muted aid should be substituted for competition, muted struggle."

Friday 5th.

The nights are thankfully star-lit, the days are thick with fog, damp and depressing. A quiet day, my sick are increasing. I do not consider that the men are fit to do long duty in the trenches. We go in on Sunday and we are to be twelve days in the trenches!

There is no sign of a move forward and it looks like it will remain here for the winter. Miserable prospect makes one feel rather gloomy and depressed.

Nicholls rode over to see his brother who is adjutant to brigade of heavies. He saw a 15-inch howitzer moved about with ease in sections and can be assembled in six hours. Six officers and 92 men attend solely to this gun.

Saturday 6th.

Walked out to the next village on the way to Bethune and went into the church and sat down in a corner for nearly half an hour. Not a soul was there, the quiet atmosphere and shallow light was very acceptable. The windows were the most beautiful that I have yet seen in France, the colouring of the glass was exquisite and the design very tasteful, just allowing sufficient light to enter without permutating the glass. I saw 52 sick people this morning.

At 6pm William turned up much to my delight. I was going to have a bath, so he had one after me. He seems curiously free of vermin despite deficient bathing and very seedy billets.

After our bath we scratched together quite a hearty meal. Mutton chops and chipped potatoes which William fried with great skill. Then bread butter and jam and prunes and ended with a good bowl of café-au-lait from the farm. Sat round the stove and had a chat before he left.

Sunday 7th. Trenches right of Redoubt.

Back to the trenches. The colonel, major, Nicholls and self, rode our horses so far to Vermelles then walked on foot to our trenches. Boards made it easier.

We spend three uncomfortable days up here. We have a very poor dug-out hardly strong enough to withstand a whizz bang and low and small. No dressing station at all.

Frightfully cold but found my trench coat a veritable treasure and discovered that I can defeat cold feet by pulling on two empty sandbags over each foot and tying round knees.

No rations arrived, we had to wait until 11pm when orderly arrived with bread and leg of mutton but nothing else. However, we were famished.

At 11.30pm some straw arrived which we put down on the floor and the all four of us lay down.

Monday 8th.

Disturbed five times in night owing to minor casualties including one man injured by our own bombs. At 6am I had to go down to the firing line to give morphine to a man shot through the head. It was very difficult to carry a stretcher along the trench.

The trench I was in was very unsanitary and smelt badly in places. Saw men's arms sticking out of the parapet, only partially buried bodies were beginning to taint the air. Could see Hohenzollern Redoubt through periscope, or either the Dump.

A thanksgiving for all souls, 1915.

"Lord, for the light of love that never paled, for radiant dreams no dawn can ever slay, for sweet-shared hours that knew no might-have-been, for laughter ringing down remembered years, for faith unbroken, hope that never failed and youth that shall not feel time's disarray, we thank thee; and for death that came between, too bright and swift for any need of tears!" *(Angela Gordon)*

Tuesday 9th. Trenches right of Redoubt.

Had an excellent night and was not disturbed despite brisk bombardment; or rather artillery duel which started much to the enemy area. Just as we were going to sleep shells (crumps) dropped fearfully near.

Whale oil served out to men and ordered them to put on feet daily against frostbite.

Germans bombarded us heavily both with whizz bangs and crumps; we had many very near us.

We are now working our reliefs as follows: we are in the firing lines for three days – in Vermelles for three – then in reserve for three – three days again in the firing line. Thus nine 'days up'. After this we hope to have at least a week somewhere in billets well behind the line. This will be the divisional arrangement for the winter.

Bombing is now the prominent form of attack in trench warfare. In our earlier days bombs were thrown promiscuously and now bombing has become a science and organised throughout. Bombers are detailed off and trained. Sap trenches are run forward in front of the fire trench for bombers. Like everything else we have copied all from the Germans.

Wednesday 10th.

A terrible night, rain came down and it was not long before it began to come through the wretched roof and drip steadily onto one's miserable bodies and soaking our blankets. My trench coat in which I always sleep came in well with my mackintosh cape over it.

There was a 'singing mouse' within the walls – at least that was my diagnosis, a curious noise it made due to laryngitis or some obstruction in the throat.

We were relieved at 1pm by the Queens, made our way down the trenches while violent shelling by the enemy was still in progress but none of their crumps found our trenches until after we had gone when one fell and overturned one of our machine guns, killing the corporal.

We had very few casualties these three days. We took over an hour to get through the trench and I felt very fatigued after struggling through the thick mud. We have an empty house in Vermelles with braziers of coke keeping us nice and warm. I am sharing with Nicholls.

Delightful night took off breeches and put on pyjamas, which was strictly against orders.

Thursday 11th.

Felt very depressed and ill yesterday owing to my liver. Today, thanks to a pill, I feel very well.

Saw 76 sick which took me from 10am until 12:45 pm. Culwick found four lice in my breeches! Most difficult to avoid getting these pests.

Friday 12th.

Began to rain heavily at night and the wind blew fiercely. Had to get up and move my bed into another sector of the room owing to rain coming through.

Our battalion is getting worn out, not with fighting but simply by being used for work parties. They have no chance of getting their clothes properly dry, nor to obtain a sufficient amount of sleep as these work parties always take place after dark.

The Germans have battalions of labourers and these no doubt do a great deal of the work, which is with us carried out by our soldiers. Surely it would be much better if we had organised something similar and left our men to do the work of fighting men, keeping them fit and in good condition.

One cannot but feel that we are carrying on the war in a very amateurish way as compared with the Germans. Our organisation is so bad – one has only to be in contact with the orderly room for a time to see how orders are sent in so often only to be washed out a few hours later. It makes one feel very depressed at times.

Walked into Sailly Labourse this afternoon and saw ADMS re: my leave. Think I may get away about the 24th or 25th of this month..

Saturday 13th. Vermelles, trenches (opp the window)

Miserably wet day again but cleared up at midday and we started up at 3pm for our new line of trenches.Luckily our men have been supplied with full wellington boots and I was able to get a pair which fit very comfortably.

What a journey we had. At first we set off gaily along floor boarded trenches but unfortunately these came to an end and then we wallowed through the most appalling trenches I have yet experienced. The mud was often nearly up to your knees. The parapets were falling in and the telephone wires lying about the floor and sides entangled our feet at every turn.

A drizzling rain added to one's misery and finally the guide gave the final touch to the picture by taking us the wrong way. The result was that we met companies coming out and had to wait until they passed. It took us nearly four and a half hours to complete the journey.

Our trenches here are terrible – they beggar description with mud. My dugout has only one redeeming feature, it is fairly safe. For the rest it is dripping wet from the roof. I put my ground sheet under a small table and lay on that in my great-coat with a blanket over me, but I was miserably cold and suffered also from cramps in leg muscles.

Sunday 14th.

A fair amount of whizz bangs but otherwise quiet. Good news arrives that we are relieved tomorrow and after two days in trenches near Vermelles, the whole division goes back to rest for ten days or so. Thank God!

Monday 15th. Trenches at Vermelles.

Slept the night not with the major in our dugout – one miserable experience there was quite enough – but in the dressing station with four of my men. I can't say I slept well but anyhow I had a dry wooden form and a brazier of coke kept us comfortably warm.

The mud and slush – up to one's knees in places – remain despite working parties, but boards are being put down and things ought to be more comfortable for the men soon. The four companies were relieved early and we (headquarters) made a very good journey out of the trenches taking two and half hours to get out.

We now hold the trenches at Vermelles. The poor men are so glad to get back to nice dry trenches, plenty of straw. I have my dressing station in Vermelles itself occupying the cellar of a partially shelled house. Corporal Culwick etc occupies the room upstairs.

Tuesday 16th.

Slept on stretchers in cellar but the brazier of coke gave me a headache.

The warmth of the coke fire has rejuvenated countless flies which had settled on the walls for the winter. These now fly slowly about and keep dropping down your neck and are a real nuisance.

Made long walk this afternoon to Mazingarbe and managed to get rid of headache. Found a large zinc receptacle, which I got Culwick to clean out and in which I had a most luxurious bath. Leeds has gone for his holiday. The Boulogne route is now stopped for those on leave and instead we go by Havre and get eleven days' absence instead of the original nine.

Ethel[29] invites me to Flower House, and I am so looking forward to seeing all of them again but so far have not arranged the date of my leave.

Wednesday 17th. Trenches Sailly-Labourse.

The prospect of Christmas dinner was discussed last evening after our evening meal.

Our colonel who had just returned before the war having done nine service years in central Africa, told us about an Xmas dinner he ordered one year to be sent out to Somalia from Fortnum and Masons.

The dinner was ordered in November but did not arrive until the following June. The colonel described very amusingly the state of the turkey etc after its protected pilgrimage, the haggis alone held up its head and they enjoyed it.

The general of our brigade complimented me on the comparative absence of sickness in my battalion. I understand our battalion has the lowest record by far in the division for sickness and of course someone has to take the credit.

As a matter of fact I attribute the low cases of sickness to great measure to my treatment of many 'feet cases' with my formalin. Some of the MO of our battalions have been sending as many as 50 or 60 a day to hospital.

Culwick stuffed straw under my stretcher which counteracted the draught of cold air which otherwise circulates beneath you. Slept well.

Relieved by Essex after great delay and waiting about in freezing cold but our horses were waiting in Vermelles and a fast trot soon sent the blood coursing round.

29. *Ethel Bullmore. Sister (next of kin) Flower House. Southend. Catford.*

Thursday 18th.

As far as billeting goes our luck is turning. The Priest's house is at the disposal of our mess and the colonel and adjutant sleep there, while the major and I once again are lucky to get the same rooms in the farmhouse as we had last time. There is a lovely bed also for me this time!

ADMS called a meeting of us medical officers and 'strafed' us re the sanitary conditions of the billets. I expect he himself has been getting 'strafed' by the DMS.

Friday 19th.

I have been busy all morning going around platoon billets.

Had a parade of men's feet in the afternoon then enjoyed a comfortable read in my billet.

Our whole division is now out and will be out for 21 days when our battalion goes back to a place called Ames, which is near St Hilaire.

Saturday 20th.

A quiet morning going around billets.

After lunch set out for Labourse to try and find William. After much searching, found him at Labourse cleaning his harness after this painfully cold ordeal. (It, the harness, was freezing all the time.)

We got excused stables and went and had some café-au-lait together then back to my billet at Sailly Labourse where we scraped together sausage and bacon etc. And after making an excellent fire we sat around and had a good chat and feed.

Sunday 21st.

Had an excellent night despite the hard frost. Had satisfaction of seeing Major Wilson get up at 6am preparatory to going forward to get billets at Ames, it always accentuates the pleasure of lying in a warm bed when someone is dressing in the same cold room.

Monday 22nd. Ames.

Got up at 5:30am and lit the stove and then retired to bed until it burnt up. Culwick brought in two eggs and some coffee from the farm and I enjoyed a good breakfast.

Bringing up the rear of the battalion I started at 7am walking by my horse as it was freezing. We passed through Labourse, Verquin, Chocques but because of dense fog it was quite impossible to see anything.

After leaving Chocques we halted in bright sunshine and had lunch and the General (Fowler) joined us with Trever his aid, they had some of our food. Trever was a great admirer of George's[30] *(brother)* drawings which he had seen in Edinburgh.

We had sent forward from Sailly all men suffering from bad feet etc. These went up in a motor lorry and we were scarcely troubled by sick men falling out en route. Indeed, only one man fell out of the battalion during the march of 17 miles. Arrived Ames at 3:15pm and the little village looked charming.

Tuesday 23rd.

The village is charming. The houses are thatched or roofed with rustic red tiles. It is not a village with just one street but is intersected by many lanes.

Most of the houses have nice gardens and orchards. The surrounding country is undulating and almost hilly and there is a nice brook which runs down the valley and turns two or three water-wheels within the village.

The people were also nice and seemed really pleased to see us. For myself I have a billet in the house of a man who runs a small brasserie and I enjoy a particularly clean bed and a hospitable host.

I would love to visit this little place in the spring or summer. They use dogs and horses a good deal to do their washing and thresh the corn. The former run round in a circle attached to a pole and the latter works on a treadmill. The dogs look well cared for and happy

Wednesday 24th.

A drizzling day. Inspected billets which are now from a sanitary point of view quite commendable. Trench latrines and incinerators complete the picture.

30. *On 9 July 1943 at 5.00pm German Dorniers dropped bombs on East Grinstead. The Whitehall cinema was showing 'Hopalong Cassidy' to an audience of mainly children, although some adults were also taking their places for the feature 'I Married A Witch'. Despite the air raid being sounded, many decided to stay, and the cinema took two direct hits. George's wife, Isabel and two daughters, Elizabeth and Erica were killed. I was privileged to have a short phone conversation with a lovely lady, Joy Crum, George's granddaughter. She told me her mother Charlotte was present that evening and survived the bombing, only to be injured in her leg by machine gun fire from a plane strafing the High street. George remained in East Grinstead until his death in 1945.*

Large cake from Ethel made by her cook. Excellent, but a pity that it has come now.

Thursday 25th.

The MO from 36th Field Ambulance took over at 9am so I was free. Indeed, my 11 days starts this morning. Packed in morning and after lunch set out for a long walk going west.

Found soon delightful countryside, well wooded and quite free from khaki. I passed through three or four villages. In the area a fair sprinkling of French soldiers and I couldn't help admiring their bright uniform, compared with our dull brown clothes that make everyone look the same, a dismal show of the worst.

Thinking that people were looking at me somewhat suspiciously I thought it best to make for Ames where I arrived about teatime.

At 8:30pm Corporal Turner came with me in the mess cart to Lillers. He very good-naturedly offered to show me to the station.

A nice hotel just opposite the station enables one to put in an enjoyable hour and at 10pm I reported to the transport officer and at 10:45pm the train started. Only two of us were in the carriage at first but soon we had six. Very comfortable carriages with good light and well heated.

Friday 26th.

Passed the night well with several short stops. A severe bellyache developed about 3am owing to bottled broad beans the night before and this pained me severely until 11am when it passed peacefully away.

About this time, they ran us into a siding and the men were able to buy coffee etc. I took the opportunity to make myself a cup of tea thanks to my spirit stove and tin with which I had thoughtfully provided myself. The tea and hard-boiled eggs, cake and sandwiches made a most refreshing breakfast.– Shaky writing is due to the vibration of the train and not to drink.

Passing through the outskirts of Rouen, we could see spires of a Cathedral, the town looked beautiful in soft sunshine and the well wooded hills rising on all sides makes one long to visit Rouen in the springtime of peace.

I really enjoyed the journey and did not find it tedious except the last hour owing to the fact that we proceeded at a snail's pace through the Havre docks arriving eventually at 6:30pm.

By stroke of good luck, I managed to get one of the last cabins, sharing it with a lieutenant colonel.

Saturday 27th. Havre-Southampton-Flower House

Woke about 2am with a desire to vomit owing to a heavy roll but settled down and slept very well until 6am when the boat slowed down and the break in the monotonous drone of the screws awoke me.

We began to dress thinking we were at the end of our journey. As a matter of fact, we had only slowed down to pick up pilots and there was another of ours joining before we entered Southampton.

We passed two or three hospital ships lying at anchor and very beautiful, the slender girdle of green fairy lights that encircled each boat was reflected in the still waters of the Solent.

By a stroke of luck I got off the boat first and got a good seat in the train, but no heating was on and the journey was terribly cold. Arrived Waterloo about 10:45am, drove to St Pauls, arrived there at 11:30am.

Very comfortable to recline on the sofa and tread on carpets. Hot bath and all the luxuries. Cecil arrived at 6:30pm from Canterbury looking very fit in khaki.

Sunday 28th.

Night in a comfortable bed, breakfast in bed! Angy came over.

Monday 29th.

Ethel, Joan and I went up to town and we did some glorious shopping. Lunch at Piccadilly restaurant was very poor. Then more shopping and tea and home for dinner.

Alice Whyte taught me the House of Commons. (solitaire card game)

Tuesday 30th.

Met Angy at Le Gobelin where all her guests had a very good meal which was well served-cooked. Theatre at 2:30pm at "the Globe" Peg O' My Heart[31] which was most excellent. Home for dinner.

DECEMBER 1915

Wednesday 1st.

Day at home until evening when I went up to see John, 11 New Square.

---

31. *Peg O' My Heart, play by J Harley Manners that opened on Broadway in 1912 starring his wife Laurette Taylor. It ran until 30 May 1914 then enjoyed a long run in London.*

Lincoln Inn, where he stays in a beautiful flat with Albert R[32].

Dined on Cheshire cheese, 'lark and beef steak pie', old Sherry and old Beer. John is very normal, looking well. Home by 10pm. *(John was recovering from a breakdown)*

Thursday 2nd.

My day this, I went up to town, Ethel, Joan, Alice Whyte, and self at 10am. Ethel and I separated and shopped, lunch at Scott's.

Met Angy after all, went to Mavournier at Her Majesty's with me. Tea at Formosa café in Piccadilly; I had arranged for a table at Café Royal upstairs and we had a good dinner there.

Friday 3rd.

Nice quiet day at home and I really believe it is the most enjoyable way of spending the day. All bussed to Bromley for tea, Alice was very charming.

Saturday 4th. Southampton

Joan left at 10am for Canterbury with Cecil. Ethel and Alice[33] saw me off on the 1:45 pm train. I had an appalling journey to St Pauls stopping between the stations and crawling, arriving at 2:45pm!

Angy met me and we drove to Waterloo and had tea. Found the 4pm train mostly full and was told to wait for the 4:30 which was nice and empty. I found a carriage with one other officer, a Canadian. I felt very miserable and agreed with the Canadian who said: "It's alright coming home but it is hell going back."

Arrived Southampton at 6:50pm and made my way to the embarkation officer who selected about six of our batch of officers and told the remaining of us that there was no more room on the boat, and we must embark at 10pm on the Veronnia. So, we went to the hotel and had an excellent dinner and smoke.

Went on board later, we now hear that the boat would not sail until 7am the following morning! Very comfortable bunk and excellent sleep.

32. *Albert Rothenstein/Rutherston. Artist. Slade School of Art. One of the 'Three Musketeers' with Augustus John and William Orpen, they indulged in what was known as precocious and extrovert 'Sladey' behaviour. Changed name to Rutherston in 1916 to sound more Anglicised. Brother of William Rothenstein. From 1916 served with the Northamptonshire Regiment in Egypt and Palestine. (Tate)*

33. *Sister Alice. 1865-1946 married Robert Henry Bicknell. (The Fothergills. A first history)*

Sunday 5th. Train Havre-Lillers.

Awoke to find we were moving out about 7:10 am but we did not get up as we soon encountered a heavy swell, so I forfeited breakfast and read till 11am when the sea became calm. So, I dressed and had coffee.

Not many officers but quite a few civilians. I noticed we were not escorted by a destroyer. I had one officer pointed out to me who was returning for the fifth time!

He was wounded at Mons, again wounded at Ypres. Then he went to Dardanelles and was wounded before he even landed and had to return home. He later was sent to Loos and was the only man out of a party of 50 who was left. He is now returning after a normal leave.

Arrived Havre about 1:30am. I am writing this from Hotel Tortoni where I will stay until late tonight as we must meet the 'leave boat' and go by their train. I am now a day late.

Monday 6th. Lillers.

A motor bus took us to the station at 12pm and we found the train waiting. It had no first-class carriages; the second class was already occupied with two a side.

My hope of a comfortable journey now ended, I had to get in somewhere so chose a second class with five others.

It was raining in torrents and we had to wait until the 'leave boat' arrived before starting. The boat eventually turned up and it was annoying to think the officers from it had started a day later from town than I had and here we are getting into the same train at Havre.

Train started at 4pm, what a journey! How difficult it is to sleep when you haven't got a corner seat! Nevertheless, I had some refreshing periods of unconsciousness.

The whole journey was a nightmare, not even a lavatory on the train. Arrived at Lillers exactly at 1 am thus it took twenty-one hours to travel from Havre to Lillers.

It was pelting with rain when I arrived. I got a bed at the estaminet opposite the station and slept very comfortably.

One of my train companions was a gunnery officer of the Gordons – 15th Division. He had been through the Battle of Loos on 25 Sept and was most interesting.

The 21st and 24th Divisions were the ones who were sent up to support the 15th etc and who gave way so miserably.

Tuesday 7th. Ames.

Left my baggage at the estaminet and after a good breakfast set out on foot to L'Ecleme two miles away where the 36th Field Ambulance was stationed. Here they lent me a car and with it went back to Ames to take over again from McClaylar who had been doing my work. He was a very robust Scotsman full of loud laughter and cheerfulness, but very 'Scotch'.

A man was explaining to me the other day how to pronounce the name of that fortress 'Przemysl' He said: "You don't sound the 'P' at all, it's a silent P, like the P in 'bathing.'

Raining hard all day.

Colonel away to look over the new trenches which we are going to hold. They returned about 9pm, very wet.

I went to bed about 8:30 pm as I was very tired after travelling from England. Slept badly owing to slight liver and had terrible dreams being pursued by huge billows of gas from attacking Germans.

Wednesday 8th. Busnettes.

Got up at 7am in rather a bad temper which I worked off on Culwick as soon as he put his head through the door.

It was a beautiful morning which was lucky. Gave one or two donations away, said goodbye to my hostess who had been very hospitable.

Our drums and fifes had been brought up to us from Armentieres, so we were able to march out of the little village in some style to the lilt of a very lively little march which was played exceedingly well.

We marched through Lillers without stopping, and arrived at our destination Busnettes about 12:30 pm. This is rather an uninteresting little place situated in low-lying land, which is now flooded with water after the recent rains. We have nice quarters in the estate and a bed.

Went on walk this afternoon and successfully lost my way and had to make for Lillers from which I retraced my way along this morning's route, arriving about 5pm feeling much better for the exercise.

Thursday 9th. Bethune.

Had another bad night with nightmares and then sleepless until almost 6am when Major Wilson turned up from leave. He had fared even worse than myself and arrived at Lillers about 5am out of a train eight hours late.

Got up at 7am and got my sick off by lorry and then we started away by 9am for Bethune in drizzling rain. We followed a long and tedious route along by-roads and it was bitterly cold. I walked most of the way. About 15 men fell out and were taken on the 38th Field Ambulance which was behind us.

Arrived feeling miserable at 1pm but was cheered to find an excellent billet.

I have a nice well-furnished bedroom with carpets, chairs, table and washing stand. I bought a bag of coal and soon there was a nice fire burning before which I could dry my waterproof leggings.

Walked into town and bought envelopes and paper.

The French seem to have taken a knock in Serbia and in the Adriatic by the Austrian fleet. The good news from our side is long deferred but everyone is full of confidence. Greeks seem determined to stay neutral for the present.

Friday 10th. Givenchy (trenches)

An excellent night. Culwick called me with tea at 8am and then lit my fire by which I dressed in comfort. What oh!

Battalion marched off in the morning. Nicholls and I were to go up in the afternoon, so we walked into

Bethune and got lunch then mounted our horses and rode along the canal to Givenchy.

Then on to a point where we dismounted and proceeded on foot to our battalion's position.

The firing line is three feet in water and despite thigh boots they are most of them wet through. They are in for 24 hours which is quite sufficient. Indeed, I do not think they could stand a longer period.

I inspected two platoons who had just come out and they were in a dreadful state, poor chaps. We had all their feet rubbed and they were supplied with dry boots and socks, had hot tea etc.

My dugout has two feet of water on the floor, the bunk is fixed to the wall and so my bed is at any rate dry and I have had a good night.

A good deal of shelling, but none in our trenches so far. Machine guns play down the road, but the fire is indirect and high.

Passages from 7th Battalion East Surrey Regiments war diaries.

Friday 10th. Givenchy.

We took over trenches on the right, two coys from 2nd Royal Welsh Fusiliers on left, and from 20th Royal Fusiliers. It was a very difficult relief as the two left coys could only relieve at night, but relief was successfully completed at 9pm. The trenches are practically all under water, but otherwise it is very quiet, the enemy are active with machine guns on the various roads but otherwise are very quiet.

Saturday 11th.

The Buffs hold the line in front of the Ducks Bill, we take on and hold the Warren and the Marches, the Queens are in support in Le Plantin. The West Kents in reserve at Le Quesnoy. Our battalion headquarters moved to Windy Corner and we share a house with the Queens.

A mine was set by us near the Ducks Bill but although it was lighted at 4pm it has yet not gone off. The Buffs are unable to occupy the front line until something happens as it is dangerously near them.

Sunday 12th.

The mine that failed to go off yesterday went off at midnight, there was no retaliation, the Germans only sent up a few red lights.

Monday 13th.

We were relieved by the West Kents and went into the brigade reserve at Les Quesnoy, about two and a half miles back.

Saturday 11th. Givenchy (trenches)

Not much doing, very quiet

Rather poor night, too many men in the dugout and air decidedly thick in consequence.

A cat and her kittens have made my dressing station their home, afforded me some entertainment during the sleepless hours.

Half a dozen times I saw the shadowy form of pussy passing out into the night and returning with a fat mouse each time. She drops each rodent in front of her offspring. Raining, water rising.

Sunday 12th. Trenches.

Have shifted my sleeping quarters and taken over the colonel's dugout. The HQ has gone down the line. Had quite a good night though somewhat cold. Rats and mice are abundant. Am now messing with Major James, excellent company.

Dugout two feet in water, water rising.

Monday 13th-Tuesday 14th. Les Quesnoy.

Our platoon in the firing trench had to stand with water which in most cases came above their thigh boots.

Their predicament was so piteous that at 3:30am when they had done twelve-and-a-half hours the colonel rang up and ordered them to be relieved, I was ordered to go down to Le Plantin and see that their feet were attended to.

It was beginning to freeze and of course pitch dark. The platoons were in a wretched state. Most of them were soaked through, trousers and socks and it was a blessing we got them out at half time.

We had some fire braziers of coke going and in front of them we rubbed their feet with grease and gave soup etc. I have had about six cases of trench foot during these two days, none of them very severe, though I have sent them all to hospital.

The general of the brigade, a damned old busy body, came around and cursed everybody. He cautioned me against getting trench foot in the regiment; quite disregarding the circumstances. Like so many of the 'Sods' in the higher command. We have had no casualties since we came here.

The Public Schools Battalion, from whom we took over, whose six days in the trenches was their baptism of warfare since arriving in France. They were a quiet source of amusement since they were full of the dangers of the position and warned us against all sorts of non-existing terrors, dangerous roads etc.

We were relieved in the evening and I stayed back to see to the feet of the platoon in the watery firing line. They were in good condition.

Marched with Major James to the estaminet corner and then mounted my horse and rode to Quesnoy, a little straggling village where we have quite nice house and beds.

Rather a cheery evening, conversation became somewhat elastic and the major said: "My first is an ejaculation, my second is I can be found in a kitchen and you can suck my whole." He explained that the answer was an orange.

He told us how a gentleman, after dining too well, attempted to retell the above to a friend. He said: "My first is an ejaculation, my second is I can be found in the kitchen and you can kiss my dick*(scrubbed out)* arse because I am a lemon." Then Nicholls asked us: "What made the lobster blush?" and he told us the reason, because he saw the oysters close up.

The conversation then resumed its normal level.

Walked out with Nicholls to see his brother's battery. They were 8-inch howitzers and we saw them fire directed by aircraft; we also saw a 12-inch howitzer on the rails ready to fire.

Wednesday 15th. Essars.

We marched off about 9:30am and arrived at Essars, a small village about half an hour later.

We took over from the Berks and were disappointed not to go back to Bethune for our billeting, but this is our furthest move back in the sequence of moves.

In the afternoon the colonel, adjutant and self walked into Bethune which is only three miles away and there we did some shopping, had tea etc at a very nice place and afterwards the colonel and I looked in at the cinema show which was not very exciting.

We three then went to a newly-formed club for English-Allied officers and we had a very decent dinner and arrived home about 10:30pm. Excellent night in a nice bed, sleeping in the same room with Major Wilson.

Thursday 16th.

A good number of sicknesses are to be seen. Indeed, my whole morning was well occupied in seeing the sick. Had a walk in the afternoon and wrote letters. Not much encouragement to go out as the country around is quite flat and uninteresting and so hopelessly full of khaki.

How one loathes the sight of these dismal khaki uniforms! How tiring constant saluting! How hateful the whole concern.

General French has been replaced by General Haig.

The Allies are now apparently thrust back into Greece. There is talk of a big German offensive in the west.

Friday 17th.

A present of tobacco and toffee from the Grasmere Red Cross Guild of Bankers, with a dear picture postcard of Langdale Tarn. Very kind of them!

Also cakes from Miss Dickinson, dear soul. Written to Nellie.

Indoors most of the day feeling rather rotten. Visited a child in the house opposite, it was rather a dear little boy of five with a croup, which made me anxious in case it might be a Dip case *(Diphtheria)*.

Saturday 18th. Essars.

Feel very seedy with a sore throat. ADMS came around some of my billets and strafed mildly about things of minor importance.

Then he was saying goodbye, saying that he thought he had better depart before he made himself too unpopular. He was quite entertaining, but I feel too seedy to appreciate him today.

Went to bed this afternoon feeling rather desperate regarding trenches tomorrow.

Vomiting, temp at 4:30pm about normal with one of my thermometers, I felt so certain it was raised that I sent for our last remaining thermometer and this gave a reading over two degrees higher!

Major Wilson insisted on sending for a medical man from Bethune. Doctor Kelly soon arrived and was very kind, promised to see me in the morning.

Sunday 19th. Bethune French Red Cross Hospital.

Temperature rose during the night. Kelly saw my sick and then took me by car to the above address. I was very glad to get into a nice little bed in a big ward with 18 other beds.

Throat very sore, temp began to rise about midnight and as it rose I felt more restless, uncomfortable and a craving for more heat. The night sister sprayed me with coldish water, I felt much easier indeed.

My temp as it afterwards transpired was then at one-hundred-and-five, which wasn't so bad for tonsillitis and the spraying reduced it to 103.

Monday 20th.

Temp morning 105, pulse 104. Temp evening 102, pulse 100.

The above was copied from my chart, one is bound to feel a bit sceptical about the 105 temp, especially with one's experience as to the ordinary hospital thermometer, that there should only be a difference of four beats between my pulse when temp stood at 105 than at 102, points to some inaccuracy?

Passages from 7th Battalion East Surrey Regiments war diaries.

Sunday 19th. Festubert.

We relieved the 8th Fusiliers in the trenches, relief completed at 7:30pm. The front line consisted of groups of islands being the only dry spots in a once front trench. There was no communication to the rear except over the open at night. Two (half coys) in the front line who were relieved every twenty-four hours from the village line Epinette.

Tuesday 21st.

There is an old support line between our islands and the old British line in which we lit fires, which successfully drew the enemy as he constantly shelled there.

Wednesday 22nd.

A gas attack was made by us in front of Givenchy at 9pm. It was not successful, as earlier in the day a gas cylinder had been burst by a bomb which the Germans evidently smelt, as soon as we started sending over the gas the Germans at once lit fires sent up very lights and started a heavy shelling, from a spectacular point of view it was a great success but owing to it not being a surprise it isn't thought that we did much damage.

Tuesday 21st.

Temp 100 morning and 99 evening.

This is the first day on which I have felt capable of writing up my diary.

The soreness of the throat would have been bearable but reading and writing became an impossibility by reason of a continuous headache which increased always with a rise in temperature The hospital is kept only for short illnesses and I notice most of those present are suffering complaints like my own, viz toxaemia[34] brought on by overeating and insufficient exercise to work them off.

Most of such complaints are put down here; as well as everywhere else as tonsillitis, as in my own case, but there is no germ responsible for 80 per cent of such attacks. They are mostly the effects of poisons generated and pent up in the liver and body generally. These attacks really express a very healthy and timely awakening of the body to its true state. The attacks mainly illustrate Nature's method of getting rid of toxins. She does not do it by means of delicately balanced synthetic preparations, she does it, my dear boy, by oxidation – she burns 'em up – hence the rise in temperature etc.

Wednesday 22nd.

Lieut Robinson runs this show, a queer, charming little man of 42 with sharply cut features and a manner which at first might appear abrupt but which later, when you realise it, to be mainly a normal mode of delivery, betokens nothing which is not sympathetic and painstaking.

The two nursing sisters are delightful. It is wonderful how people can keep so cheerful despite living so long among sick people. My only adverse criticism has to do with the understaffing of orderlies etc. It seems to me we would benefit by an increase of orderlies and one wonders why on earth they don't get more men.

Today it was discovered that I have developed a thick scarlatina-like rash all over me. I attach no importance myself as I remember having it with my last attack, in consequence they think I should stay in bed which is a pity.

However, the appearance of this rash has now given a considerable amount of interest among the medical men.

Some kind; thoughtful presents from people at home today. A letter and knitted scarf from Carine Thorne, she is invalided with a dilated heart. I shall make a point of visiting her and Jimmie on my return.

_____

34. *The symptoms suggest trench fever. High temperature, headache, painful legs and rash.*

94

Thursday 23rd. Bethune hospital.

"It is the property of things seen for the first time, or for the first time after long, like the flowers in spring to reawaken in us the sharp edge of sense and that impression of mystic strangeness which otherwise passes out of life with the coming of years." R L Stevenson.

It looks as though I may have to spend my Xmas here. This rash blocks the way. It is still there and my temp is normal.

Sister had the ward decorated this afternoon with huge festoons of ivy. I never saw such lengthy festoons of ivy; they and sprays of green palm leaves show up against the yellow and white walls and ceiling.

I hear our battalion goes out of the firing trench tonight into Epinette where they are still considered in support trenches and will carry on work parties for three days. After that I hope they may be billeted at Bethune for eight days. It's raining now, and I'm very comfortable in bed.

Friday 24th.

I got up after tea and felt most terribly weak, low, and depressed. This happily wore off considerably as time went on and I got to bed feeling much better.

At midnight a military band came into the hall below and played all sorts of jolly waltzes for nearly an hour. It felt quite cheerful and Christmassy. Some of our convalescent 'invalids' came out in their hospital pink pyjamas and danced with the nurses in the hall. It was very laughable though when the band left us, the lights were turned out. Silence returned. I heard them strike up again some distance off with some familiar Xmas hymns and it reminded me so of old Grasmere *(childhood home)* that the tears sprang to my eyes. For I could imagine myself back again at Allan Bank[35] in bed and I could hear pa's window go up with its cheerful creak and then the few words he spoke to the band before dropping down his subscription wrapped in a bit of paper Then the crunch of the gravel and voices as the village band moved away.

Saturday 25th. Xmas Day Bethune hospital.

The rash has disappeared and though still weak I feel very well. Well, here we are Xmas Day. 'Peace and good will towards men!' We spent

---

35. *Allan Bank, Grasmere, is now owned by the National Trust and was once home to William Wordsworth. It holds the diary of the doctor's father, George, with frequent mentions of Regie as a child.*

quite a nice day, a simple luncheon and in the evening, things became quite festive. The table was dressed up with flowers and about 12 of us sat down to soup, turbot, turkey and cauliflower, plum pudding and dessert, stout, beer, and lemonade. The dinner was nicely served too, the food wasn't just slopped on one's plate.

After dinner the sister brought in half a dozen half bottles of hospital champagne so that all together, things quite hummed. We had a good gramophone with a good many indifferent records and there was a piano nobody could play. There has been a rather puzzling patient here since last Monday. He was sent in as a hysterical case *(shell shock)* and indeed he looked in most ways entirely so, although, there were also present indications of nerve trouble in the legs which looked undoubtedly organic. He had no temp and pulse was normal, he complained of profound loss of power on one side, pain numbness etc.

Sunday 26th.

Well, last night I was just getting off to sleep when he suddenly fell out of bed onto the floor and when picked up he was dead. It would be interesting to know the true diagnosis.

Doctor Robinson, the head surgeon here, diagnosed the above as Landry's Paralysis having seen a similar case where no temperature occurred. General Scott and the ADMS visited the hospital this morning. The general made personal enquiries all round, the ADMS was rather amusing and apologised profusely and jokingly for strafing me the last time we met, which was the same day I came in here. Went to a concert in the afternoon given by the French mission. We had a free box as an invitation to the ill and wounded at this hospital.

I was handicapped by ignorance of French; the turns were too long and encores too liberal.

Passages from 7th Battalion East Surrey Regiments war diaries.
Thursday 23rd. Epinette.

We are relieved in the front line by West Kents. We went into brigade support at Epinette, the men were in ruined houses and were comfortable. Very few working parties.

Friday 24th. Our artillery kept up an incessant fire as a forerunner to Christmas Day.

> *Saturday 25th.*
>
> *No fraternizing this year[36] although the Germans tried to make peaceful advances by showing the white flag. Our artillery consistently pounded their trenches all day and night. A certain amount of retaliation took place but not nearly as much as we put over.*

Monday 27th.

I feel very much better today and the weakness in my knees is disappearing. Doctor Robinson says I may go back tomorrow, this will suit as we come out of trenches tonight and return to Essars for four days.

Nash from the 36th Field Ambulance who has been doing my work came to see me.

Tuesday 28th.

Returned to Essars by mess cart and took over from Nash who was quite fed up with regiment life. Found Nicholls just returned from leave and very cheery.

Also found that I was just in time for another Xmas dinner which the colonel had postponed until they came out of the trenches. We had quite a good dinner with turkey, plum pudding, and plenty of etc.

Wednesday 29th.

Busied myself among the billets and made paths over the mud to the latrines by stealing from the heaps of stones which lay on the roadside.

In the afternoon Nicholls and I walked over to Bethune and went to the divisional pantomime which was wonderfully good. The men dressed up as women and allowed great amusement.

We had dinner at the Bethune club afterwards and it was quite a farce owing to appalling intervals between the courses.

Thursday 30th.

Nothing to note, went on walk, wrote letters etc.

---

36. *Commonwealth War Graves Commission records show a total 64 war dead for Christmas Day 1915 (voltaire60. Great War Forum). Taking into account earlier wounded men who died of wounds or illness that day makes it a very low number of deaths along the entire front line. Although there was no official truce and no fraternising allowed, did the opposing front line soldiers have their own unwritten rule, 'Live and let live'?*

I played Patience in the evening, and tried Streets of Venice, which was shown to me the other day.

Friday 31st. Windy Corner trenches.

The arrangement of the trenches here is rather extraordinary, platoons are dotted about.

This time I have my dressing station just by the battalion headquarters and I am sleeping at HQ myself.

We are hopelessly far away from the firing line but considering all things, it is probably the best place for the dressing station.

We rode here this afternoon. It was raining hard, our route led us along the Le Bassee canal most of the way.

This is a half-ruined place like Vermelles, the extraordinary thing is that this house remains perfectly intact and never seems to get shelled. Perhaps it is partly hidden. Anyhow it is rather nice to occupy a house when one is in the firing line.

We sat up playing Patience and talking before a nice fire. There present, the colonel, Major Wilson, Major James, Captain Nicholls, myself, a machine gun officer and a liaison officer.

At midnight our field guns opened rapid fire just to show there was no ill feeling. The Germans scarcely replied, and things settled down. Thus, the old year went out and the new year came in. Not to the merry ringing of church bells but to the roaring of countless guns.

Passages from 7th Battalion East Surrey Regiments war diaries.
Wednesday 29th.

Men were busy house-maiding the various keeps in our area. The divisional concert troop were doing a pantomime in the municipal theatre Bethune, called Aladdin, considering that there were no females it was wonderfully produced. The theatre was crowded with troops from all corps.

Friday 31st.

We took over the Givenchy trenches from the 9th Royal Fusiliers. At midnight all our field guns fired salvos to announce the new year, the Germans replied on our front with three salvos from one battery which did no damage. Then everything was quiet.

> *The month has been quiet but very wet, our casualties have been very slight and sickness wonderfully slight considering that often the men have had to stand up to their middles in water.*
>
> *Strength 31 Dec. Officers 30, OR 1,048. Casualties, Killed. Officers nil, OR four. Wounded, Officers nil, OR six. Sick hospital, Officers one, OR forty.*

JANUARY 1916.

Saturday 1st. Windy Corner.

A disappointing year. Have made feeble efforts to live up to my ideals, for the most part have sunk into materialism, not of the grossest type, thank God, but still as a performance the show has been a failure.

The war is my excuse. It has been impossible to altogether choose a method of living. One has had to compromise. The fruitarian diet has had to be abandoned. It has been impossible to read anything serious or thought provoking apart from literature bearing on the war. I have found it impossible to follow theosophy except on rare occasions. The war dominates everything.

Thank goodness I am so saturated with theosophy that I must always be influenced by it, if only to the extent of being provoked from sinking to any humiliating level of thought or deed. But I suffer from a spiritual dryness which I fear cannot be relieved until this frightful war has ceased.

What a terrible future lies before us. The advance in spring for instance – what a frightful business to look forward to, and, how many of those around me as I now write will be here to tell the tale?

I wonder whether I shall live through it! I feel perfectly fearless and resigned about it. We are indeed 'on the knees of the Gods!'

Things quiet and no casualties. Rain and wind got up until it blew a gale. Remained indoors all day. The Colonel went on leave, leaving us after dinner.

Sunday 2nd. Windy Corner, Quesnoy.

The Germans were very much in evidence today. They started by blowing up two or three mines and damaged some of our trenches burying 16 men in one place.

Then they bombarded our trenches with high explosives, it was a wonderful sight to watch, the lyddite (high explosive) bursting in every direction, licking the ground with tongues of yellow and black smoke. They also sent over a good many rifle grenades and we had five slightly wounded from one of these and I also attended four Buffs.

While this was going on they put 5.9-inch high explosive shrapnel just to the right of Windy Corner. It burst with a terrific report but caused no casualties and none fell on our HQ.

I went up into the observation station and watched things for a time. We eventually fired all our howitzers and field guns on the enemy lines and guns etc; there was pandemonium for some time, the afternoon was quiet.

We are now changed over every 48 hours which is a great nuisance.

The West Kents took over from us. The relief was bungled as usual and we didn't leave Windy Corner until 8:30pm. We rode, Major Wilson, Nicholls and self, through inky darkness and drizzling rain driven by a fierce wind. Arrived at Quesnoy at 9:30pm. Hot soup and sausages

Monday 3rd.

A very comfortable bed at the top of the house. At 2pm set out on horseback to Cormette to see William. Cormette lies about three miles from Bethune and it took me an hour to get there. Found Bartholomew there buying a horse or recycling one from Major Russell the CO of KEH.

Bart congratulated me, and when I asked him why; he said: "For being mentioned in despatches. I saw your name in the Times the other day! I said: 'This is the first I had heard of it' and thanked him.

William looked very fit and we walked over to Hinges, a small village close by and had coffee together. He was very fed up with the life there and told me how all the men cordially dislike the CO who does nothing for their pleasure and overwhelms them with fatigues, even on Xmas Day.

In the evening after comfortably getting into slacks and slippers I had a message to go down and see Lieutenant Anns who with C-coy was billeted on the canal bank quite near Bethune. I took Leeds with me and led by an orderly we set out through inky darkness.

The orderly took us along most appalling roads and byways where shell holes crowded into one. I must inevitably have fallen had it not been for an electric lamp which I fortunately brought with me. Found Anns with flu. Found my way back by a much better road arriving soon after 10pm.

Passages from 7th Battalion East Surrey Regiments war diaries.

Saturday 1st January 1916.

A quiet day. Last night we shot six German revellers, they were quite drunk and walking about on top of a crater. The colonel went on leave in the evening. Major Wilson taking over command with Major James second in command.

Sunday 2nd.

The enemy exploded a mine just north of the Le Bassee canal, which started a heavy artillery strafe on both sides, which lasted till the evening. The enemy put over mostly heavy shrapnel 5.9-inch but did little or no damage. We were relieved by the West Kents and went into the brigade reserve at Le Quesnoy.

Tuesday 4th. Windy Corner Quesnoy.

Had rather a large dose of sick men because in addition to our own men I had to see a whole lot of RE (*Royal Engineers*) also some West Hants and Buffs. Went around billets through a sea of mud.

Rain began to come down in a regular drizzle in the afternoon and we therefore decided not to go up to trenches on foot. We mounted our horses at 5pm and rode up at a walk arriving at Windy Corner about 6pm.

It appeared that during the relief nine of our men were hit by a rifle grenade and were dressed by Carson, MO to West Kents from whom we are taking over, none of the wounds were serious. Slept on a stretcher quite well except for the traverse of rain into the back of my shoulder all the night.

Wednesday 5th. Windy Corner (trenches)

A beautiful sunny morning, so curiously warm for time of year. Had to send a message to ADMS re my renewal of contract. Nicholls invited me to send it to him at Bethune – six miles away or so by pigeon.

So, two identical messages were written on very thin soft paper and these were each rolled neatly up and pushed into a little cylinder of aluminium which was clipped to the foot of two birds. That the message arrived safely is proved by me getting an answer to my note. As a matter of fact, I had hardly dispatched the note when the ADMS turned up. He was alone and asked me to go around the trenches with him.

He was evidently fulfilling some red tape ordeal as our tour of the brigade trenches was a mere joyride and we did not even glance at a latrine.

The trenches were very narrow and broken down and going was difficult. I saw nothing interesting except a row of trees near Givenchy church which were absolutely 'polled' and evenly pruned to the smaller branches by shell fire of various kinds.

Thursday 6th.

The bad men shelled Le Plantin most of the day. We had one or two platoons there and had one killed and three wounded with shrapnel.

Major James asked me to walk up to Le Plantin with him in the afternoon but when we had gone halfway the enemies' shells began to fall so uncomfortably close that we turned back, the subject of our journey being unimportant.

We changed headquarters with West Kents, and we now occupy quarters to the right of Windy Corner, we are not too well billeted and more exposed to shelling.

Have received a letter of congratulations from Mrs Cross for being mentioned in despatches, so I suppose it is correct, although I have not yet seen my name.

I have now got to inject my wounded with a vaccine supplied to me as a preventive against gangrene etc.

Friday 7th. Windy Corner

We had large working parties on duty today and I had a correspondingly large hunk of sickness to deal with. It is rather disgusting having to, as it were, drive the men back to duty. Instead of being able to sit down and in a friendly and sympathetic way, interview and treat your patient, you have in the greater proportion of cases to steel yourself and pit yourself against your patient. All the time I continue to feel so sorry for them because they indeed have a dog's life.

I went out with Major Wilson this afternoon to see some keeps and we nearly got dished by a shrapnel. They were shelling parallel to our road and before trenching off at right angles we, at the last minute, decided to wait for the next shell just to see which way they were putting them.

Just as we drew up against a wall it came and burst above us, the bullets came pelting down into the road, but we were not hit.

But the most important event of the day took place this evening when I 'got out' the Streets of Venice.

Saturday 8th.

Because of an enemy aeroplane which was flying over us this morning, they shelled our old headquarters now occupied by the West Kents. There was no direct hit, though the outhouses were much damaged, one shell took the roof off my old dressing station en passant and smashed into a room where there was much bully beef stored. It was amusing to see the twisted beef tins, reminding one of the Three Men in a Boat[37] episode.

Unfortunately, a captain in the KEH who oversaw village machine guns was standing within the doorway of the house and was badly hit. Visited Givenchy Keeps with Nicholls this afternoon.

Passages from 7th Battalion East Surrey Regiments war diaries.

Tuesday 4th.

We relieved the West Kents in the trenches at Windy Corner again. Nine casualties from rifle grenades.

Wednesday 5th.

The enemy shelled Le Plantin all day mainly with 5.9-inch high explosive. One man killed and four wounded. Four more casualties from rifle grenades.

Friday 7th Working parties under RE all day. Major James went on leave.

Saturday 8th.

A fine day, the enemy had an aeroplane up all morning and consequently shelled the village line rather heavily with shells of all sizes. They also shelled battalion HQ at Windy Corner, doing considerable damage to surrounding buildings. One of our water carts was smashed up, the horses being killed.

---

37. Three Men in a Boat – humorous account of a two-week boating holiday from Kingston upon Thames to Oxford and back. (Jerome K Jerome, published 1889)

Sunday 9th Essars.

There was a lecture on gas helmets at Bethune 3rd Battalion. I arranged for Carson to do my work and sent for my horse to meet me at HQ Windy Corner.

In the meantime, they started to 'crump' Lone Farm, the field ambulance ADS, where the road led down. My groom was prevented from coming up by reason of the shelling, so I made my way down parallel to the road but 300 yards to the left of the farm.

It was wonderful to hear the shells approaching over my head and crashing down close to the farm. The shooting was very bad I thought. As each crump landed its huge black smoke rose into the air, I had to crouch to expose as little of my body to the splinters which fell around me.

After about 25 shots they at last landed one as I thought on the high walls of the courtyard and a huge cloud of red brick dust rose in the air. I knew that they had splendid cellars so did not fear for Captain Milne and his RAMC men who I knew were there. After that or after a few more misses the firing ceased so I rode on to Bethune.

The lecture was given by an expert on gas. He said the efficiency of the helmets against gas was proved absolutely. He said the Germans were using gas now which was composed of Chloral Phosgene – phosgene being the gas produced when chloroform is exposed to air and has a delayed action on the bronchial tubes.

Monday 10th.

I hear Colonel Wilson, our ADMS, is leaving and being promoted to corps. Went on a nice long walk this afternoon to Lacon, entered church and saw some rather curious old stained-glass windows. Got home for tea.

Tuesday 11th.

Went into Bethune in a mess cart with Corporal Turner and bought an acetylene lamp for mess.

Met Goldsmith of 38th Field Ambulance. He told me that Milne at Lone Farm was only grazed on the leg, but three or four of the men have since died of wounds. If they had only remained in the cellar, not one would have been hurt.

Letters of congratulations from Ethel, Joan and Alice, with a small paragraph from the Dalton Guardian. Beautiful sunny weather and as mild as spring

Wednesday 12th. Essars.

Nothing to note, a fine, sunny quiet day. The colonel returned from leave.

Thursday 13th. Festubert trenches.

We rode up to the trenches or rather to Festubert, arriving about 7pm. It was moonlight and one could see that the village was a mass of ruins.

Walked from there to so-called trenches. As a matter of fact, they are all 'breastworks' on this line. It is delightful to have no trenches to struggle through and now that the water has been drained so successfully and trench boards laid down, it is comparatively comfortable.

Also, we have a long extensive view of both German and English lines. We can see the shells bursting exceedingly well. I am sharing a dugout with Nicholls; it is quite dry but so low that you must crouch to get in. There is a supply of straw.

Watched good strafe of German trenches this afternoon through my powerful glasses.

Friday 14th.

No casualties so far, a good deal of shelling. Thousands of rats, one ran over my head during the night, also mice. I am rather anxious about my trench coat as the MO of 8th Fusiliers who was occupying my dugout had his gnawed through one day.

A mouse fell into my Po (chamber pot) during the night and after splashing about for a time managed to scramble out thanks to the tin being somewhat battered in places.

Saturday 15th.

There was an artillery strafe arranged for today at 10am, a 12-inch howitzer, 9.2-inch and all the other smaller ones were going to fire for two hours but so far nothing out of the ordinary has occurred. It is cloudy so perhaps it has been postponed.

This is a Patience I find very thought provoking – 'The Scorpion's Tail', two packs. You choose one of these rows as your tail. Turn up one card at a time from the pack. If it is an ace, put it up, if it won't go on the exposed cards. Building down in alternate colours it must be put on a tail. Portions of sequences may be moved; a space may be filled by any exposed card or sequence of cards.

Sunday 16th. Epinette.

A letter from Cross. Profits for last quarter ending Dec 30th were £290. He says the Commission is paying us a very small proportion of what is due to us for panel practice. Cross says they now owe us almost £300. He paid into my account £120 leaving surplus to pay income tax, which will be £100.

We have over 2,000 on our panel but he says that out of these as many as 1,400 applied for medicine during the year. This is a very high proportion and I don't see how the powers that be can under this circumstance lower our capitation fee. The West Kents took over from us in the trenches. Nicholls and I left together before the relief was complete and after a rather sweaty walk because of my trench coat we found our HQ. It is a farmhouse and very comfortable, the kitchen making a splendid room for mess with good fireplaces and with a roof intact. One feels very secure here.

The Kents were here three days ago, a six-inch shell crashed through the kitchen window and buried itself in the floor. Fortunately, it didn't explode, and the cook was unhurt.

Slept on a stretcher and was beastly cold all night. The cold air passes beneath the canvas of a stretcher and although you may pile a mountain of clothes over yourself, your back always remains as cold as ice.

Monday 17th.Bellerive billet.

Many things strike one's attention in this war and the life out here. One is particularly struck by the extraordinary lack of truth exemplified by the reports of events given by eye-witnesses and particularly by those handing on the report by hearsay.

There is somehow a universal tendency and desire to exaggerate all details to a stupendous extent. It is therefore not surprising that extraordinary rumours are always going around. At first one attached huge importance to every tale but now I scarcely ever take the slightest interest in such rumours.

We hear and have heard for months at short intervals that – the Kaiser is dead – that the Crown Prince is wounded – that we are going to the Dardanelles. These are the most frequent reports.

When the war is over, the French in the north of France will find themselves up against another enemy, 'the Rat'. The trenches have proved ideal breeding grounds for him. The crevices among the sandbags, the dead and the ruined houses are happy hunting grounds for him. While he finds a never-ending supply of food thrown lavishly around by the troops.

This wholesale waste of food is one of the most stupendous things possible to dismay me. I have seen portions of trench parapets built out of unused corned beef tins. I have seen heaps of biscuits rotting in an old billet; while the amount of good wholesome food which daily finds its way to the incinerator is enough to satisfy any thinking person that we are a very amateurish Army in more than one direction.

Thursday 18th. Le Perriere, billets.

Well we were relieved at Epinette by the 22nd Welsh Fusiliers (33rd Division). They had only been out two months and were very keen and cheerful. I hope their keenness will continue but I am quite sure their cheerfulness will diminish.

The adjutant, Nicholls, had to go on to Bethune with Major Wilson who by the bye was given the DSO the day before yesterday (*Distinguished Service Order*). So, I acted as adjutant during the relief and in consequence had a good deal of fun thrown at me afterwards.

Well, we marched on the 17th to Bellerive, stopping on the way at a small farm near Hemlin. I dismounted soon after starting and walked the eight miles enjoying the exercise and being able to keep warm, which is more than I can do when riding behind a battalion.

Only three or four men fell out with sore feet and the journey was a very pleasant one and the weather delightfully spring-like. We are now going back for sixteen days of so-called rest. At Bellerive we had a very nice house as HQ and comfortable beds. It started the next morning at 10:30am and the battalion marched independent of the transport. I had a horse ambulance behind me and managed to get through the journey very well, thanks.

Wednesday 19th.

Drizzled with rain but the march was pleasant along the canal for the most part. Arrived about 12:30pm. HQ is a farmhouse with rather limited accommodation and no fire or stove in the mess room. We managed to hire a stove and are now very comfortable.

For myself I am very lucky: I have two delightful rooms in a small very clean farm, a most comfortable bed with a table, chair, and pegs on the wall. Culwick, Leeds and others occupy a barn behind the farm and are also very well contented. Leeds is now and in future acting as my servant, he is splendid and lays himself out to make one comfortable in every possible way.

Thursday 20th.

Busy with billets, improving latrines, building paths through mud to same. I make use of the prisoners for this purpose. They of course prefer such work to being tied up by the hands as is done in first field punishment.

At 2pm Colonel Nicholls and I rode to a place near Ham where General Joffre[38] was going to inspect some of our 12th Division. We were kept waiting for over two hours and I felt sorry for the brigade which was on parade as they must have felt the bitter wind very much. However, the general eventually arrived with a string of other motor cars and was introduced to our general by Field Marshal Haig. The Old Man passed quite close to me and it was rather inspiring to see the man who moves the pieces in this stupendous and ghastly game.

We arrived home about 5pm and I just had time for a cup of tea before setting off on bike for Gonnehem six miles away, where by arrangement met Colonel Goddant CO of 38th Field Ambulance and he took me in his car to Fouguieres where we were going to have dinner with the 36th Field Ambulance to celebrate Major Turner's DSO.

The 36th Field Ambulance have formed a rest station there and the mayor of the village has lent them his house. It is a splendid chateau with some beautiful panel paintings and capacious rooms.

Everyone was very nice, I received congratulations from all sides. The dinner was most excellent. On returning to Gonnehem I resumed my journey back on the bike. What a ride! No lamp, mud inches deep and slippery. At Busnes, which was only one mile from home, I took the wrong turn and after wandering about on the most appallingly muddy

---

38. *General Joseph Joffre. 1852-1931. The French general served as Commander-in -Chief of French forces on the western front from the beginning of the war until the end of 1916 when his political position suffered after Verdun and the Somme. (Wikipedia)*

roads for half an hour was relieved to recognise our village once again, it was 1:15am before I got back.

What a 'cushy' time I might have continued to have with the 36th Field Ambulance had I remained with them – the Prince of Wales[39] billeted in the chateau before them and their quartermaster now occupies the 'Prince's' bed.

The mayor who owns the house is a most distinguished old man in appearance. He is a staunch loyalist too. After dinner he came in and made a speech. He spoke so slowly and distinctly that I could understand nearly all he said.

Friday 21st.

My stretcher bearers are now handed over to me during the time we are 'down', and I must arrange parades for them. Lectured this morning to them in a barn and then sent them on a route march.

This is the anniversary of my joining the service and I now have the right to 'putting up' another star on my sleeve.

Saturday 22nd. Perrier.

Wrote last week to the manager of Dalton bank for advice re investments and for a statement of my balance in the bank. Heard from him today: deposit £1,067.11.8 – current £105.4.8 – total £1,172.16.4.

Am taking a good deal of sweat over billets, and have now got them into very good order.

Sunday 23rd.

A most gorgeous day, brilliant sun which became quite hot as the day went on. At 11am Colonel Nicholls and I set out on horseback to a town which lies on the canal about seven miles away. The colonel usually rides like the devil and on this occasion was no exception, so we arrived about midday.

We went over to the Cathedral. It is a grand building, especially outside with a very beautiful tower. The inside was as usual disappointing, the

---

39. *Prince Edward, later to become Edward VIII, joined the Grenadier Guards in June 1914 but never saw active service. He was said to have been desperate to go to the front and fight but was banned from doing so by Lord Kitchener in case the future King was killed or captured by the Germans. He had to make do with visiting the men on several occasions at different locations each around five miles from the front line between January and September 1915. (Telegraph)*

pillars were 'plastered' in colour to represent real stone and the vaulted ceilings were papered blue with golden stars instead of fresco work. The false ring about everything prevented that awe and reverence which one is accustomed to when inside large and beautiful buildings. There were two or three very wonderful stained-glass windows, full of life like figures and exquisite colouring.

We were just in time to witness a French soldier being decorated with the Médaille militaire. The ceremony took place in the Gran Plaza, English and French troops paraded. There was a band, town councillors, a French colonel and the victim – a youth who had lost an eye from a wound. The colonel fixed on the medal, kissed the soldier on both cheeks and the band played the Marseillaise.

Everyone clapped their hands. Lastly, with the band playing a good march, all the troops marched past the hero and gave him eyes right as they passed.

Monday 24th.

The post brought me a notification from Holt that sixty pounds had been placed to my account as gratuity for a year's service. I noticed they had also deducted five pounds-eight for income tax.

Johnson the divisional sanitary officer came this morning and went round the billets with me, he was very pleased with all I had done.

Tuesday 25th.

Several officers were sick. Funny thing is how one gets more sickness when down at rest in billets.

We had a brigade route march, saw sick at 7:30am and we started at 8:30, about six miles and quite enjoyable as it was a glorious day and the march was not too long.

Wednesday 26th.

Found out where William is and sent a parcel down to him this morning with Leeds. Also planned for going over in the afternoon. I found I had so much to do that I couldn't get away.

The divisional manoeuvres were billed to start tomorrow. The HQ kept us in the dark as to details regarding time of starting etc. At 8:30am they sent to say it was cancelled and now at 10:30am as I write we have received orders to be ready to start at two hours' notice.

Went to bed with clothes on and slept badly, expecting to be called up every minute. Nothing transpired, the night passed quietly. We must therefore begin from today.

Thursday 27th.

They tell me this is the Kaiser's birthday, so perhaps we expected activity on the part of the enemy, which may account for our division being kept on the 'qui-vive' *(state of alertness)* because we are still kept on two hours' notice.

Had a quiet stroll along a country lane and was amazed to see so many signs of spring. I remember how in Dalton I used to eagerly watch for the buds on the hawthorn to burst and I call to mind that in 1913 I saw buds breaking on March 7th – the earliest of any spring.

But fancy here on January 27th seeing the hawthorn buds green and already bursting in sheltered places! All kinds of undergrowth now green, young nettles sprouting, lilac buds full green.

Friday 28th.

There is apparently great activity on the German side and ours. We can hear guns firing. Our manoeuvres have been postponed and instead, we are out on two hours' notice which looks as though the higher command are a trifle uneasy.

I walked over to William's troop this afternoon, about three miles away. He was out but they told me he had gone into Lillers to take two horses to be shod. So, I walked toward the town, and it was not long before I spied him approaching. He was looking very fit. We went to a little farm and had coffee and a good chat.

I took a short cut home along terribly muddy roads and arrived just in time for dinner.

We were supposed to go to bed with our clothes on. My bed looked so comfortable that I decided to relieve myself of military discipline and my clothes and with a sigh of relief sank into my 'cushie' couch and was soon asleep.

Saturday 29th.

I think I have a case of typhoid; it is mild and atypical *(irregular)* but the rash is well marked. This is the first case I have had in my battalion.

Walked out to canal bank and watched for some time a competition among our snipers.

Lieutenant Anns had painted a very life-like head and they shot at it at 200 yards. The first and best shot put six shots through the face out of ten. They were using the sniper scope, a telescopic lens.

Orders have now come in that the manoeuvres start tomorrow. Had a talk with Captain Turner who came over to my billet to go over mess accounts. He was butler to Lady Romney[40] and was with her when she died. He found her lying halfway down the stairs, she had heart disease and fell. He travelled up and down Europe with these people.

Afterwards he was with Lord Wolseley[41] until he died. The old gentleman became very whimsical during his later years. He (Turner) had to place his piss pot outside the window on the ledge every night. Sent Major James to hospital with laryngitis.

Sunday 30th. St Hilaire.

Fine, but with a thick fog. Started at 8pm from Busnes, which was the rendezvous. The show was supposed to be a divisional manoeuvre for two days. It was so raw and cold that I got off my horse and started to walk. I walked all the way about 20 miles or more and arrived perfectly fresh and quite ready to go for miles. Of course, I carried no pack, rifle or ammunition.

It was a most monotonous and depressing march because of the fog which absolutely shut one in. It was very disappointing as I knew we were passing through some pleasant woods.

At one o'clock we halted for one hour and I had a pork pie of the colonel's, it was thoroughly appreciated. Also, some coffee which Captain Turner got from a neighbouring farm.

Only one man fell out altogether and was too unwell to go on. About 25 left their companies but I collected them behind my medical cart and by use of encouragement managed to keep them together until the end. We arrived about 6.30pm.

---

40. *Lady Frances, Countess of Romney (1844-1910)*

41. *Field Marshal Garnet Joseph Wolseley, 1st Viscount Wolseley, KP, GCB, OM, GCMG, VD, PC. Governor of the Gold Coast, Governor of Natal, Governor of Transvaal. (1833-1913)*

Monday 31st.

I had expected the worst of billets and, indeed, had the original programme been carried out and we had gone on to our destination we
might have fared badly. As it was, I had a two bedded room with the
major which was most luxurious with a full height mirror and perfect
bed.

We got up at 7:30am and did not start until 9:30. I collected all the
people with sore feet etc and left them behind to come on slowly in the
afternoon under an officer.

We marched direct home, seven miles and arrived in time for lunch.
My feet were not blistered, merely bruised through walking over so
much paved road, which being so uneven and unyielding is always most
trying for the feet.

Passages from 7th Battalion East Surrey Regiments war diaries.

Friday 21st.

*Parade, mostly in orchards. This has now been stopped, so the only
place for our men to parade now is on a muddy road. Lieutenant
Fothergill RAMC made Captain.*

Friday 28th.

*Enemy reported to have bombarded the whole of the 1st and 4th
Corps front, also aeroplane reconnaissance. Great amount of railway
traffic in the direction of Le Bassee, Hulluch. Enemy blew up mine in
front of the chalk pit and attacked under cover of a cloud of smoke. It
is reported that we have the situation well in hand.*

Sunday 30th.

*Divisional manoeuvres. The 37th Infantry Brigade marched as a
brigade. We did twenty miles and went into billets at Ham, St Hilaire.*

*Casualties for month: Officers killed none, wounded one, sick one –
OR killed one, wounded 30, sick 36.*

*The following officers, NCO and men have appeared in the London
Gazette as having received rewards for gallant conduct – DSO (Dis-
tinguished Service Order) Major A.H Wilson – MC (Military Cross)
Lieutenant J.S Hewat – Croix de Guerre Sergeant F.C Evans – DCM
(Distinguished Conduct Medal) Sergeant F.C Evans – Mentioned in
despatches Lieutenant R.H Fothergill.*

February 1916.

Tuesday 1st. Le Perriere.

There were no parades today and the men were given a complete rest. Cold and frosty but beautiful and sunny.

Quite common to find young leaves of hawthorn. The little garden in my billet is quite gay with red daisies, primroses, primulas and blue periwinkle, while the rose trees are full of young leaves. Had a nice walk.

Wednesday 2nd.

Have one or two men with certain symptoms of typhoid. One man in particular – Private Wilson, who has run an evening temperature for some days, so dull, apathetic, some spots on abdomen, diarrhea at first. The temp however is not typical, I have sent him 'down' today to hospital.

The old lady of my billet is very hospitable and often offers me a most excellent cup of freshly ground coffee. Most wonderful however is her volatility which is particularly abnormal in that it reaches its height in the early morning. At 5:30am she is up talking as hard as the devil.

Thursday 3rd.

A message from KEH came and told me that William was coming over in the afternoon, so I sent Leeds down to Business to buy cakes etc and got my bedroom ready. It was very disappointing that he never turned up after all. The weather has been terribly cold the last two days.

I don't think I can remember having ever enjoyed my bed so much as I have done since coming here. The cottage is silent as the old people retire early. I have a nice light at my side and rolled up in a sleeping bag. I enjoy a delightful read.

Leeds wakes me in the morning with a pot of tea and some boiling water.

Friday 4th. Le Perriere.

According to divisional orders I took a scabies parade today and examined the whole battalion by companies.

The men stood with their sleeves rolled up to the elbows and their trousers to the knees. Then I walked along and found only one doubtful case.

It was rather disconcerting to see some of the designs tattooed on their arms – beautiful women with meagre clothing etc.

Colonel Silver the new ADMS came over and went around the billets and seemed very satisfied.

Saturday 5th. Ham-en-Artois.

During the last few days, we have heard rumours that we should be moved within a day or two to take over the line near Quinchy. Last night we received definite news that the division was not yet 'going in' and following orders we packed up our belongings and marched back to the above place about four miles away.

It was a lovely morning and we made a very cheerful show with our band playing in front. We took over from the Sussex whom we passed en route.

This is a delightful village with recreation rooms for the men, canteen and estaminet. We, the HQ are also in luck's way. We have 'The Abbey' as our billet, a most charming place. It was a monastery until six years ago but now belongs to a private family. It consists of a main chateau built of limestone with picturesque turrets jutting out and attached to the building is another long building lower in height ending with the church. 'Oh' I have not got estaminet.

The whole set of buildings is very old and pleasing. Inside there is an abundance of plain oak panelling to the rooms. Nicholls and I share a room upstairs. Outside is the monks' recreation ground consisting of a large field with high walls behind which on two sides opens to the country beyond, though guarded by a deep moat.

Sunday 6th.

We now hear all sorts of rumours re the movement of our division. Some say we are going out of the 1st Corps before the end of the month. Then there is a rumour from a parson that we are going to Salonika. So, there you are.

Anyhow, it is very pleasant here and I don't mind if we remain here until the end of the war. Nicholls and I walked into Lillers this morning – three miles away – and got our hair cut. Mine was cut by a lady barber and very well done too.

115

We have the Brigade Major Trever and Captain Stewart for dinner, so we bought oysters and some pate.

Our horses met us in the town, and we rode home together. Our brigadier, Fowler[42] has been removed by the Corps CO!

The dinner went very well, and Stewart was very humorous. He told us of a court martial he had just been to where the charge against the prisoner was for 'continually sleeping at the post.'

I was called in this morning to see a little boy aged five next-door. They had sent to Lillers for the doctor, but he replied that he couldn't see his way to come over as it was Sunday!! I found he had diphtheria. The parents produced some anti-dip serum in some miraculous way, and I gave him a good dose. The child seemed bad.

The next thing that happened was that during my absence at Lillers the mother got anxious and hearing I was out got some other MO in. I don't know who he was.

Two hours after my injection he gave another one and from the look of the empty bottle it must have been a very big one too! I never referred to this when speaking to the parents, but I think it was undoubtedly too much for the child: he died last night.

The authorities are evidently casual re certifying death because I have not been asked for my signature and Mons Dutrec says the civil doctor – who refused to attend the case because it was Sunday – will most likely sign it up.

When a death has occurred in a family it is customary to place a huge cross of straw on the road in front of the house. The cross is quite five feet and two feet thick with sprigs of evergreen on the top.

Tuesday 8th.

Found some beautiful violets in the old monastery garden – deliciously sweet violets, they were as big as wild pansies.

This afternoon Mons Dutrec and I took our electric lamp and explored a subterranean passage leading out of the monastery.

---

42. *Sir Douglas Haig replaced Field Marshal Sir John French as Commander-in-Chief of the BEF (British Expeditionary Force) in December 1915. Possibly because of this Fowler relinquished or was removed from command of the 37th Brigade in January 1916. He saw no further active service on the Western Front.*

The tunnel is solidly bricked, broad, and high enough for a small cart and horse to pass along it. Indeed, it is said that the monks drove along it this way as far as another monastic house to which it led some miles away!

Unfortunately, we found it bricked across about fifty feet from the entrance.

It seems the monastery was founded in the 11th century by a Benedictine sect. Mons Dutrec and I then entered the church which was full of tawdry ornaments but there was one beautiful picture – an oil painting of Madonna and child – which looked out of place among such cheap surroundings.

Then an ascent of the old tower rewarded us with a magnificent view in all directions.

Wednesday 9th. Ham-en-Artois.

Patience card game invented by Mons Dutrec – 'The Dutrec Patience'.

I asked Ethel to send me some Players Navy Cut pipe tobacco out, free of duty. I had to pay one pound and Players sent me 6lbs post free. This works out at 3s.4d a pound – John Players & Sons, Nottingham.

Walked down to Bourcq this afternoon and had tea at the 37th Field Ambulance mess. Colonel Silver and Major Richmond also came in for tea.

Thursday 10th.

There are quite several artesian wells around here and the water is excellent. Three or four of these wells have been allowed to form the centre of a few ponds. In these watercress is grown. We have it every day for lunch.

This morning General Scott inspected our battalion at Bourecq and decorated some men with DCM.

I rode down to Lillers and was lucky in being able to get a tooth stopped. The stopping, or some of it, had come out.

I do not feel particularly optimistic about the excellence of his work. He never put any carbolic over the cavity he had prepared for filling and I fear I can only look upon this work as a makeshift. However, it was a good thing to get done and may save me a toothache.

Friday 11th.

Nothing to do today. Rained heavily all day, indoors nearly all day. Nicholls in bed suffering from influenza. Findlay taking his place.

Holt advised me that I have a balance with them of £142.11.1. I think £30 of this – half my gratuity – should have been sent to Cross.

The Army & Navy (club) account shows that from 12 Nov 1915 until 4 Feb 1916 we were debited £9.12.6 entirely for whisky, we have paid £2.15.0 so we owe £6.17.6. In future I shall get whisky from Christopher & Co Ltd, 43 Pall Mall, near Army & Navy.

Saturday 12th.

Beastly day again. A walk along a muddy road in the afternoon for exercise. Saw a few civilian patients. Nicholls temp 100 at night, at 3am he complained of so much pain in back and became so restless that I gave him morphine by mouth. He slept until morning.

Sunday 13th.

Nicholls temp 99 morning. Pain better, seems better though drowsy. Cannot find anything definite although I had thought of kidney calculus.

Nice sun at intervals.

When I came in from afternoon walk I found William here! It was very jolly to see him again.

There is a sort of pantry between the mess and the kitchen and here we had tea. Afterwards, we had a walk and returned for dinner, which I think he enjoyed, especially as I was able to give him some whisky and soda, coffee, and Benedictine.

He told me that he and five others had been selected from the KEH to do 'outpost' duty in the trenches. He will have certain points in the enemy lines to watch continually through powerful glasses and will make immediate reports of movements etc.

I am very glad he has found some useful and interesting employment. At the same time, one cannot but feel anxious for his safety.

Monday 14th.

A very wild day. Attempted to take a walk after lunch but it started to rain in torrents, and I was forced to retire.

Lieutenant Charter is now acting as adjutant, he plays the piano very well and as there is quite a good one in the mess it has been a wonderful treat for me. He played some of Schubert, Nocturne, Impromptus etc.

Tuesday 15th. Bethune.

Marched away from Ham at 9:30am. Decided to send Nicholls to hospital, his temp was 101 last night and in spite of castor oil I failed to get his bowels open. Funny case, similar in some ways to three or four cases I had at Perriere. I left him behind to be picked up by ambulance.

I had arranged for my 'crocks' i.e. men with 'bad feet' etc to be taken by lorry, but owing to transport difficulties they had to walk, and so, I had a miserable crowd of limping men behind my medical cart.

Our new brigadier came along and strafed me for letting them struggle!

I walked 11 miles and kept warm by doing so. Arrived Bethune at 2pm.

We have the same billet as we had for one night when marching back from rest last December!! I remember how comfortable I thought my bedroom was then. I think it even more so now. I have a bright fire in the hearth and am writing now in front of it. With a nice table on my left with my books neatly arranged on it by Leeds, he is looking after me extremely well.

We are kept in the dark as to our movement after leaving the trenches. It is extraordinary the number of different places we are said to be destined for. It will be most exciting when we finally do know.

Wednesday 16th.

We hear we are not going into trenches until the 21st, so I shall have the luxury of my comfortable room for a few more days. Raining and very cold.

Had the most excellent hot bath at some public military baths where a few bathrooms are set aside for officers. A great treat to enjoy a full-length bath after so many wooden tubs.

Visited Nicholls in hospital and found him well, though still with temp and weak.

I felt cold, shivering with a developing cold, treated by careful dieting and a hot bath and kept inside afterwards.

Thursday 17th.

I woke up this morning feeling very fit and quite free from a cold.

The terrible loneliness of my life which I felt so keenly during the times of peace and even now when we are away from the trenches. The yearning for the soul whose love and sympathy must vibrate in unison with mine. The intuitive feeling that 'she' exists even though 'she' may not happen to be on this side of the 'veil'.

All my thoughts on the above seem to be beautifully expressed in the following poem by Sarojini Naidu.

HUMAYUN TO ZOBEIDA (from the Urdu)

You flaunt your beauty in the rose, your glory in the dawn, your sweetness in the nightingale, your whiteness in the swan.

You haunt my waking like a dream, my slumber like a moon, pervade me like a musky scent, possess me like a tune.

Yet, when I crave of you, my sweet, one tender moment's grace, you cry, "I sit behind the veil, I cannot show my face."

Shall any foolish veil divide my longing from my bliss? Shall any fragile curtain hide your beauty from my kiss?

What war is this of Thee and Me? Give o'er the wanton strife. You are the heart within my heart, the life within my life.

Friday 18th.

Learnt yesterday through division that the Russians had captured Erzerum. *(12-16 February 1916)*

Wet and cold. Read a good deal of theosophy. How one longs for the end of the war! At times one longs for victory thinking only of the great principles for which we are fighting, realising how evolution shall be helped forward by such an issue.

Again, in a less exalted mood, one yearns for an end so as to be free from the general discomfort and hardships.

Sometimes, the thought of broken hearts at home makes one anxious for peace, and often one pants for an end if only to escape the tedium of answering salutes, and forever being surrounded by our monotonous khaki uniforms.

Saturday 19th. Bethune.

It was rather funny at dinner last night, we happened to allude to Leamington and the colonel asked whether I knew the place. He said he was at school there.

It turned out that he was not only at school with uncle but had actually stayed the night at granny's. He said she had poulticed him for bronchitis. He knew Aunt Flo, Beth, and mother by their names!

Visited Nicholls at hospital and he is now convalescing. We took a stroll; he is very weak still and will go home on leave Tuesday.

We are off tomorrow, probably to Annequin and then into the trenches for a few days. After that, who knows. Mons Dutrec says to Arras.

Letter from Ethel; Cecil at Malta.

Sunday 20th. Sailly Labourse.

Last night I had just got into bed when I heard an aeroplane, 11pm, which I realised was German after five successive explosions in different parts of the town showed they were throwing down bombs. There were however no casualties, although some premises were damaged.

Captain Jones returned to the battalion this morning. He was shot through the tongue and neck last summer at Le Touquet, curiously enough I was orderly officer at the 36th Field Ambulance when he was brought in.

They think a tremendous lot of him here as an officer and his men are extraordinarily fond of him. We left Bethune at 2pm in bright sunshine and arrived Sailly at 4pm. Got a nice bed in room with major.

Monday 21st. The Quarries, trenches.

The battalion started at 8am. Colonel, major and self, started about 10:30 riding to Vermelles. It was bitterly cold.

We walked up from Vermelles and entered the trenches 20 minutes later. The trenches were greatly improved since we were last in this zone, trench boards all the way.

We reached our HQ after a good walk. I have a deep dugout and stretcher with plenty of sandbags. I share it with the liaison artillery officer who is on duty here for two days.

In the afternoon I went around the support and firing lines with the colonel. It was most interesting. Through the periscope I saw the remains of our poor fellows still lying between the lines where they had lain since September 25th.

I also looked over into a recent crater through a small peephole, a deep pit – 30 feet with all manner of wreckage strewn about.

During the night we had five casualties from rifle grenades and snipers, one fatal through the head. Very cold during the night, bitterly cold.

Tuesday 22nd.

Our corps sniper, Rule, is reported to have shot a sniper on the Hogs Back (trench). If there was any doubt about it, the probability of ending his career was made certain by our trench mortars which wrecked the position from which he sniped.

Horribly cold today and heavy snow for two or three hours – the first I have seen since we came to France which has whitened the whole country and enhanced the enemy's trenches – a wintery scene indeed!

We avenged the aeroplane raid on Bethune by a flight of 29 machines over Dom the following day. Each of these aeroplanes dropped two bombs of 120lbs!

Today we hear officially that yesterday the French brought down five German aeroplanes and one zeppelin!

The Russians have advanced from Erzerum and taken Mush.

Bad headache, probably from fumes from my brazier which are always so poisonous. Royal Irish Fusiliers under instruction by us, two companies, left this morning.

I am told that we are springing a mine at 9am. The colonel and I watched from a very good position. A trembling of the ground first warned us and then the cloud of smoke and muffled roar, but it was too far off for detail to be observed.

Wednesday 23rd. The Quarries.

Bitterly cold with hard frost. We came out of the firing line today and the Kent's relieved us. We went into support trenches but owing to lack of dugouts we were obliged to crowd up to make room for the Kent's HQ.

Their MO, Moore, of the 36th Field Ambulance shares my dugout and my aid post.

Luckily our casualties were small, being confined to odd sniping cases. Otherwise it would have been impossible to carry on. Snow falling fast.

Thursday 24th.

There are four mild cases of trench foot. Exceedingly hard frost, we wear four sandbags on each foot here in the dug-out as feet are very cold.

Walked down to D-coy who occupy 'Straw trenches' about one and a half miles back. Bad headache owing to fumes from brazier.

Friday 25th.

Freezing hard. What a change from weather a month ago when it was delightfully mild with the promise of early spring everywhere. Three or four more trench feet.

A battalion of Royal Irish Fusiliers (16th Div) has taken over from the Kent's and now occupy the HQ dugouts around us.

The MO has just arrived with his panniers. It is their first experience of holding a bit of line as a battalion.

Saturday 26th.

More snow last night and the country is now white and wintery. The trenches cannot be distinguished from a distance.

The Royal Irish Rifle Battalion is now holding the front trenches and we are in support.

They are most entertaining with their brogue and granite expression. Their adjutant came into my dugout this morning and was very droll. They have only had one man hit. He was hit by a bullet which pierced the back and front of his helmet and grazed the top of his head en-passant. When hit, he dashed away and has not been heard of since! Much to everyone's amusement.

Sunday 27th.

This morning as an officer of the Royal Irish Rifles was firing a rifle grenade, it exploded and killed him and wounded another officer. A very nice fellow and I had been treating him for a carbuncle. Two deserters came over into our lines during the night of 26th – jolly men too.

An officer of the 36th Field Ambulance told me that owing to vacancies having occurred lately in MO appointments to regiments the division had sent around to all the field ambulances asking for volunteers to fill these posts. He told me that not a single officer volunteered! I thought it rather a disgraceful fact. And yet, a large sprinkling of distinctions goes to the field ambulances.

Personally, having been mentioned in the last despatches, I am quite satisfied but have met a good many medical officers of our division who were never mentioned and I think that every regimental MO who has worked in the trenches for six months should be entitled at least to the above humble distinction.

Monday 28th.

Snow is practically gone and the rise in temperature is very welcome, especially at night.

The brigadier has given me another aid post in Lone trenches and then our congestion up here is considerably diminished.

Got out of the trench this morning and screened by a hedge, was able to get a magnificent view as I stood on high ground. To our right lay Loos hidden by the rising ground upon the top of which stood out the well-known Tower bridge *(Tower bridge. Pair of pithead gear towers.)*

Tuesday 29th.

Bethune Walked down to Lone trench *(Lone Tree[43])* this morning in the open because the relieving battalion was coming up. Extraordinary amount of rifle bullets and shrapnel lying about.

'She's a finished musician don't you think'. 'I hope so: I was afraid she was going to sing again.' (Tatler)

Very glad to get back to my billet – the same as I had last time in Bethune. Leeds had gone down in advance and had lit a good fire in my bedroom and got me some hot water.

Our tour in the trenches had not been very pleasant. The extreme cold and frequent falls of snow were something which we had not hitherto experienced.

43. *An account is given in The Donkeys (Alan Clark) of a cherry tree near Loos, known as Lone Tree, between the British and German lines. In April 1915 an officer of the Seaforths led a night patrol to the tree. He climbed it to place a Union flag. He was lit up by a flare and machine-gunned. He was suspended on the tree for some days despite attempts to recover his body. Guns ranged onto the tree in an effort to bury the body, branches were blown off with no direct hit, leaving a tall stump. The flowering cherry was replanted in 1995, the 80th anniversary of the battle of Loos, close to the original position of the tree.*

I had only three trench feet that were bad to send to the hospital. The minor cases I treated myself and they were all able to march home.

Today, I understand the Buffs had numberless cases. There is no doubt that the frequent and systematic rubbing of the men's feet – three times a day sometimes – under the supervision of platoon officers, has greatly reduced the occurrence of this affliction.

Passages from 7th Battalion East Surrey Regiments war diaries.

Saturday 5th.

General Fowler went home giving up the Brigade.

Monday 21st.

Occupied trenches (frontline) in front of the Hohenzollern, namely Mud trench, Sticky trench, Hogs Back, West Face and Kaiserin. Also, the first support line, Northampton trench.

Tuesday 22nd

Enemy snipers are very active, also enemy rifle grenades and trench mortars. A recent type of small aerial torpedo was also sent over. A Bosch sniper on the Hogs Back crater who had proved very trouble-some to the 8th Royal Fusiliers was reported by our sniping officer to have been first shot by Corporal Rule and then blown up with his small 'fort' by trench mortars. Alert period for gas attack as the wind was favourable to the enemy.

MARCH 1916.

Wed 1st. Bethune.

Nothing to relate. The town seems livelier than it was and a good many more people have come back to live. It is possible to buy fresh fish at reasonable prices.

The great facts which theosophy lays before humanity are:-

"The soul of man is immortal; its future is the future of a thing whose growth and splendour has no limit.

The principle which gives life dwells in us and without us, is undying and eternally beneficent, is not heard, or seen or smelt, but is perceived by the man who desires perception.

Each man is his own absolute lawgiver, the dispenser of glory or gloom to himself, the decreer of his life, his reward his punishment.

These truths which are as great as is life itself, are as simple as the simplest mind of man."

(From the Idyll of the White Lotus by Mabel Collins)

Thursday 2nd.

Had a bath in the town. Visited club which has been enlarged by taking over the next house.

In the afternoon I went to the divisional cinema where the divisional brass band played extremely well.

Friday 3rd.

At daybreak this morning the 36th Brigade sprung a mine under the German trenches – the Chord – part of the Hohenzollern Redoubt. They occupied the crater and German trench.

A tremendous bombing contest ensued but they held what they had taken, but they had 400 casualties.

I understand one of the main enemy mining galleries was exposed by the assault. The position overlooks a large part of the German lines.

Started to walk out but was driven back by rain.

Saturday 4th. Sailly Labourse.

Last night 200 of our men had to go by motor lorries up to the trenches and help to consolidate the position taken by the 36th Brigade. They had no casualties but came back soaked through with snow and mud.

At 9am we received orders to march at 11am to Sailly Labourse. The above 200 were left behind to rest until this afternoon, the rest of us marched through a blinding snowstorm.

We are now ordered to take over the trenches which include the piece recently captured and I expect we shall have a lively time of it too!

Very wintery, the whole country once again covered in snow.

Passage from 7th Battalion East Surrey Regiments war diaries.

Monday 4th.

This morning we were hurriedly moved up to Sailly Labourse, preparatory to relieving the 6th Royal Sussex on the Hohenzollern front. This was rendered necessary owing to Germans attacking the new position with the resultant heavy casualties.

Sunday 5th. Hohenzollern Redoubt craters.

Spent rather a comfortable night in the mayor's house, the major and I sharing a room. He had been away at Bethune busy with six court martial cases and he arrived about midnight.

I was up at 6am and saw my sick at 7am. Rather a lot and I was sorry for the poor chaps, but I cannot possibly send trivial cases to hospital.

At 9:30am we set out for Vermelles which I walked with Leeds beside my horse. A shell burst very close to us indeed, I thought it was coming right on to us.

At Vermelles Leeds and I walked on the top and so avoided the trenches, they are once again in bad order owing to the parapets slipping in.

I am back again in the same old dugout and have had a very busy morning as we have had a good many casualties of a minor type.

Our battalion is holding our newly captured position on the top of the craters and we have been badly hammered ever since we took over.

Captain Martin who returned to us last night after six months away after being wounded at La Touquet, was buried by a shell half an hour after entering the crater position. He is suffering from a bit of shock and a slight wound.

I am in the same dugout but the colonel etc are nearer the firing line and so I shall have to get my food here as best I can.

Ever since we came in there has been a constant dribbling of casualties into my dugout.

Monday 6th.

Mostly whizz-bang wounds or people suffering from the effects of being buried.

Tuesday 7th. Hohenzollern craters.

These two days; Mon-Tues, have been terrific days. The enemy threw shells into the craters, rifle grenades, mortars, the poor boys suffered much. It was snowing and freezing cold.

Wounded kept coming down in a steady stream and any sleep was out of the question for me during the two nights.

In the late afternoon I was asked by the Northants Pioneers to see a man in C crater who had a shattered limb. I made my way up and passed through some bits of trench which were partially blown in. One had to keep low in order not to be exposed above the parapet.

Then into the crater, what a sight! A huge basin 50-yards wide or more and 50-feet-deep, covered in debris and dead bodies of Germans.

Around the further lip were our brave boys. A small path ran around it, of cover there was none as there was no time to build dugouts.

I found my man lying among some corpses, his left limb was hanging by a few tendons and although he was obviously dying I could not leave him.

My stretcher bearers of the coy were knocked out and so I had to get three volunteers to help me. A rifle grenade came over and exploded with a deafening report close to me, wounding slightly three or four men.

Captain Richards shouted to warn me that the Buffs were 'going over' at 6pm which would mean a bombardment of the crater.

I could not get my casualty away by then and I heard the German machine guns playing on them as they advanced, and our artillery commenced an intense bombardment.

After an immense struggle, myself holding one end of the stretcher, we got out of the crater and fought our way through the narrow trench expecting to be crumped at any minute. The poor fellow however expired before we had gone very far. I felt nonetheless very glad that I had done my best for him. I made my way back to the aid post through the appalling din of the bombardment and got back safely.

Wednesday 8th.

I had to make another visit to this crater this morning for a man with a fractured leg, things were quiet then and I had an uneventful journey.

The Buffs attack on Tuesday evening was a failure and they were beaten back. Last night the Bosch attacked C crater, we easily repulsed him.

We came out of the firing line this morning and went into support trenches further back. It had been a terrible night of snow-sleet and our men were in a sorry state. We had 140 casualties during the three days.

The bursting of the crumps among our men has undoubtedly a terrifying effect and when no actual wounding takes place men are often killed by the concussion, or if not too close are absolutely 'knocked out' and their nerves entirely shattered.

Again, they may be buried by a falling parapet or die from suffocation.

Yesterday our corps sniper, one of the pluckiest men in the battalion, foremost in reconnoitering in front of the trenches etc was knocked over by the concussion of a German 5.9-inch and converted into a helpless wreck, unable to speak or co-ordinate any of his movements.

Of course, I see the worst side of the thing, all the 'funks' find their way to me. But, you have only to visit the trenches and craters to realise what splendid fellows – officers and men – are there in abundance.

I saw them in C crater; they all looked worn out and showed every sign of nerve strain but nonetheless determined. This is the worst form of fighting – sitting still, waiting to be shelled and unable to hit back!

---

*Notes

3rd–7th March

At 9:37am brigade commander, Brigadier-General L.B Boyd-Moss reported that the situation was satisfactory, the craters having been captured, consolidation started, and the triangle crater had been captured, in this they found the entrance of the German gallery system.

Observation of the enemy lines back to Fosse 8 had been gained, some of the Chord had been taken and much of the rest destroyed.

German artillery from 6 to 8am caused many casualties. The battalions of Bavarian infantry regiments were withdrawn during the night of 4/5 March. The 36th Brigade was relieved by the 37th Brigade on 5 March and the 6th Buffs and 7th East Surreys took over.

German attacks on C-crater at 8pm, 9:22pm and 10:35pm which were held off with the help of the artillery.

Germans recaptured triangle crater and entrance to the gallery system making precarious the British hold on the new craters, time was needed to clear the British galleries and start mining.

Another attack on the triangle and the chord to block Big Willie by the 6th Buffs was planned. A party from crater two up the south face of the triangle to block Big Willie, a second group to attack from crater two up the north face to the chord. A third unit to attack from crater A to the Chord.

When the first party attacked along the south edge of the trian-gle crater the men sank up to their knees in mud and were machine gunned and hit by German hand grenades.

The enemy attacked and pushed the party back to crater two where the fighting developed for two hours until the Germans retreated. The second and third parties met at the chord but retreated when they ran out of hand grenades.

The Germans again attacked crater one but were held off by one machine gun until reinforcements arrived.

The failure of the attack and the weakness of the start were reported at 6:55pm and a company from 6th Battalion Royal West Kents went forward; they and the artillery managed to repulse the German attack.

Between 6th and 7th March the 37th Brigade lost 331 men.

::::

Among the attacking men was acting Corporal William Cotter VC[44] of the 6th Battalion The Buffs, part of the 37th Brigade. His unit

was attempting to take the triangle crater. They went over on 5 March to relieve the men who had begun the attack three days earlier. They were counter attacked by the Germans but with the help of artillery they resisted the attack.

::::

Over the winter of 1915-1916 the 170th Tunnelling Company Royal Engineers, the unit being made up of civilian sewer workers from

---

44. London Gazette entry. William Cotter.
"When his right leg had been blown off at the knee and he had also been wounded in both arms, he made his way unaided for 50 yards to a crater, steadied the men who were holding it, controlled their fire, issued orders and altered the dispositions of his men to meet a fresh attack by the enemy.
For two hours he held his position and only allowed his wounds to be roughly dressed when the attack had quieted down. He could not be moved back for 14 hours, during all this time had a cheery word for all who passed him. There is no doubt that his magnificent courage helped greatly to save a critical situation."
Corporal Cotter died of his wounds at a field hospital on 14 March. He was posthumously awarded the Victoria Cross for bravery in action.

Manchester and ex-miners taken from the infantry units such as the 11th Welsh, 8th South Wales Borderers and 2nd South Staffs, dug several galleries under the German lines in the area of the Hohenzollern Redoubt which had changed hands several times since September 1915.

In March 1916 the west side was held by the British and the east side the Germans, with the front near a German trench called the Chord. The land in between had been turned into a crater field and the enemy had a clear view of the British positions from Fosse8.

The British line was held by outposts to limit the number of men in danger from mines and also from the mental strain of knowing that the ground could erupt at any time.

The 12th Division was chosen to attack and take the crater field and gain observation from crater lips to Fosse8 and try to end the danger of mine attacks. Four mines, the largest yet sprung by the British were detonated on 2nd March and followed by two battalions, took the new craters with Triangle crater which had not been seen until the attack and a good part of the Chord, the rest being obliterated.

The entrance to the German galleries was found in Triangle crater and the 170th Company crossed no man's land to demolish it. Germans counter-attacked to recover the Triangle crater which was retaken on 4th March. The re-taking of the galleries by the Germans threatened the new positions of the British who attacked the Triangle but failed.

The British infiltrated the enemy galleries from one of their own and demolished the system on 12th March, removing the threat of more mine attacks.

On 18th March the enemy surprised the British lines with five mines which were dug through the clay layer above the chalk forcing them back to the original front line.

By 19th March both sides occupied the near lips of the craters. The allied casualties between 2nd and 19th March were over 5,400. By the time the 12th Division was relieved on 26 April had risen to over 6,400 with nothing gained. Brigadier-General Cator 37th Brigade commander decided that attempts to occupy the craters should end *and the near lips held instead as the craters were death traps to howitzer and mortar fire.*

The 170th Tunnelling Company started work on the mining of the Hohenzollern Redoubt on 14th December 1915, by the end of the month had sunk six shafts.

Two sections of the 180th Tunnelling Company were attached to the 170th and began another three shafts. They carried out mining in the clay layer to distract the Germans from the deeper mines in the chalk layer. It was estimated that the German mining was six weeks ahead of the British mines.

The mines were intended to destroy fortifications and the men in them. Excavated material being chalk was easily identified, some was used in the front line, but large carrying parties removed most of it out of sight of enemy observers and reconnaissance aircraft.

The shafts were dug well back from the front lines and driven forward with galleries at intervals, silence being of the utmost importance. When the tunnels were close a small mine would be dug to collapse the enemy workings and then resumed to the target area, a chamber would be dug and loaded with explosives ready to be fired.

The mental strain on the tunnellers and the men above in the front line must have been unbearable knowing that a mine could be detonated at any time beneath them.

Over the winter the British efforts overtook the German mining and it was planned to destroy the enemy galleries. Four mines were planted beneath the Redoubt to be exploded just before an attack on the Chord.

Chamber A was loaded with 7,000lb of ammonal, chamber B 3,000lb of blastine and 4,000lb of ammonal and chamber C 10,550lb.

Chambers A and B were predicted to make craters 100 feet wide and 35 feet deep. Crater C 130 feet wide and 35 feet deep. The smaller fourth mine had been planted under the side of crater two and was predicted to leave an even bigger crater. (Wikipedia)

::::

132

Second Lieutenant Angus Campbell (qualified mining engineer) was in action with No4 section of the 170th Tunnelling Company from October 1915 to July 1916. He was working with his section which included 86119 Sergeant S. J. Davis and 86111 L.Cpl Thomas Langford in tunnel F4 which was known as Bart's Alley, around one mile from the Hohenzollern Redoubt and Fosse8.

They broke through into a German mine and found it packed with 2,500lbs of explosive, primed and ready for detonation. Campbell cleared most of his men and alongside Davis and Langford disabled the mine and removed the explosives which were packed in 25kg wooden boxes with every available space filled with 1kg packs, they worked underground for more than 20 hours.

For this Campbell was awarded the MC and Davis and Langford the MM.

Campbell made a detailed report with drawings of the German mines, most likely the first come across and therefore gave good information on the enemy's method of mining warfare.

Having survived the War, in March 1919 Campbell died in the Spanish flu pandemic most likely weakened by the lung damage caused by his experiences of underground mine warfare.

L.Cpl Langford had a rather colourful army record leading up to becoming the holder of the Military Medal. On at least five occasions he was charged with being AWOL and absenting himself from duty. He received several episodes of field punishment and demotion through the ranks. Including CTB (confined to barracks) with loss of pay. Sergeant Davis was a witness on several of the charges against him.

On 27th April 1917 at Hulluch he was badly gassed, spending three months hospitalised in Scotland before returning to his unit. He was placed in reserve in 1919.

Thursday 9th. Support trenches.

My stretcher bearers were splendid and worked night and day. Old Culwick worked until he nearly dropped and looked very drawn this last morning. Poor old chap, he told me he will be 53 in May! He called himself 37 when he went to the recruitment office and to avoid rejection he dyed his hair before presenting himself. His hair was white and grey, he told me with a burst of laughter that the dye turned it yellowish-green and was rather obvious! The recruitment sergeant nearly collapsed laughing.

And now we are in support trenches and I am confronted with a terrible lot of trench foot, or rather sodden feet which if not immediately treated will become trench foot[45]. Not many sick.

Friday 10th. Hohenzollern craters.

Last night, or was it Thursday night? The Bosch attacked all our craters with bombers. The Queen's and West Kents drove them back and our artillery cooperated very successfully.

I stood on some elevated ground and watched the attack, a wonderful sight! The livid red flicker of the bursting bombs with their sharp reports. The flash of our shrapnel bursting over the enemy lines, accompanied all the time by the barking of our 18-pounders behind us, the slow roar of our eight-inch shells as they sailed over our heads.

I continue to write at 12:30am. A huge enemy mine has just been sprung in the Loos area, there was a prolonged and muffled boom and my dugout rocked and shook.

The enemy must have sapped rapidly towards our C crater because they are reaching it with their bombs. Already I have nearly a dozen casualties, none of them severe.

Passages from 7th Battalion East Surrey Regiments war diaries.
Sunday 5th.

The battalion relieved the 6th Royal Sussex in the front line today, opposite the Hohenzollern. We found the front line considerably altered owing to the craters in front of and in the enemy lines – the Chord.

Monday 6th.

The battalion has been reminded of the fact that there is plenty of life still left in the Bosch, all the craters, saps and trenches being

---

45. *"Often and often I noticed that a battalion with a first class MO was always a first class battalion, had the smallest sick parade, fewer men falling out on a long march and the lowest quota of casualties from trench foot." (Memoirs of a Camp Follower, Capt Phillip Gosse RAMC.)*

heavily bombarded. Enemy trench mortars seem especially active. A mine exploded at 12:05am to the right of our line.

Tuesday 7th.

An attack was made by the battalion on our right (6th Buffs) on Triangle crater, which lies to the south of A crater with a view of taking the Chord and consolidating the new position.

The Germans apparently arranged an attack for the same time and a deadlock ensued. The Bosch made three attacks on C crater held by the 7th Surreys. One at 8pm, one at 9:22pm and one at 10:35pm. All were repulsed by the garrisons of the crater – A-coy, Captain B.C Richards in command. Communication was good during the attacks and very effective shrapnel barrages were put up by the artillery on Cross trench and Little Willie.

All our lines were heavily bombarded and Russian Sap leading to C crater was almost filled in. Northampton trench was made almost impassable during the day.

Wednesday 8th.

All available men repairing the damage done on the previous day, but the Germans materially interfered with the work by shelling Northampton trench, C crater and West face with field guns, howitzers and heavy trench mortars.

In the afternoon we were relieved by the 6th Queen's and moved to the reserve trenches.

Saturday 11th. Hohenzollern craters.

A long night at last ended. I might have slept peacefully from 4am but through a false report I waited up for some stretcher cases which never arrived.

I think I am too sensitive for this MO job. It has a depressing effect on me to see our men coming in mangled and wounded, it is against one's softer inclinations when one has to return to the firing line the more timid of our men who come down with trumped up symptoms.

The mental agony that such poor fellows must suffer must be impossible to truly realise and I don't marvel that self-inflicted sometimes, though very rarely, occur. And yet, as an efficient MO one must be hard and allow no man to escape his share of the firing line, except he be – in one's opinion – too ill to carry on.

To favour some is to be unfair on those brave fellows who are holding the line, many of them feeling far from well and all of them intensely tired and overwrought.

Sunday 12th.

A very disturbed night again because of the wounded. D-company's trenches were crumped steadily all afternoon and Northampton trench badly broken in. One shell struck a dugout and the man inside had left leg blown off and right foot, he was also severely cut about the head. He was found with his mangled limbs in contact with the live coals from the brazier which had been upturned. He did not die until he had been taken some way down the trenches.

At 3am I dressed four or five wounded, a batch resulting from an accident with one of our own bombs. Then Leeds and I revived the brazier with charcoal, and we talked about milk, his trade, cows and meadows full of lush grass and golden buttercups.

We discussed the Jersey and Alderney and several other classes of these gentle creatures, we forgot all about the war. Instead I went with Leeds with his milk to the little town and we jogged along delightful country roads at six o'clock upon a glorious spring morning, between brilliant green hedgerows and with birds singing on every side.

Monday 13th. Hohenzollern support trenches.

We were relieved by the Queens. The relief started at 2pm and was not completed until 8:30pm! We have had many casualties since Feb 21st, the time we came in, the brigade has had 800!

They say the craters we hold are very important and if we can only consolidate them we shall dominate the German positions around the Fosse 8.

Tuesday 14th.Reserve.

Although we are out of the firing line craters we still carry on with the same dugout. It is a gorgeous day with delightfully hot sun. I am writing this on the disused railway, screened from the Bosch lines by a hedge enjoying the sun and the song of larks on every side. Once again spring is reasserting itself after the terrible setback. The poor undergrowth which had sprung up at the beginning of February has been cut down by the recent frosts and growing leaves of hawthorn are blackened and withered.

In an article on the Great War, Leadbetter says: "Horrific as it is, it has yet lifted thousands upon thousands of people clear out of themselves out of their petty parochialism into worldwide sympathy, out of selfishness into the loftiest altruism – lifted them into the region of the ideal."

Wednesday 15th. Reserve Hohenzollern.

Lying in bed at the present moment, I am thinking how interesting it is to consider such a small matter as the bare walls of my dugout – 15 feet deep, steps lead down to this particular dugout. The roof inside is supported with thick wooden beams and the interior of the room is also strongly strutted with timber.

The walls are naked and consist of beautiful hard clay, in its upper part smooth homogeneous, in its lower layers intermingled with fine particles of chalk. If the dugout were still deeper we should find ourselves entirely surrounded by white chalk. As was the case in our dugouts about a mile away where the clay came much nearer the surface.

An exquisite day, I saw my sick in Lancashire trench, about 15, and then visited some mild cases of feet which I am keeping in a cellar in Vermelles looked after by Culwick.

Basked in the sun for a couple of hours in the afternoon behind a bomb store and watched the enemy 'crumping', or trying to, our reserve trenches. I was standing about 400-500 yards away and screened from the enemy by a hedge.

I heard the shells coming and watched them burst – veritable coalboxes! – they had no direct hits.

Thursday16th. Craters.

We are relieving the Queen's. They have had only 31 casualties since they took over from us the day before yesterday. Aerial torpedoes being used by the enemy into craters – terrific explosions – practically no casualties.

As usual the poor Surreys caught it hot during the relief. Whether the enemy spotted a relief was in progress I don't know, but they certainly dropped shells among us, and I had a dozen wounded very soon. They threw heavy trench mortars into craters but each time they did, our artillery retaliated very effectively and stopped them.

Friday 17th.

A terrible night, repeatedly out to dress cases. One man hit by a bullet which entered below the right scapula, came out behind the clavicle, then entered below the lower jaw and came out through the tip of his nose.

Another man got a bullet through open mouth and it entered above the tonsils and where the devil it went then goodness only knows. Certainly, there was no exit wound and no paralysis, though he complained of pain in the back of neck. Bombing went on all night or until early daylight. Next the enemy threw shells so near the battalion HQ (one within a few yards) that they had to move down here

Saturday 18th. Craters.

Well, despite many casualties we have held onto the craters and now thanks to the engineers etc they are comparatively safe. A parapet has been built up as well as a parados (*bank of earth*), the latter protects us from anything that bursts in the bottom of the crater.

The enemy have thrown in a good many minenwerfer, which are aerial torpedoes. These are most fearsome things, not so much on account of their killing qualities since they are very local in effect as the outer case is so thin as to do no damage on bursting. The noise of the explosion is absolutely terrific, and I have men with fractured eardrums due entirely to the explosion.

Poor Robinson was killed last night in C crater. He was in charge of some mortars. Such a nice boy, it is terrible to see them go one by one.

Captain Jones also died in hospital, hit in the buttock by a small fragment of shell. It must have penetrated the intestines. He was thought of fondly in the battalion; his men were dedicated to him.

Last night was quiet on the whole. I was up only twice.

The craters which we now hold give us the dominating position and the Hohenzollern Redoubt is no longer a German Redoubt, but English.

Until however, we have strengthened it and got a sufficiency of well concealed loopholes, we shall not feel the benefit of the gain.

Sunday 19th.

Things being so quiet, I was tempted to write up Saturday 18th diary in the morning. "We little knew what was about to happen!"

All was quiet until 6:30pm on Saturday when suddenly the enemy began to shell fiercely on reserve trenches and a few minutes later their intense bombardment became general into our four craters, support and communications trench. It was not surprising when A coy rang up to say the German infantry was attacking craters!

At once we gave the SOS signal to the artillery and they put up a barrage of shrapnel between the craters and the enemy lines.

Suddenly our dugout rocked, and we knew that a mine had been sprung, and at once our telephone communications with the craters was cut off. Messengers then came in asking for reinforcements for the craters and the Queens were sent up from the reserve trenches, Worcestershire's took their place.

Wounded now began to come in and I worked off and on until the early hours of the morning. The enemy tried to silence our field gun batteries by pouring gas shells into Vermelles though without effect. The bombardment was kept up by both sides for about two hours. The enemy sprung the mine under C crater and nearly all those in it were buried alive. Only a few escaped and among them, curiously enough were the three coy officers all of whom got out alive.

Captain Scott of D-coy did some magnificent work from B crater, rallying his men and reorganising the defence. He will undoubtedly get high distinction.

The result of all this was that the enemy successfully drove us out of three of the craters. They did not however occupy any of the craters but began to consolidate themselves on their side of the craters while we did the same on our side.

It was madness trying to occupy the cavity of these craters – they were just basins into which the Germans could lob their minenwerfer and large mortars.

Monday 20th.

We were relieved in the afternoon by the 5th Berks. Leeds and I set out on foot across country enjoying the freedom of movement. The fumes from the gas shells still lingered about among the batteries and my eyes were quite sore.

Dinner was ready for us when we got in, but we were all too tired to enjoy it. The colonel fell asleep after the soup. I dropped off after the meat course.

This tour of the trenches has caused us about 400 casualties! Lots of good fellows have been killed including a dear little stretcher bearer of mine who was buried in the crater when the Germans sprung the mine.

This afternoon I went over to Labourse and met William and we had some grub together and a talk. He has been doing observation work for (the artillery) and going on working parties. He looks extremely fit.

Spent the evening with Captain Scott the hero of the crater scrap, such a nice boy, good looking and aristocratic. He gave me an interesting, modest account of the events. He did remarkably well.

Tuesday 21st. Sailly-Labourse.

A quiet day, very few sick.

William came over this afternoon. He had been on working party and brought me back the nosepiece of a gas shell. We had an interesting talk and arranged to meet at Bethune. He told me that two men from our 12th Division were shot behind the chateau (occupied by the KEH) – Desertion from the ranks. He was on night guard and heard the whole thing.

---

*Note on executions

20/3/1916. G/1799 Pte Beverstein, Abraham. Age 19. (alias Harris, A) 11th Middlesex Regiment. Desertion.

21161 Pte Martin, Harry. 9th Battalion, Essex Regiment. Desertion. Labourse communal cemetery.

There were two executions carried out on 19 March:

15/13211 Pte McCracken, J F. Age 19

15/890 Pte Templeton, J. Age 19. 15th Royal Irish Rifles. Mailly Maillet communal cemetery extension. (25/30 miles from KEH billets)

In September 1914 Abraham Beverstein of East London joined the army using the name Abraham Harris. He had not told his parents. He was 18 years old, their only son. He wrote home: "I was very sorry to leave you, and very sorry to see you cry, but never mind, I will come back one day, so be happy at home."

In the spring of 1915, his battalion moved to France. By the end of the year, a telegram to his parents reported he was "suffering from wounds and shock." (mine explosion)

In January he was able to write: "I am feeling better, so don't be upset." He went back to his unit. Later he wrote again:

"Dear mother, we were in the trenches, I was ill, so I went out and they took me to the prison, and I am in a bit of trouble now, I will have to go in front of a court." This was the last they heard from Abraham.

In April they received a letter from the senior officer in charge of infantry records.

"Sir, I am directed to inform you that a report has been received from the War Office to the effect Pte G/1799 Middlesex Regiment was sentenced after trial by court martial to suffer death by being shot for desertion, and the sentence was duly executed on 20 March 1916.

I am, Sir, your obedient servant."

In his statement to the court where he had no representation Abraham explained: "I left the trenches because three rifle grenades exploded near me. I was deafened, and my nerves had gone a bit."

He was seen by a MO who told the court he had found him suffering from no appreciable disease and told him he was fit for duty.

A soldier saw Abraham at the farm where he was billeted: "Harris told me he had just come out of hospital," the soldier said. "He had no greatcoat or hat and was covered in mud. He stayed in the billet all afternoon sitting by the fire warming himself."

By the evening Abraham was arrested.

The owner of the farm told the court: "He said the trenches were being bombed and he left them and was going to England."

Abraham said: "I felt nervous and lost my head. I thought I would stay at the farm for a few days and go back to the company when they came out of the trenches." Those were the words that condemned him. The court was convinced that he had intended to desert.

Sylvia Pankhurst, a campaigner for human rights and social reform, knew the family and took up their son's case. She published his letters in her magazine Dreadnought and protested against the injustice of executing a 19-year-old volunteer who had endured eight months in the trenches and had only just come out of hospital with injuries and shell shock.

Passages from 7th Battalion East Surrey Regiments war diaries.

Monday 13th.

The enemy seemed to have connected up their Saps behind the Chord forming a new front line. We blew up three enemy mine shafts opposite A crater early in the evening of the 13th and considerable bombing ensued, nothing to report.

In the afternoon we moved out to the reserve line, one company in Alexandra trench, front line.

Saturday 18th.

Enemy shelling with 4.2-inch howitzers and field guns continues during the day. The enemy started a heavy bombardment on craters, front line, and support lines. This was the prelude to a determined attack on all craters, held by us and the battalion on our right, the 6th Buffs.

5:30pm. Intense bombardment opened on the whole front, trench mortars, minenwerfer, rifle grenade, shrapnel and high explosive.

5:40pm. All wires with the exception of B coy and Quarry wire cut.

5:50pm. Message by Corporal Cushon A coy to say that C and B craters were being badly smashed. He had volunteered to take this message from the craters through what seemed certain death and after delivering it returned to duty in the front line.

6:20pm. Two mines were sent up, one on the left lip of C crater and one between B and C craters.

7:05pm. Captain Scott reported No4 crater occupied by the enemy. They had come into No4, but he had bombed them out and established bombing posts overlooking B crater. No3 crater reported "all correct".

7:35pm. Half coy Queens sent to reinforce the West face. Blocks had been established in Russian Sap and Sap12.

> *9:25pm. Captain Scott consolidating round No4 crater.*
>
> *10:58pm. Enemy reported trying to crawl down Russian Sap and also reported holding near the lip of C and B crater.*

Wednesday 22nd. Bethune.

We marched out of Sailly Labourse at 11am and reached Bethune by lunchtime. Our battalion looked very meagre. It went in from rest about 800 strong and marched back about 400.

Here I have struck a palatial billet, a well-furnished bedroom with eiderdown quilt on bed and lovely linen sheets. The headquarters mess is par ici and also very comfortable.

Thursday 23rd.

Did a bit of shopping and according to a previous arrangement went to Hotel de France at 2:30pm to meet William. But he evidently was unable to get leave and did not turn up.

Major Wilson went on leave on Wednesday evening.

I hear corps commander General Gough is leaving and a Guardsman, General Kavanagh taking his place.

Friday 24th.

Snowed hard all night and is still snowing as I write at noon. Once more we seem to be in the grip of winter, it is very depressing.

However, I am glad I didn't put in for leave and I intend to wait until spring is really with us before I go home.

I have visions of some glorious days in the Lake District, the music of mountain streams is in my ears and the intoxicating odour of bursting buds is in my nostrils.

Saturday 25th.

Just heard we are not returning to damned trenches tomorrow, so I have another delightful 'louse' in bed to look forward to.

Visited a rifle grenade factory this afternoon and watched the molten metal pouring like cream from the furnace. The whole process was most interesting.

Sunday 26th.

Translation of German document 20/2/16 found on a German prisoner recently captured: "Committee for the increase of the population"

Sir. On account of all the able-bodied men having been called to the colours, it remains the duty of all those left behind, for the sake of the fatherland, to interest themselves in the happiness of the married women and maidens by doubling or even trebling the number of births.

Your name has been given to us as a capable man, and you are herewith requested to take on this office of honour and do your duty in right German style.

It must be pointed out that your wife or fiancé will not be able to claim a divorce, it is in fact hoped that the women will bare this discomfort heroically for the sake of the war.

You will be given the district of - - - - - - -

Should you not feel capable of the situation you will be given three days in which to name someone else in your place. On the other hand, if you are prepared to take on a second district as well, you will become a "Seckoffizier" and receive a pension.

An exhibition of women and maidens as well as collection of photographs is to be found at our office. You are requested to bring this letter with you.

Your good work should commence immediately, and it is in your interest to submit to us a full report of results after nine months."

(German barrack room humour)

Monday 27th. Vermelles.

In spite of a bed luxuriant enough for a hothouse exotic, I must candidly admit I slept badly in it. I undoubtedly sleep better on a hard bed or floor provided I am sufficiently warm.

Had to give evidence in a court martial case, the prisoner had come down to me during the time we were opposite Hohenzollern. He was obviously terrified, so I excused him from duty and wrote him a note to take back to his Coy. He however slunk away towards Vermelles and remained in a dugout for two days until discovered.

Leeds waited for me and then we got a lift on a lorry to Noyelles-lès-Vermelles. The driver of this lorry told me he only did three miles on a gallon of petrol and he drove about 700 miles a week! Here I am in the bowels of a brewery but have a kind of bed.

Tuesday 28th. Brewery.

Made one or two walks to Noyelles-lès-Vermelles where we have two coys. Things are quiet. The man I gave evidence about at court martial got 88 days imprisonment and I was so glad he wasn't sentenced to be shot.

Feel fed up with the trenches, never felt so sick of the whole thing as I do today.

Wednesday 29th.

Lovely sun shining, but cold. Visited 18-pounder battery and had a nose piece of shell opinionated on and pronounced safe.

Enemy aircraft came over and I had to get into gun pit until it cleared.

At 10pm we heard of enemy preparations for attack on our right – 16th Division – and were warned to be ready to move up during night.

That is the position as I write, everything points to attack because they have mined under our front lines and are reported to have cut both ours and their own wire in front of trenches. Also, they are said to be massing behind the line.

Took Leeds with me to Noyelles-lès-Vermelles and on the way told him something about the teachings of theosophy. He is very intelligent, and I hope I may interest him in it.

Thursday 30th. Trenches.

Well nothing happened, the night was undisturbed. A lovely day; I started up trenches at 10am, looking at nine more days!

Leeds and I walked up more or less slowly. It took us an hour or greater to reach the aid post. Trenches were a foot deep with water but only in places. They were enormously improved to what they were when we last held this portion of the line nearly six months ago.

Am sleeping in aid post which is some way behind HQ. A splendid view of the Dump which now lies on our left.

Feel terribly tired of these trenches. Feel like an imprisoned animal. You can't walk far in case casualties should come down.

So far things have been quiet except for the terrific crash of trench mortars and minenwerfers.

Friday 31st.

Had two casualties during the night which wasn't much considering the number of trench mortars they fired on us. Our poor battalion has dropped into it again!

The Bosch blew two mines in the evening and we sustained three killed, while about 20 were badly shaken and buried by the debris. The large trench mortars they used accounted for a good many bad casualties and altogether I was kept busy nearly all night.

Our new draft of 101 men on Wednesday therefore had a rough baptism.

The noise of explosions from the Hun's mortars and minenwerfers beggars description and one can readily understand what a morale effect they must have on any but the most phlegmatic.

However, tactically, the enemy gained nothing by last night's mining. Indeed, we are probably in a better position or shall be tonight when we have finished our saps to the two new craters he made but did not occupy.

Passages from 7th Battalion East Surrey Regiments war diaries.

Sunday 19th

Relieved by 5th Royal Berkshires. Moved Sailly Labourse.

Monday 20th.

Our losses during the period 7-18th were: Killed 34, Missing 22, Wounded 243, Shock (hospital) 39, this included Captain Jones, died of wounds 12th.

(Commonwealth War Graves records show Captain Jones 16/3/16)

Wednesday 29th

A wire from the GOC (General Officer Commanding) informed us that 2nd Lieutenant Cook had been granted the Military Cross and Private Venables and Private Hewitt the DCM.

These were given for good work on 7 March 1916. A welcome draft of one officer, Lieut Marshall, and 101 men arrived today. Most of the men were 1st and 2nd Battalion and almost all had been cut before.

> *Thursday 30th.*
>
> *The battalion relieved the 6th Royal West Kents in the front line this morning, holding from Rifleman's Alley to south of Swinburn Loop. A quiet day. A few mortars fell during the night and we retaliated.*
>
> *Friday 31st.*
>
> *Quiet day. The enemy blew up three mines, one at 7:15pm and two at 7:32am, all three were at the Hairpin.*
>
> *The enemy attempted to bomb from the two craters on the right leg of the Hairpin but were bombed back. A sap is being carried out to the lip of the new crater.*

APRIL 1916.

Saturday 1st.

A perfect day. Not a cloud except the cloudlets caused by the hundreds of anti-aircraft shells. Really, trench life becomes almost enjoyable when things are quiet, and a glorious sun allows one to enjoy a bask in some sheltered nook.

A very broken night on account of wounded who kept dropping in and I was brewing tea at 3am. Two mines went up during the night causing as usual my dugout to sway and the wooden supports to creak and groan rather ominously.

The enemy were pretty lively with their trench mortars and it was wonderful how few casualties we had.

Another of my stretcher bearers was killed.

Sunday 2nd. Support.

By Jove! What a day! A cloudless sky and scorching sun.

We were relieved by the Kents and went down to trenches lower down. I have a dugout at the end of a cul-de-sac so that I am for once undisturbed by passers-by and just outside a cleft in the parapet gave me an ideal seat, a perfect sun trap. Three days here, what bliss!

A letter from Cross, poor man, he is fairly working – 26 confinements in 10 days! Surgeries packed and the locum not very popular.

Cross, with his foresight, had bought a large supply of drugs which have now reached a fearful price – Potassium Bromide, usually one-shilling-eight pence per pound now thirty-shillings; Sodium Saline, one-shilling-two pence now twenty-seven shillings; Paper, four-shillings a ream, now eight shillings etc.

Monday 3rd. Support.

Never before have I seen larks in such abundance or enjoyed their singing as much before. Man is no longer an enemy to them, penned down as he is in the trenches, the green tracts of pasture that wend between the rows of trenches are theirs without question.

Have just seen rather an interesting thing. I saw the shell of a crump with the naked eye about twenty feet before it reached the ground and exploded, needless to say it was uncomfortably near in front. You can scarcely hear a crump approaching when it is coming directly for you. You just hear a sort of drunken shaky oscillation of some heavy body – it is most terrifying; you seem to feel its approach rather than hear it.

On the other hand, when a crump is approaching at an angle you hear its train-like roar growing louder. Next you see the cloud of smoke and debris rise in the air followed by the actual sound of the explosion.

Tuesday 4th. Support.

Got up about 6:30am and taking advantage of the early morning mist which obscured us from the Dump and Bosch trenches, Leeds and I got over our parapet and had a hunt for 'nose pieces' along the open ground. Found one or two new specimens and found some fairly useful shell holes. Also put up a brown owl which was sitting on the ground.

It was planned that the sappers should spring two mines which they had prepared under the two left German craters. The mines were to go up at midnight. We, the brigade, made tremendous preparations for the occupation of the near lip by the Queens and one of our corps was to clear out our own first line which would be blown in by the explosion.

At midnight, to the second we felt the two mines go up, there was comparatively little strafing after it and our artillery which opened was scarcely answered.

Wednesday 5th.

The show last night was not a great success. We occupied the near lip of the first crater, but the Bosch were the first to get into the second crater. The Queens were too slow and feeble. The crater which we occupied was taken by the Surreys who were in support.

148

Thursday 6th. Firing line.

Leeds has been telling me something about milk dealing and the tricks of the profession.

His company buys cream at three shillings a quart then retails it to customers at eight shillings a quart. They are allowed to add, if they want to, a preparation made from an Indian root. This gives ordinary milk a rich creamy appearance, the stuff itself being of a reddish colour costing fourteen shillings a bottle for 20 ounces.

Leeds has also done canvassing for his milk company. The agents supply them with addresses of new people settling in a place and for this information they receive in some cases 10d or in others ten shillings if they, the new residents become customers.

An interesting fellow, Leeds – for a long time he was with a smart West End fruiterer in Bond Street, he used to canvas for them. He told me that he would gain the custom of a rich family by paying the chef or head cook between five and ten pounds, then after that they would get two shillings in the pound on all orders

Friday 7th.

A little rain during night which has made the trench boards exceedingly slippery. Walked around a portion of the firing line with Anns at 4:00pm.

To my surprise William turned up, he is sniping from Rifleman's Alley and I feel very anxious as he has no 'plate' *(protection)* and has to look over the parapet to shoot. He thinks he got a Bosch this morning.

Have given him my life preserving medal which I have worn since the beginning of the war. It was blessed by the Pope and given to me by Fisher.

We had tea and afterwards walked a little way down the trench and had a talk. Shrapnel and heavy stuff began to fall so close that we returned to my dugout. A trench mortar burst very close this evening and put out our candle.

Good news from Tigris – five lines of trenches taken and 6,000 Guards advanced. We blew a large mine this evening. It is a perfect race to mine and countermine.

Saturday 8th. Firing line.

Things were very quiet all morning. This afternoon took Leeds with me as far as Rifleman's Alley hoping to find William, but he had gone.

However, I found a sniper in the observing post and he showed me a Bosch through the telescope. His head and shoulders were just visible, he was dressed in keeping with his surroundings on the Dump – slate coloured cap, blackened face, and dark clothes, so that; even with the aid of a telescope it was most difficult to spot him.

William thinks he may get leave in about a fortnight, so I think I must postpone mine so as to try and get home with him or thereabouts.

I have finished Intrusions of Peggy (*by Anthony Hope*) – very entertaining. Am now reading Marcelle (*by Hampden Burnham*).

Sunday 9th. Firing line.

They gave us a terrible dose of trench mortars last night. I watched them coming over in the dark, a track of sparks making it easy to follow their course up and downwards just like a Roman Candle, only instead of ending in an innocent display they end with a most appalling crash which has the most nerve breaking effect on those near it. The Bosch however doesn't happily land them often in one's trenches, we have extraordinarily few casualties from them.

Had a crump 30 or 40 yards off me this afternoon and once again saw the shell before it reached the ground.

Mines are now a daily occurrence and do not lead to much excitement as they are mostly blown in order to destroy or with hope of destroying each other's mine galleries.

Thank God we are relieved tomorrow by the Suffolks.

The question of leave is exercising my mind just now. I love to think of spending a divine fourteen days among the Lakes and I don't want to go until the larches at least are gorgeous with their exquisite green. I fear therefore, that I shall have to endure another tour in the trenches in order not to arrive too soon.

Nellie writes to say spring is very backwards this year. I am torn with a desire to get home and away from these festering trenches and this desolate country which is void of all vegetation that looks just the same now as it did in mid-winter.

Monday 10th. Annequin.

Oh joy! We were relieved soon after 11am by the Suffolks and Leeds and I were soon walking down the trenches. How delightful to tread the broad road and revel in a long horizon.

This is the first time we have billeted here. There are numbers of heavy batteries all around and the village occasionally enjoys a few shells meant for the gun pits in the vicinity.

On the whole the village has been left alone and there is quite a good population including women and children.

Lovely sun shining, took a stroll and found a quiet place away from the tractor track on the edge of a marshy piece of ground where beautiful marigolds grew among the sedges.

Tuesday 11th.

It Rained today for the first time in days. Had a bath at the 'coal pit'.

Wednesday 12th. Billets.

Wet blustery day. Sent Leeds over to try and find William at Vermelles. He found him occupying one of the cellars which I had used for some sick cases about a month ago. William turned up this afternoon and we had a walk together and a good chinwag over old times at Grasmere. Walked back to Vermelles with William.

Major Wilson left for England to be invested by the King with his DSO.

Order from division tonight – "all leave stopped"! So, my plan of getting home on the 22nd falls through. It may happen that leave will be reopened in a week or two, in which case I should not complain as I should rather get home in May. At the same time, it looks as if it means a push somewhere or other.

Thursday 13th.

Got in touch with William who was still living in the same cellar at Vermelles. He came over for the afternoon, it was blustery, rainy, and cold, we had to sit inside. However, we talked of old times at home – very old times.

Lived once again together so vividly in the past that one really felt the physical glow of some of the happy days we summoned before us, instead of being surrounded by half shelled houses and all the debris of war.

We are only conscious of beautiful mountains rising on every side, of musical mountain streams and quiet lakes!

William is still sniping; I hope no harm will come to him. Gave him my St Christopher medal. *(refers to Apr 7th)*

Friday 14th.

I woke up feeling rotten and therefore thought the best plan would be to walk it off. I therefore walked to Sailly Labourse and saw ADMS about my leave and other matters. Then pushed on to Labourse and by the railway to Bethune. It was as much as I could do to trail my legs along.

At Bethune I went to a lecture on gas and gas shells which was interesting. Walked all the way back to Annequin, found William there but I went straight to bed and William talked.

Restless night, temp 102. The battalion moved out at 10am and I got the ambulance to give me a lift to Bethune where I went straight to bed.

Saturday 15th.

Got Major Phelan of 37th Field Ambulance to send an officer – Lieut Sheldon – to see my sick for me.

Temp 101, Leeds most attentive, has looked after me extremely well.

Sunday 16th.

After a bad night I am glad to find my temp has dropped to subnormal this morning. I shall therefore return with the battalion tomorrow to the trenches.

Have had poor old Corporal Culwick[46] passed by the ADMS for PB duties *(Permanent base duties, medical),* he has been breaking up very fast lately and has now for all practical purposes quite lost his nerve.

It is extraordinary how this form of warfare tells on the nerves, no one realises this better than the Germans, they have brought psychology to bear on the war in a way which we have not. Their flammenwerfer[47] *(flamethrower)* and minenwerfer *(short range mortar)* are undoubtedly methods of frightfulness meant to play on the nerves.

Felt cold and shivering towards the evening and went to bed. Undoubtedly, I am feverish. Nicholls just turned up, as did Captain Martin and Devenish.

---

46. *513 Cpl Culwick. Alexander. Discharged on 17th June 1916 under paragraph 392 Kings regulations (xvi). No longer physically fit for war service. Silver war badge no 12470. (Forces war record)*

47. *Flammenwerfer. Portable backpack M16. First used Verdun 1915. An account in 1917 suggests use on the Somme. Recorded use at the Battle of Argonne Forest 1918.*

Monday 17th. Support.

A bad night with stiff neck and general restlessness, felt weak and listless.

Got the ambulance to give me a lift as far as the Chateau Vermelles, the ADS of the 37th Field Ambulance. Found refuge there and rested for an hour before walking up to trenches with Leeds. Made quite a good lunch but about 4pm I began to feel cold so I went to bed at 5pm. I was disgusted to find myself with a temp of 100, headache over one eye and rather irritating cough.

Tuesday 18th.

Got through a miserable night somehow but awoke to find myself free from fever and also no headache. I wonder what I shall feel like this afternoon.

It was a quiet night, no casualties for us and only one slight case for the West Kents. Headache this afternoon.

They periodically put a few 4.2-inch shells round about here each day.

This afternoon, while I was lying down I had the satisfaction of hearing one – a dud – come whistling towards us and then fell with a dull thud in the soft earth. Next one pitched on the parapet just outside my dugout, burst with a loathsome crash which sent a load of earth down into the dugout and did not improve my headache.

The RAMC men came rushing down into my dugout panic stricken. Why they left the aid post I don't know because it was perfectly safe against 4.2-inch

Wednesday 19th. Hohenzollern support.

Miserable drizzling rain and not at all warm. Very quiet on the line.

In the afternoon I developed a wracking headache and temp, also sore throat, and irritating cough.

Thursday 20th. Trenches.

I feel very weak. Same headache and temp in afternoon

Passages from 7th Battalion East Surrey Regiments war diaries.
Saturday 1st.

Continual work all day clearing out the saps and repairing damage done. The day passed fairly quietly. Our casualties due to the mines blown the previous evening amounted to about thirty.

> *Monday 3rd.*
>
> *Relieved by 6th Royal West Kents and moved to support lines. Occupying Curley Crescent.*
>
> *Wednesday 5th.*
>
> *Captain Cook left for England on special leave for an investiture at Buckingham Palace. At 5:30am two mines were blown at the Hohenzollern, no activity followed.*
>
> *Saturday 8th.*
>
> *We were shelled today for a considerable period and retaliation was given. A new form of hate was introduced today by the Bosch, viz a shell in the form of a canister containing a virulent acid, this was forwarded to the brigade. About 8pm a large mine was blown in the Hohenzollern, some activity followed.*

Friday 21st. Chocques hospital.

Felt all right, except run down until afternoon then wracking headache, temp 101 made bed the only place possible.

My ambition was to stick it until Tuesday when we are going back for a month's rest. The colonel however, came down to see me and was very sympathetic, practically ordered me to go down to the hospital. He then wrote to ADMS and told him I was going to the hospital. I must say, a deep dugout is a cheerless place when you are feeling really ill and I was glad to have the matter settled for me. So, we packed up and Anns very decently came down to the ambulance with me in spite of the rain.

It was indeed raining hard and I never remember the landscape looking more dreary and melancholy than it did in the fading light which was just sufficient to silhouette against the skyline, the battered church, and roofless houses of Vermelles village.

I took Leeds with me. I got a car to Labourse where I saw Kelly who was apparently offended with me ref my row with 38th Field Ambulance which unfortunately involved him. However, he was quite ready to make amends.

I left in a car for officers' home Bethune. Arriving there we found the hospital was full, so they sent us on to Chocques. It was pouring with rain as we arrived at No-1 CCS (*Casualty Clearing Station*)

154

It is a large French chateau with some magnificent rooms. The one I am in, on the ground floor, is panelled with white wood and the ceiling has some striking mouldings.

When I arrived, my temp was normal; I had not been in bed long before it started to rise.

This is a much nicer place than the officers' hospital at Bethune. The food is much better and with etc's in the way of clean toilets, towels etc. are all there.

Sunday 23rd.

A glorious spring morning with sun streaming in through the open window. The songs of thrushes in the garden, no sound of a gun or rifle to remind one of the trenches.

My temp this morning still over 100 and a good deal of pain in chest. Spitting up a lot of purulent stuff, my throat is also sore and inflamed, back is also painful.

The Padre came and visited us yesterday and invited us to attend celebration this morning. He looked so genuinely earnest that I accepted. Four out of five in the ward attended.

Feeling worse this afternoon and fever which I quite thought I had gotten rid of has returned. This is now the 12th day of the fever.

The MO advises me to go down to base tomorrow, he suspects typhoid, but I think by my sputum that TB is just as possible. Feel tired and quite unconcerned whatever it shows itself to be.

Monday 24th. Red cross hospital.

Leeds[48] packed my belongings and I gave him some Francs for my medical staff and told him to explain to them that if I had been somewhat irritable of late it has been down to me not feeling well.

---

48. *283 Pte Leeds, William Arthur. MM. Enlisted 22/08/1914 East Surrey Regiment. Occupation on enlistment – Canvasser and collector for dairy. William was of slight build, being 5ft 3in and weighing 8st. 25/05/1917. London Gazette issue 30095 page 5193 – The Military Medal was awarded to Cpl W A Leeds for acts of gallantry and devotion to duty under fire. On the 15/01/1918 reported missing presumed dead.*
Report dated 19/02/18. Cpl 283 Leeds previously reported missing now reported prisoner of war and in German hands. There is a record in the 1939 register of a William Arthur Leeds, newsagent in Seven Oaks Kent. Possible death in 1943 aged 58. William's personal details are the only ones recorded in The Doctor's diary.

Soon after midday I was taken by stretcher to a car and driven to Chocques station where I was transferred to the Red Cross train. I was lucky to get the middle of the three bunks as it gave one an uninterrupted view through the window against which I was lying. My bunk was well hung on great spring levers, very comfortable.

The first portion of the journey no one knew our destination, which might have been one of four or five places, then we learnt that we were going to Rouen.

A long weary journey, the worst of ventilation. Felt very ill and my cough troubled me incessantly.

Tuesday 25th. Rouen No 2 Red Cross hospital.

Arrived Rouen about 5am, feeling too ill to write much. The doctor thinks it has been Influenza tracheitis which has left me very weak and my temp was normal.

I have a room all to myself, most comfortable, charming nurses and sisters. Food cooking is absolutely first class: "Do you want whiskey, wine or beer?"

Wednesday 26th.

Headache, burning eyes, sore throat and constantly wracked by cough with expectoration of yellow purulent matter.

The MO, Major Hudson diagnosed influenza with a patch of bronchial pneumonia at left base.

My own diagnosis which I have kept to myself is acute gout. I believe the whole thing has been an acute intense acid toxaemia, the lack of exercise in the trenches, the impossibility of dieting oneself, the meat diet after a year of fruitarian food. All has culminated in the attack.

After a successful saline purge headache left me but temp remains 100. The sisters and nurses are awfully nice and do anything for one.

Thursday 27th.

Temp normal for the first time this morning. I feel better except for sore throat and irritating eyeballs. Major Hudson says I must stay in bed.

I managed to shave myself but felt very weak after I had finished. Major Hudson reports my sputum to be full of pneumococci.

Friday 28th.

A bad night as usual, woke at 2am to find my eyelids stuck together owing to them becoming involved in the attack. Temp is practically normal this morning, I feel very exhausted even when lying in bed, also depressed.

Doctor Hudson says it is undoubtedly a case of influenza tracheitis. He is such a nice man and has a smile which is attractive as it is unexpected makes one forgive him anything – even his previous diagnosis of bronchial pneumonia. He is keeping me in bed today.

Saturday 29th.

A good night, the first I have enjoyed for days. Feel much stronger in bed but am still coughing up a lot of purulent phlegm. This hospital in peacetime is a seminary.

Yesterday evening the sisters and men were having a choir practice and I enjoyed some really splendid singing in the way of anthems. One nurse has a fine voice!

Got up and dressed at 1:30pm. After enjoying a bath, I was taken to the balcony on the sunny side of the building. Here I lounged in a fine Morocco chair in the blazing sun. I feel extraordinarily weak and when walking my boots keep hitting one another at every other step.

Sunday 30th.

One succession of cloudless days and as hot as mid-summer. Dressed after lunch and sat on the balcony, feeling very low and depressed. Was glad to go back to bed at about 5:45pm.

Does not appear to be much likely-hood of getting back to England on sick leave. Feeling shaky and coughing is troublesome.

Passages from 7th Battalion East Surrey Regiments war diaries.
Saturday 22nd. Hohenzollern.

At 7:30am we exploded a mine near the end of Russian sap and C crater. It is thought that our mine was quite successful in that it blew in the enemy's galleries that were undermining Russian sap.

We had no casualties and very little damage was done to our trenches; all the debris went over the Bosch lines. Raining hard all day.

> *Our men are worked to death, keeping things in repair, making new saps, loopholes etc in craters. The brigadier is offering a week's leave to any man bringing in a prisoner and a weekend for a dead one – new.*
>
> *It is thought that the Germans have carried out a big relief lately and it is of the greatest importance to find out who is in front of us.*

MAY 1916

Tuesday 2nd May.

Feel much better, the Archbishop of Rouen whose house adjoins this building allows us to roam about his garden. It is just a rough piece of land, but it is a fairyland of fruit trees in full blossom and you get one or two delightful peeps of the hills surrounding the town.

Heavy rain at intervals with thunder.

Wednesday 3rd.

Pulse only 64 and temp 97 and I feel quite well. Got a pass to Rouen and accompanied by Lieutenant Barrington of the Gloucestershire's we walked down.

I had a smell around, the cathedral was wonderful with some superb old glass windows. The building as a whole is spoiled from the outside by an atrocious wrought iron spire which was recently created on the top of the rear tower.

Thursday 4th.

Feel quite well again although I still cough, and my nose runs, and I have also lost all sense of taste and smell. Doctor Hudson promises to send me away. My kit however has not yet arrived, which is a nuisance as it contains my souvenirs

Friday 5th.

Got leave to go into town this afternoon and at 2pm I set off alone.

First, I visited Saint Owens, a lovely Gothic building with beautiful stained glass. Then I went into the church of St Maclou which is said to be an exquisite specimen of Norman architecture. It is absolutely wonderful.

I wandered about unheeded inside and seeing a small door in the solid masonry I pushed it open with some difficulty as it was jammed with all sorts of debris lying on the floor.

However, I opened it wide enough to squeeze through and shut it behind me. A narrow flight of stone steps invited an exploration and I started upwards. I climbed and climbed and every now and then I came out into the open and was rewarded with some magnificent views, especially when I reached the highest portion of the tower and could see the Seine winding up the valley towards Paris. A most beautiful sight.

Indeed, I thought it one of the most beautiful cities I had ever seen. Such a lot of trees throughout the town and the greater proportion of houses appearing to lie in their own grounds, even in the heart of the town. I found a pigeon's nest with two eggs in it. There are also some jolly old houses, 15th century, with balconies running outside reminding one of the houses in Chester.

Saturday 6th.

Doctor Watson says he is sending me somewhere tomorrow, convalescent camp I think.

The CO advised me to send in my application for leave directly. So, I shall forward it to the DDMS Rouen and hope he will allow me to go to England.

Cloudy, cold and rainy.

God! How I loathe the thought of those trenches now that I am away from them. Haven't I really done my share by having worked for ten months in them?

Just finished 'The Tenant of Wildfell Hall' by Anne Bronte. Have enjoyed it immensely. She had apparently never met a 'real' man, the male characters are the type of sporting rake and the hero is a very poor specimen of English gentleman.

"Heaven and Hell of the Christian doctrine"

If there is a life of happiness on the other side of death it is earned in some way, either by resisting temptation or by positive well doing.

If we do earn the heavenly life it seems very hard that some die in infancy. They had no choice. Or perhaps it is that such anyone, having done no wrong, shall enter into heaven. Then it is very hard that others should have to live a long life full of temptations and dangers.

Surely the heavenly life must be earned, for that earning equal chance be given to each. It is not equal chance when men are born so differently, one a savage or an imbecile while another is endowed with all good tendencies and favourable opportunities.

Nor can it be that little is expected from one and much from another, for that is to say again that this life is needless, to believe that it is right that some should pass here a life of pain and ignorance, and others one of pleasure and joyous life, yet both reap the same result.

Nor will it do to say that one receives a higher seat in the supernal (*Belonging to the heavens of divine beings*) world, because of his greater difficulties hear, for then, one may demand that each receive an equal chance to reach the highest Christianity cannot answer the problem because she does not teach the doctrines of reincarnation and karma.

If a man knows himself to be in a world of law and himself. To be neither a victim of some caprice nor a puppet of blind chance, he has the strength wherewith to work.

Monday 8th. No 9 General Hospital.

Oh! Oh! Again! Once again, we move on.

I have met a lot of men here from different regiments. One 2nd Lieutenant from the Gloucestershire Regiment aged 22 asked me whether I should like his photo which I accepted. One meets so many nice fellows and perhaps never see them again. "Ships that pass in the night and speak to each other in passing, only a signal shown and a distant voice in the darkness, so, on the ocean of life we pass, only a look and a voice, then darkness again and a silence." (*from The Theologian's Tale; Elizabeth by Henry Wadsworth Longfellow*)

I also met a KEH officer – Havelock Sutton[49] – who has been in hospital for sixteen weeks with a wounded foot. He comes from Formby and knew the Longs whom he had met at dances at the hall.

The ambulance car took me to No 9 General Hospital. It consists of a multitude of huts and is situated on the edge of a huge forest of Scotch firs. There are some twenty RAMC officers in our mess, some of them residents, the majority birds of passage like myself.

---

49. *Lieut Havelock-Sutton, George Henry. Awarded MC for distinguished service in connection with military operations in France and Flanders. Wounded 14 January 1916 at Le Cauroy, rifle grenade wound to leg in 19 places. Later Capt Flying Officer. Died 30/7/20. Depot (Halton camp) RAF St Michael and All Saints Church. (KEH website)*

160

Tuesday 9th.

I did not expect to get a good night's rest because I had to sleep in a tent! My kit has not yet arrived from Bethune, so I have no 'flea bag' or clean clothes. However, in spite of a very low temperature I managed to keep quite warm and had quite a comfortable night.

Quite a different set of medical men here from what one meets among the field ambulances. They are an older lot; one also meets men eager to get up to the front and waiting impatiently to get sent up.

Others again like myself have had the experience and are in no hurry to go back. Personally, I am waiting to get leave – my fourteen days – and shall almost certainly get it within a week. How splendid to get home. I feel far from well. This morning despite a slight drizzle of rain, I walked into the forest for two or three miles. It was delightful, the quiet hum of the wind through the trees had the most smoothing effect.

I felt I could have laid down and dropped off to sleep in five minutes, but it was too cold. Curious how cold it has become. 25 degrees lower than it was a week ago

Wednesday 10th.

The beauty of the country over which one can ramble absolutely beggars description. Yesterday afternoon I walked for miles with a forest of Scotch firs immediately on my left and a mixed wood on my right where the exquisite green of the jolly oaks contrasted strikingly with the sombre colours of the firs on my left.

This afternoon, as I write, I am lying in this mixed wood reclining on a soft bed of heather with a glorious sun above me. I watch the sunlight flickering among and through the young and translucent leaves of the beech trees and the birds sing around me.

I am reading a delightful book – 'Ships That Pass in the Night' by Beatrice Harraden (*suffragette*) – a book full of the most beautiful thoughts. Being, by nature, I have often lamented at having to work for my living, but this book points out what a privilege and blessing it is to be able to work and shows how so many people are denied this privilege by reason of illness.

To be cut off from active life and earnest work was a possibility which never occurred to me

Thursday 11th. No 9.

I have a medical ward to look after and I simply go around and see any new cases that come in.

On average my work can be got through in half an hour! And then as far as I can see, there is no reason why one should appear on the scene again during the day. Except perhaps to look in at any bad case you may have.

There are 12 of these hut hospitals and altogether they can accommodate 12,000 cases, and if they also make use of the YMCA huts, they could put up about 15,000 cases.

This afternoon Captain Sparrow, who was at King W College IOM, whose brother showed me over his study one day fourteen years ago and practices in Southampton, and I took the train to Rouen and then went on board a little steamer that runs up the Seine eight or nine miles to Bouille.

Although there was no actual sunshine, the day was bright and warm. It was a great treat. The woods were indescribably gorgeous, beautifully wooded hills running down towards the banks of the Seine ending abruptly in blue grey-cliffs of limestone. There was a striking contrast where dark yew trees and young beeches grew together. The distant woods were absolutely enchanting, in the foreground, houses with gay gardens full of laburnum and wisteria made a pleasing contrast. In Bouille we went ashore for half an hour and had a cup of coffee.

Bouille, our first stop on the left side of the river, seemed very picturesque and I was sorry we couldn't see more of it. We passed close to a German enclosure and could see the prisoners playing games and working. Cold and rain.

Saturday 13th.

Cold and showery, I went into town with interpreter who is a wine merchant in Bordeaux. Bought a large bottle of eau-de-cologne (fourteen francs). It has gotten much dearer.

I took him to lunch at a restaurant opposite the left front of the Cathedral. The lunch was three francs each and it was the best lunch I have ever had. The cooking was superb, the dishes most artistically arranged.

Enquiries at Red Cross hospital for my kit which is still heaven knows where!

Sunday 14th.

Weather so cold and gloomy but the darkest weather cannot rob the woods of their glorious colours. I walked to the left, skirting the pine woods.

Coming back, I felt so fatigued and 'done up' that I could scarcely get home.

Monday 15th.

I am now seeing the early morning sick at the No 5 General Base Camp. I have to be there by 7:30am. I see about 30 or 40 of all different regiments.

Bitterly cold. I feel at times very low and depressed, nor can I get clear of the 'cold' in my nose, also I keep expectorating a lot from my trachea.

Charlie Hannay notified me that he has paid into my bank £11.18.2 – my share for two quarters' rent. Went to a play this evening, most amusing and very well acted for amateurs. The men dressed as women were extraordinarily grotesque; especially the heroine, a six-foot corporal of very graceful proportions dressed becomingly in a blue silk costume and with a very deep voice, It was extremely clever.

The hospital band played surprisingly well.

Tuesday 16th.

Have not had my leave granted to me yet and am beginning to feel anxious because leave may be stopped owing to increasing activity of the enemy on the front.

A warmer day with glimpses of sunshine. Am writing this as I recline on a fallen tree in the midst of the pine forest. It is beautifully still; and the birds sing so joyously. It is difficult to believe oneself to not be in England as I lie in a glorious sun among some long grass on the side of a little wood. The same trees and the same blackbirds singing away.

There is a wonderfully varied flora, I have already found a number of unfamiliar flowers and I can see by strange leaves the promise of many more species quite unknown to me. Solomon's seal, Lily of the valley, some large Spurges and a beautiful red Milkwort are common.

Wednesday 17th.

Another glorious day! Have had a fair amount to do with seeing sick – a motley crew – and inspecting drafts going up to the front. The Schorm-shankers *(lead swingers)* are troublesome here.

In the afternoon I got away from my work about 2:30pm and walked through a part of the forest coming out among beautiful cornfields which grew right up to the forest. A delightfully peaceful glade separating a portion of the cornfield from the deep forest invited me and, sinking into some soft grass bathed in sunshine, I read and thought for more than an hour.

I found a curious grasshopper or cricket which burrows in the ground and is, I think, responsible for the endless chirruping which one hears in passing through the meadows here.

Thursday 18th.

Still perfect weather and too hot for these loathsome khaki clothes. Oh! for peace and civil life again!

I went into Rouen this afternoon and bought a thin vest, socks and drawers. Then I found my way into the magnificent 15th century church of St Owen with the idea of mounting the tower.

The Sexton showed me the little oak door, up I went. Endless steps brought me to a narrow stone balcony which was built around the whole building immediately beneath the lower edge of the steep roof. I followed this ledge as far as the main tower and after climbing through a narrow opening was able to finally reach the belfry by a narrow flight of stairs. From here I had a magnificent view all over the town. I now descended the stairs but much to my annoyance found the door at the bottom closed!

I knocked and knocked but it was greater than an hour before, amid some commotion and the grating of a rusty lock the door opened and to my horror, I found myself standing – cap on! – about six feet from the floor of the church overlooking a lot of reverent and kneeling people.

Everyone looked so startled at my sudden appearance through a door which it seemed had not been opened since the 15th century, that I felt almost afraid lest they might mistake me for one of their patron saints. Well, the Sexton, by the aid of a chair helped me down and seemed to think the whole thing rather a joke. The last thing I saw of him was trying to conceal his smothered laughter behind one of the pillars.

Friday 19th.

I am now doing the work for the MO of the 5th General Base Depot who is away on leave. All I have to do is to go there at 9:30am and see about twenty-thirty sick.

Occasionally during the week, I may have to run up a line of men – drafts – going to the front and pass those that are fit. This usually takes about ten minutes to do. A medical board held once a week on doubtful cases.

This is all this MO has to do. It is extraordinary how easily some of my counterparts earn their daily pay! He has also at hand a dentist, an oculist and an ear specialist, while any surgery of the most trivial kind is sent to the hospital and all the venereal cases sent to the venereal hospital.

Saturday 20th. No 9 hospital.

This has been the busiest day that I have had since I came here. I inspected some drafts and then inspected the two camps. I had finished my work for the day by 10:30am!

It is of course disgraceful keeping a medical man on to do such work as this. It would be excusable to keep said posts entirely for temporarily sick or convalescent men like myself. But for men to hold the position permanently or for months at a time speaks volumes for the bad organisation of the RAMC.

The civil population at home are now under-doctored in hundreds of districts, here are practitioners doing a few hours work a day which might be equally well done by a couple of intelligent NCOs.

I felt so jolly fit and energetic today, that, in spite of a blazing sun I set out and enjoyed a glorious walk of nearly 13 miles through deep woods, along level plains and dusty roads. Beautiful scenery, ever changing and some novelty in the flower world at almost every turn. Having missed tea, I decided to go down to town where I had a good dinner and half a bottle of wine at the Cathedral restaurant and arrived home rather tired at 10pm.

Sunday 21st.

Another sunny day with pleasant breeze. With the return of magnificent health, one's outlook on life becomes so much stronger and healthier, wholesome and vigorous thoughts replace the weakly and more selfish ones.

I had been planning to get myself appointed to some duty or post at the base. Now I am all for a speedy return to the trenches. It is fine to feel these nobler desires surging in one's breast. Although I must have a peep at Old England first of all and I await somewhat impatiently for my leave to be granted.

I have heard a good many opinions as to the meaning of the word 'Blighty' as used by the men meaning England, viz a 'Blighty wound' means a wound which is severe enough to get you to England. I read now that Blighty is a 'Tommy' corruption of 'Baladi' which in Arabic (not Hindustani) for 'country my'.

Monday 22nd.

If ever I survive this tremendous war do not let me forget to grow ranunculi's in my peaceful garden, they have got a whole border of them in the garden of the mess. It is extraordinary the variety and brilliance of the colours. They are as variant as the single poppy, also they flower fairly early and are at their best just as the anemones begin to wane.

As the ranunculi have done so well I ought to say that the soil is extraordinarily sandy and what soil is among it consists of a large extent of loam such as one might expect to find seeing that this ground here is simply cleared forest land. They have enriched the soil by adding a little manure.

Tuesday 23rd.

Still waiting for leave. I would not complain of the delay only that there is more than a likelihood of all leave being stopped.

Wednesday 24th.

Have got on the track of my kit at Boulogne. It's raining hard, very cold.

Thursday 25th.

Cold and dull but nature is so fresh after pelting rain all night.

Friday 26th.

Am reading an interesting article on the birth of a new subarea, by Leadbetter.

"The principal which underlies all progress appears to be that of cyclic movements. Everything goes in impulses, it moves forward, works for a while, draws back again and then goes forward again.

The life of man is the nearest example of it. Man, as a soul comes down into incarnation, he takes a body and through that he leaves certain lessons, he develops certain qualities and then he goes back again into himself in order to digest the results of his efforts, in order to assimilate those qualities and to strengthen those powers. Then he comes out again and once more shows himself through matter, in order that a fresh set of qualities may be developed."

The scheme of evolution as applies to man is put very succinctly in the above I think. We must remember that this cyclic change is that of a spiral and not of a circle. The spiral makes evolution on progress possible.

Saturday 27th Rouen.

All leave stopped!! My hopes fall and with them my spirit. I have not had leave since November 25th. How I have been longing for my fortnight in England for months. The thought of it alone made life possible while in those loathsome trenches where one eked out the existence of a rat for so many hours of each day.

I should have gone home at the end of April in time for the emerald green of the growing larches, but sickness denied it to me. Then about 10th May I should have returned to the battalion, being convalescent, the ADMS would have immediately allowed me to go home.

But, the CO of the Red Cross hospital Rouen with the best of intentions advised me not to go all the way back to my battalion but go to a general hospital and put in for leave from there. I gladly accepted his offer with the result that here I am still. However, there is no doubt the rest here has done me the world of good and I ought really to feel very grateful.

Sunday 28th.

Am now doing clerical work at the hospital – writing up case cards from old records!

This afternoon, Paley, who practices in Newton Abbot, Devon walked with me. We skirted the forest, dropped down to St Etienne and soon came to the banks of the Seine. The river is very broad here – quite three-hundred yards across. We were ferried across for one franc and this brought us to the delightful little village of St Adriene, where we had tea in the garden of a café.

There was a fair sprinkling of khaki but a lot of French people of the lower middle class who were rather interesting to watch. Then we climbed up a steep track and visited the little church dedicated to St Adrien. The interior of this church is in reality a huge cave in the face of the limestone cliff, while from the outside the suggestion of a church has been kept up by constructing a half roof of thatch and building up the face of the cave. A half steeple or tower completes the edifice. Inside, the rough bullying solid rock makes a dim light, the carved figures and a huge pincushion stuck with countless pins because every girl who wants a 'wean' pushes her pin into the cushion Once again across the Seine we strolled home through the quiet woods.

Monday 29th.

This afternoon I took my waterproof and walked out some miles and rambled among most delightful meadows and woods, uphill and down dale, never a road did I touch and never a soul did I see. I found three more flowers absolutely new to me, My word! What a collection one might make here.

A good collection of wildflowers would indeed be a glorious thing to bring home after the war. I think the War Office ought to offer a prize for the best collection of flowers, a special medal should be given for a man who has collected specimens under fire or in front of the trenches.

Tuesday 30th.

The ADMS came to the hospital this afternoon and I asked him about my leave. He was very decent and told me to ring up his office at 5pm, which I did. Major Mitchell then took down all particulars and promised to do all he could. So, if leave is not stopped altogether I ought to get home very soon.

Felt enormously full of energy and started for a walk across the plain. Not a man was to be seen and it wasn't long before I broke into a very respectful trot which I kept up without fatigue for a long way.

'A man is as old as he feels and a woman as old as she looks.' I certainly feel like 25 today!

The men in the mess are all really extremely pleasant and the CO is also a cheerful old soul, though common and vulgar.

I have had letters from our battalion's adjutant – Nicholls – and Mons Dutrec, each of them hoping that I will come back. I don't know what to do. If I have to return to the front, I should of course prefer to rejoin my old battalion. But on the other hand, I really feel I have done my 'bit' after nine months in the trenches I am tempted to put in for something less strenuous.

Wednesday 31st.

Had rather an entertaining walk with O'Flynn whose brother has just been killed. Very sad. They were in the same division – O'Flynn in a field ambulance and his brother in a trench mortar battery.

We went down to Rouen, had tea or coffee at a really first-class hotel – Hotel-de-Poste, Rue Jeanne D'arc – then a hot bath and I changed into some clean linen which I had just bought.

Dinner at a very French restaurant, then a music hall, also very French, especially the comedian. Taxi home ended rather an amusing evening. Discovered that my application for leave had never left the Rouen office!! Beastly slack.

Passages from 7th Battalion East Surrey Regiments war diaries.

The diary reports one year of active service. The casualties for the year were as follows: Officers Killed – Six

Wounded – 18

Missing – One

Other Ranks killed – 142

Wounded – 630

Missing* – 58

Total – 855

*The vast majority of the missing were actually killed in action.

JUNE 1916

Thursday 1st. Fourteen days leave.

Ha! My leave! Am to go home this afternoon.

Here the diary is broken, let it suffice to say that I had a most enjoyable fourteen days leave.

A chill caused by remaining on deck all night, in order to avoid vomiting by staying below, brought on a slight return of my fever so that for the first week I had a return of an afternoon temperature.

Visited the practice at Dalton and received enthusiastic welcome from everyone I met.

Ethel met me, and we went to Coniston by train with dear Lassie *(Regie's dog)*. One night in Great Langdale; one at dear Dungeon Ghyll.

From there we walked via Stickle Tarn to the top of Sergeant Man, dropped down to East Dale Tarn, here we were met by Flora. I was feeling very tired and was glad to get to Eller close for tea. Delightful house and grounds with views towards East Dale and Silver How.

On to Rydal for two nights, Angy surprised us and joined us at Flora's, so we had a large family gathering consisting of Angy, Ethel, Nellie, Joan, Arthur, Flora and me.

Joan and I returned to London by the midnight.

Sunday 4th.

Alice is very charming.

Tuesday 6th.

Travelled up with Ethel, midnight train from Euston. Arrived at Dalton about 10am.

Thursday 8th.

Ethel, Lassie and I walked from Coniston, we had tea at Yew Dale Farm. Lovely new laid eggs, scones clotted cream and jam etc – Mrs Allenby's.

We revelled in the beauty of the walk along the rushing mountain streams, through the gorgeous woods with the great heaps of slate peeping out from the feathery larches. It has been three years since we last visited this dear spot and we were so pleased to find the very same people at the little Inn.

We walked slowly over the fells past Blea Tarn, Lassie had a swim and we basked beside the lake in roasting sunshine. Then on to Langdale, decided to stay the night in a cottage

Saturday 10th. Eller Close Grasmere.

Decided to walk to Grasmere via Stickle Tarn and Sergeant Man. Climbed up towards the Langdale's, knee deep through the young bracken, Lassie nosing among the green ferns and drinking at the mountain streams, myself struggling behind, panting audibly.

Then the descent to East Dale Tarn where Flora met us, reached Eller close. Nellie and Joan met us, had tea and a good hot bath.

Sunday 11th.

Visited Pa's (*George Fothergill 1833-1915*) grave and sat down for nearly half an hour bathed in beautiful sunshine. Angy joined us and we walked up to Allan Bank, still un-tenanted. Almost painful, the rush of feelings that swept through me as I stood by the billiard room and then strolled towards the kitchen gardens. The hay grass was at its best with white daisies blooming, while wild geraniums were in such abundance. The absolute quietness and wonderful peacefulness of the place cast a glamour over everything.

Tuesday 13th.

Two delightful days at Nellie's. Picnic on Long Brigg

Wednesday 14th.

Said goodbye to dear old Lassie, Joan and Alice came with me up to town. We lunched at Cafe Royal, mayonnaise salmon and peach melba. Went on to McMahon, 19 Whimple St, who finished my teeth. Said goodbye and left them feeling flat as ditch water. Caught the 4:30pm from Waterloo.

Thursday 15th. Rouen

Arrived at 12am and reported myself to the CO. He is undoubtedly an extraordinarily vulgar little man, so pompous and thinks such an enormous amount of himself.

Sunday 18th. Train from Rouen to 39th Division.

At 10:30am I received orders to leave at 12:30pm and report to ADMS at 1pm. I was booked with another officer for the 39th Division. When the other officer turned up I discovered an old Edinburgh acquaintance in Hunter. We used to play tennis at the same club, he reminded me of a rather frivolous evening in Dundee! Hunter had gone through the original landing at St Hellas, Gallipoli, of which he was deservedly proud.

Well, although we did not know our destination we knew we were in for a long journey and so we got two bottles of wine, Perrier and plenty of grub. Four of us went to the compartment. Travelled for twenty-four hours through Abbeville, Calais, Hazebrouck and finally ended at Bethune.

Mon 19th. Locon 134th Field Ambulance 39th Division.

From Bethune we took a steam tram to Locon where we reported to ADMS of 39th Division. He sent us by car to the 134th Field Ambulance, which was close by. We were just in time for dinner, found my billet – very comfortable in a small cottage and slept very well.

Tuesday 20th.

This is a very young field ambulance and has only been out since March. Therefore, only one officer is a captain and I am senior to him.

I hope it won't lead to any friction. The CO Major Hildreth is a young cavalry RAMC and I think I shall like him very much and the officers too seem good fellows.

This morning Hunter received orders to go to some other division and he left by car before I saw him.[50]

It is very strange that I should find myself back again on the very portion of the line held by my old battalion last Xmas. Indeed, I remember walking through this very village one miserable cold grey day when we were billeted at Essars. The country then was dreary and bleak, brown ploughed land as far as the eye can see. Now not a brown field is to be seen, every inch of ground is growing something, a cheerful green meets the eye on every side.

Wednesday 21st. ADS near Festubert.

"Many happy returns of the day my fine fellow." You have frittered away thirty-seven years and you have made little use of many a golden opportunity. "The spirit truly is willing, but the physical body is weak."

Today Major Hildreth has sent me up to the ADS[51]. Another officer is with me – Captain Porter. We are right in the country and it is delightful, no shelling although we are among the 4.7-inch guns and 4.5-inch howitzers. Practically nothing to do, a few odd cases dropping in during the day and one or two during night.

Thursday 22nd. ADS.

I was on duty last night, soon after midnight the Germans blew a mine at Givenchy, my bed rocked and creaked. Then an artillery duel began, the Bosch shelled our heavies in a wood not far away.

It was rather a wonderful sight to watch the flashes of our guns and seeing the German shells exploding in the wood. They must have used gas shells because the air became pungent with the familiar mustard and cress odour and my eyes began to smart.

---

50. *134th Field Ambulance War Diary.*
Admitted 17 OR – evacuated two officers and 22 OR – back to duty 37 OR.
Lieutenant Burrel reported departure for 30th CCS, Captain Fothergill reported to duty.

51. *134th Field Ambulance War Diary.*
Captain Fothergill relieved Lieutenant Harris at ADS.
Admitted 14 – evacuated 23 – remaining 28. DADMS visits ADS and relay post.

Casualties came peedling in until 6am and my servant was kind enough to let me sleep until 10:15am. This is the first really warm day we have had – a right summer's day at last.

Friday 23rd.

There is little to relate, Captain Porter and I take it in turns to do the night work. There are practically no casualties during the day despite the fact that we receive the wounded from two battalions. But at night we usually get six to eight because a good deal of wiring and consolidation has been going on at the 'Islands'.

The wounded reach us between 2am and 6am so that we can always look forward to a disturbed night. During the day there is practically nothing except a few sick, we loll about in the sun and read.

Saturday 24th.

I visited the two battalion aid posts yesterday and it was most curious to walk again along the same old familiar trenches. They have been considerably strengthened and improved since I was there.

I came back through Festubert, recognising the same old ruins which we used to pass on our way up to the trenches after dark.

Porter and I occupy a little house which has been used as the ADS mess by different ambulances for a long time.

The following has been written and stuck on the mantelpiece –

"To all and sundry
Harken! All ye whom duty calls to spend some time within these friendly walls. Others will sojourn here when you have passed.
You were not first, and you will not be last.
Therefore, take heed and do whatever you may, for safety, for comfort, while you stay.
Just place a sandbag here a picture there to make the room more safe – the walls less bare.
Think as you tread the thorny path of duty, of comfort, of security and, of Blighty. So, your successors when they come may say, 'a splendid unit we relieved today'."

Sunday 25th.

My night on duty was up as usual, off and on from 2am. Heavy bombardment going on in the distance.

Monday 26th. ADS

We are making every preparation for a sudden rush of casualties. Last night I went up with some men to the trenches to see whether we could use a trolley for evacuating wounded. We managed very well and pushed the trolley right down from the aid post as far as the ADS in 35 minutes[52].

It simply poured with rain; coming down in sheets and we splashed through mud and pools of water.

Tuesday 27th.

Our CO is up here this morning making final preparations.

Wednesday 28th.

Germans raided our or some of our 'island' positions this morning and used revolvers and knives inflicting nine casualties but took no prisoners.

Have improvised a mosquito net over my bed which works very well. These pests are very abundant and are as large as Daddy Long Legs. The idea of being sucked by these vampires is loathsome.

Today I have discovered the larvae in myriads in the semi stagnant ditches on either side of the road just outside the house. The spraying of a little paraffin on the water quickly killed them.

Thursday 29th.

No casualties today.

The DMS of the corps – Major General Pike – came here and looked round. We are all ready for the prospective 'raid', our trolley system works well.

Friday 30th.

Our troops made an attack early this morning near Richbourg. A whole brigade went over, they had nearly 600 casualties; it was a failure[53]. They

---

52. *134th Field Ambulance Diary.*
Visit to ADS re scheme of evacuation by trolley, a successful experiment carried out last night. Scheme to be used tonight.

53. *134th Field Ambulance Diary.*
Admitted, one officer – 24 OR – evacuated 30 – remaining, one officer – 34 OR.
Three officers and bearer sub-division sent to assist 132 Field Ambulance. Lieutenants Racey and Huggins assisting at ADS of 132, Lieutenant Mitchell to

ran short of bombs and had to retire after taking two lines of trenches. They brought back some prisoners.

This wretchedly cold and rainy June ends today. I see by the paper that it has been the coldest June since 1879.

JULY 1916.

Saturday 1st. ADS Marrais.

A fair number of casualties from the islands, which the Germans last shelled.

Six aeroplanes dropped bombs on Bethune this morning and were engaged by our aircraft, we put one out of action and she fell near Beuvry.

I rode into Bethune and got a haircut and made one or two purchases. I have a very nice pony, quite small and easy to mount, it takes comfortable short steps.

I am very content with my lot, considering it is war. We are very comfortably situated here behind the trenches and get sufficiently far up and busy to make one feel that one is justifying one's existence.

Read the first communique ADG *(Assistant Deputy General)*. After terrific bombardment we advanced over a line of 19 miles for 2,000 yds, the French ditto over a line of six miles.

Sunday 2nd. ADS.

Good news from the front.

Monday 3rd.

I saw one of our planes brought down today by anti-aircraft guns, the shell seemed to burst right on the plane. Certainly, the petrol tank was hit because a great sheet of flame suddenly leapt up. For a few seconds the machine kept on an even keel then dived down but suddenly righted himself and for a few breathless moments it seemed as if the pilot was still master.

Gradually however her nose dropped, and she began to descend at a steeper and steeper angle until it became quite obvious that she was

---

RAP Plum Street. Admitted during the month, 13 officers – 436 OR. Of these, battle casualties of officers and 116 OR. Evacuated to CCS 12 officers – 222 OR Corps rest station 109. Back to duty 57. Two died of wounds being carried to ADS.

hopelessly out of control. Then for half a minute we watched her, not dropping like a stone but fluttering slowly to earth like a butterfly. It made me feel positively ill to watch this horrible thing taking place and yet I was fascinated beyond words at the sight.

Well, it fell between the lines in no man's land where 600 or 700 yards separated the trenches. O'Kell the MO to the Sherwood Foresters, although comparatively elderly immediately ran out – a very plucky act! The two men were dead[54] but they got them in without themselves being hit.

And later the bodies were brought to the ADS where Porter and I collected all their belongings. The pilot had a compound fracture of the jaw; the observer had no obvious injuries.

Tuesday 4th.

After a bombardment, two coys of the regiment at Festubert went over but although they got into the first and second lines and did some good work they got badly caught by machine guns between the lines.

It is generally believed that the enemy expecting the attack had machine guns actually between the lines waiting for our men.

We had seven motor cars at our disposal and three extra officers to help. We were very busy from 1:30am until 6am and passed about 90 wounded down the line[55]. Our evacuation from the aid posts by trolleys along the rails was most successful and we had no congestion.

Wednesday 5th.

Writing now at 10:45pm. We are bombarding the trenches like hell preparatory to another attack at Givenchy. Tyler who runs a 4.5-inch howitzer battery tells me he is going to fire 800 rounds in two hours.

---

54. *2nd Lieutenant Sherwell, Rex. Age 18*
2nd Lieutenant Stewart, John Charles Miller. Both K.I.A, brought down by anti-aircraft fire in FE2b 6339 (a presentation machine – Nova Scotia) at Festubert during bombing at La Bassee. Both are buried at Lapugnoy military cemetery. (topgun1918, Great War Forum)
55. *134th Field Ambulance Diary.*
Casualties arrived about 4:30am. Total number passed through ambulance 87, five of these officers. 23 direct admissions to CCS including two officers. Report furnished to ADMS – the work performed was splendid, evacuation by trolleys worked admirably. Admitted 579 OR. All battle casualties evacuated by 12:30pm.

I wonder whether we shall come off better this time! Midnight, cannot sleep, these field guns of ours are the noisiest devils possible to imagine.

Thursday 6th.

We did: The raid was a great success, a whole battalion went over and did good execution; took a machine gun and some trench mortars and brought back 43 prisoners! I was on night duty and received 17 wounded.

Friday 7th.

The bad men must have been shelling some of our batteries away to the south with gas shells because the beastly stuff came along just as we turned into bed, everyone's eyes were streaming.

Our 134th Field Ambulance, the main body, has moved back today; to Annequin behind Bethune. Porter has been sent to take over the ADS at Lone Farm and I am left here in charge until we move. Lieutenant Simpson, a recent arrival at our ambulance is with me here.

What cold, cloudy weather for the last eight days with rain. Our advance north of the Somme is at a standstill. We are consolidating after taking Fricourt, Montauban and the French are now three miles or so from Peronne.

Saturday 8th.

I prophesy that this war ends on this date. This was written Jan 4th, 1916. The above was indeed an inspired utterance – I don't think!

However, the Allies are not doing so badly, if the war is not over the end is certainly in sight.

Sunday 9th.

A young man of the Royal Buffs was brought here this evening with a bullet wound at the back of knee. He approached our parapet from no man's land about 10:30pm, got through and he made this explanation: He said that he took part in the attack on July 3rd-4th and was wounded and became unconscious and did not wake up until this morning. He waited until dark and came in. He had some soup when he returned to our trenches and a little bacon.

When he reached me, he was sitting up strong and hearty and had a normal pulse.

I was glad an officer came down with him and wrote down his statement, because personally I am completely satisfied that the man had not been six days without food and water. It would not surprise me to learn that he had spent his time in the German trenches and as a reward for giving information was allowed his liberty.

The man was permanently disabled or most probably so, it wouldn't be any advantage for Bosch to keep him.

Monday 10th. ADS.

Porter having left this ADS and now being in charge of Lone Farm ADS, I am now in command here.

Tuesday 11th.

We made preparations for 100 casualties.

Sergeant Gardner and I examined the trolley from the south aid post to Rue De Bois ADS and settled on places for two relay posts.

The raid took place about 1:30pm and was a failure in our sector. Something must be wrong somewhere! We had only seven casualties.

This division has been in the trenches for so long – about 40 days – they are all (the men) absolutely stale and are not in a fit state to make raids. What they want is a thorough rest behind the lines; then I am sure they would 'go'. Whoever is responsible for the working of this division must simply look upon the men as machines.

The Germans have deeply studied psychology in its bearings on the war. I fear some of our commanders have never given it a thought. Oh! The unimaginative and conservative British Bull Dog!

Wednesday 12th.

A quiet day and got a short rest this afternoon. Weather horribly dull, feel depressed and morbid. The bad men put some shells uncomfortably near us about dusk. I thought the last one was a direct hit on Captain Tyler's billet in a farm 100 yards down the road, as a matter of fact it (4.2 inch) just missed the roof under which the men were lying and hit the trunk of a very respectable tree three feet from the ground completely cutting it in two. This is indeed a very dangerous war!

Thursday 13th.

Have received orders to be ready to quit at short notice and so have sent down surplus stock to field ambulance. Sorry we are moving as I don't think we are likely to strike more comfortable quarters than these for many a day.

7:30pm. Just received notice to say that the field ambulance is not going to move after all. So here we are again with a good deal of our staff sent away to Annequin.

Friday 14th. ADS.

Weather is appallingly bad and yesterday was so cold that we had a fire in the sitting room and thoroughly enjoyed it too.

Dull, cold and rainy, it has been like that for nearly three weeks. Mosquitoes are very troublesome, they take advantage of the smallest opening to get under my net and when one of these pests is sharing the enclosure with you there is no prospect of rest.

Am keeping quite well in spite of this marshy place, the country is flat and low lying, an uninviting climate at its best.

Saturday 15th.

Still very cold but an hour or two of sunshine this afternoon was cheering.

On the other side of the road is a small tobacco plantation very carefully looked after and every weed is plucked out, while the banking up of each symmetrical row of plants enables irrigation to be carried out.

Today liquid manure was freely applied. I notice that they only apply this when the wind blows towards our windows.

Six to eight leaves only are allowed to develop on each plant, at least that is what I gathered from the man with the aid of bad French.

Sunday 16th.

This morning all our guns opened on the German trenches and other objectives, even the 9.2-inch was barking. We had a rather lively quarter of an hour here when the enemy put about a dozen 4.2-inch rounds about the battery just behind.

They really had a miraculous escape and not a single man was injured, there were shell holes 12 to 20 feet from the gun pits and one through the roof of billet missing boxes of ammunition by a few yards.

The Bosch has obviously got that particular battery very accurately registered and I really think they are foolish not to move.

Monday 17th. ADS.

Took a run down to Bethune in the car and did some shopping, on to Annequin then started back but the spring of the car broke and so I marched the men out to ADS.

Went up to trenches to collaborate with MO ref our programme in case of raid. The MO had his head bandaged and showed me his steel helmet with bullet hole through the top which had grazed his scalp.

The Germans have brought up an 8-inch howitzer and shelled promiscuously around this morning. I went into one crater which was eight feet deep, the shell was evidently armour piercing and with delayed action. Such a shell has the same effect as a mine when it explodes, the resulting crater is always very large.

Tuesday 18th.

Ten pm. Have made all preparations for casualties as we are making a raid on Bosch trenches. An extra car is here to go and take up Bosch prisoners – if so be it there shall be any of them.

Wednesday 19th.

Our local raid was not very successful as our men found practically no Bosch in the part attacked and no prisoners were taken.

However, these repeated raids and bombardments will not allow the enemy to weaken his line by sending reinforcements to the Somme. In this way our raids are indirectly useful. Did not get to bed until after 6:00am.

Army general came nosing round this afternoon, which was unfortunate as the men had hardly more than had breakfast and things were not very tidy. However, it gave him something to strafe about and that after all is what most of them like to do! These people in cushy billets miles behind the firing line must try and justify their existence.

Thursday 20th.

A real summer's day at last! Not by any means perfect but still hot sun and delightfully warm with pleasant breeze.

Oh! To be among the mountains threading one's way through the green bracken, the scented ferns hanging over deliciously cool streamlets and above all, the extraordinary peace.

Mrs Besant[56] allowing to the war, says: "Well indeed might the masters refuse to give any knowledge of the forces of subtle destruction to the nations who have not yet learned the first letter of brotherhood, for imagine, the torrent of destruction had the German chemists learned to let loose the force that disintegrates the atom, leaves but a whirlpool of astral dust where men and cities had been.

The relation into which husband and wife sometimes pass where married lovers become married friends and which is sometimes but rarely outside marriage, which has all the strength, and trust and sweetness of love perfected by the sex and difference, but utterly free from passion."

Friday 21st. ADS.

Went up to see Captain Hacker MO in the trenches and had a long talk. He has lent me a book – "Germany In Defect" by Souse.

Funny thing – my eagle eye suddenly discovered growing out of a sandbag just by his dugout, the beautiful little blue pimpernel which I had never before seen. It has a tiny little peacock blue flower, which is in great contrast with its sister the scarlet pimpernel.

Saturday 22nd.

We are busy making a drain for the slops from the men's billet. Last night we stole a good supply of large red tiles from a ruined house and these are going to form the channel.

Sunday 23rd.

There was a raid last night opposite Givenchy and it was very successful although we only had 10 casualties. Very quiet in our sector and for the first time for two months the night passed without a single casualty being brought in.

Quiet day, cold and no sun, it is indeed a melancholy summer but after all it is better that we shouldn't have a glorious summer, it would be a waste out here. But next year-

Monday 24th.

Tyler invited us up to his observation post. We had a pleasant walk there and reached it without entering trenches except the last 50 yards.

---

56. *Annie Besant (1847-1933), British socialist, theosophist, women's rights activist, writer, orator, educationalist, philanthropist.*

The enemy had shelled immediately round it the day before with their 8-inch howitzer and there was a very nice unexploded shell lying there. I measured it – 24 inches from end to end and just about as many inches in circumference.

I had a good look at the bad men's lines through the glasses, things were quiet and there was little to be seen. The trenches there were very deserted and extraordinarily beautiful with most luxuriant growths of white Mayweed, blue Cornflowers and scarlet Poppies. All of these growing side-by-side – red, white and blue – are a most striking sight.

Tuesday 25th.

Cold, gloomy and heavy air. Simpson has gone to the field ambulance and Mitchell has arrived in his stead.

Wednesday 26th.

Still gloomy, no sun for days but a bit warmer and no rain. Busy making drain with roof tiles to take washing water away.

Went down to see an officer in billet who had accidentally shot himself while putting on his revolver before going into trenches, penetrated abdomen – poor chap.

Walked out among fields and found myself among a perfect garden of Wildflowers and found a delightful Orchid, Also the grass of Parnassus which I never before realised as being so beautiful with its pure white petals streaked with green lines like a Snowdrop. There were also two or three unknown flowers.

Thursday 27th.

(Borrowed 20 francs from Mitchell.)

A wounded German was brought here about midnight, he had some tiny wounds from about his face and neck but complained of inability to move his body. He was disgustingly fat, so we gave him tea and made him comfortable.

Friday 28th[57].

The ADMS of the army came here and looked around and seemed very pleased. I afterwards walked with him to Lone Farm. I think he was Colonel Firth, an authority on sleeping sickness. Very genial but very depressing person in his views on the duration of the war.

As I write at 11pm I can hear the low rumble of the bombardment on the northern Somme battlefields. Russians have taken Erzenham.

Saturday 29th. ADS.

In a drunken brawl one of our men struck another man on the chin, he fell down backwards on the pavement – resulting in cerebral haemorrhage and death. The prisoner is up for manslaughter.

Russians captured Brody and 9,000 men; we have got Delville Wood.[58]

Sunday 30th.

Perfect summer day at last.

The Padre Woodhouse gave us a service which I made a compulsory parade.

We congregated in a nice shady spot among some trees. Afterwards Woodhouse had tea with us, he had made a living in Douglas and won the Isle Of Man Tennis Cup. He knew all the Castletown folk and we had a jolly chat.

Tonight at 1:30am 100 of the 14th Hants 'go over' on a raid, our guns will bombard over Givenchy for one hour and then lift fire. At this moment we shall bombard for 10 minutes opposite Festubert. By thus directing the enemy's attention to the Givenchy sector we hope the actual raid opposite Festubert will be a surprise.

The men will carry a large straw mattress which they will fling on the barbed wire and then so protected will rush over into the enemy trenches.

---

57. *134th Field Ambulance Diary.*
Friday 28th.
Admitted one officer, 16 OR – evacuated 24 – remaining four officers, 45 OR.
Private Cunningham, J. RAMC. died at 33 CCS as a result of being struck by Private Cullen. Court martial documents sent to ADMS re manslaughter charge against Private Cullen, J. RAMC.
81534 Pte Cunningham, Joseph. Age 31. RAMC. Bethune town cemetery.
58. *Battle of Delville Wood (Devil Wood) 15 July – 3 September 1916.*

I write above at 11:00pm and we shall see. In the meantime, I am busy making arrangements for possible casualties.

Monday 31st. ADS.

The raid was a failure, they found wire in the middle of no man's land which prevented the mattress being drawn along and then the torpedoes which should have destroyed the wire did not go off. They had only 10 casualties.[59]

AUGUST 1916.

Thursday 3rd. ADS.

I wore my 'slacks' yesterday with low shoes and in consequence got bitten badly by mosquitoes In evening. My ankles are swollen and itching this morning.

Oh! What glorious weather, perpetual sun and light breeze.

Saturday 5th.

Glorious day; walked along a quiet sluggish stream or rather canal, not a soul in sight.

A riot of wildflowers, grasses and reeds and the water itself full of pure white Water Lillies and lovely green grasses.

Curious to be able to sit so peacefully thus and yet so near Festubert. Those grey flies – 'cleggs' – however alone prevented one from sitting quietly for more than a minute or two.

A new officer – Anderson – here in place of Simpson. He is from Aberdeen and his accent is very much so, which is a pity.

Sunday 6th. ADS.

The Germans shelled a battery about a mile away for two hours this morning with 5.9-inch. This afternoon I walked out and inspected the four gun-pits which were in an orchard, the shell holes were everywhere but not a single gun touched!

59. *134th Field Ambulance Diary, Monday 31st.*
Admitted two officers, 17 OR – evacuated eight OR – remaining three officers, 42 OR. Total number of cases passed through the ambulance for month 844. Of this number 202 were transferred from 101st Field Ambulance. 368 battle casualties. 465 sent to CCS. 331 to duty and corps rest. RAMC personnel, 19 cases were under treatment during the month, 10 of these were evacuated to CCS. The ambulance held two ADS, Mairas and Lone Farm. Unfortunate death of Private Cunningham on 28th was our first casualty of this nature.

Later Anderson and I strolled out, one of our aeroplanes was being shelled when an unexploded shell came whizzing down and landed in a courtyard of an isolated cottage used as a billet where it exploded very near us. Unfortunately, a man was hit by it, and I fear badly injured in the lung.

Monday 7th.

This has been a nerve wracking day. As our car had to go to the field ambulance I went with it as far as Bethune and ordered it to pick me up at the square on its way back. I shopped for vegetables and amused myself watching the country people who had flocked to the main square to sell market produce – it was market day.

I was just about to get into the car which had arrived when the enemy started shelling the place. A crash on the far side of the house just above, we started the car across the square when a deafening crash occurred. The whole square was filled with red brick dust, flying glass, carts and horses bolting and people flying hither and thither.

I stopped the car and picked up two terrified little boys covered in dust and slightly cut. It was a most harrowing sight to see the panic. Out of a stricken house rushed a woman with two naked twin children in her arms. Other women were being carried away. We then started again and missed a runaway horse and trap by a fraction of an inch. The delay in negotiating it perhaps saved us because we had not proceeded 50 yards when another much larger shell crashed at about where we might have been.

I then saw three wagons with their six horses stretched out on the road, one with a driver, while just by me was a Tommy with his leg blown off at the thigh and hanging by the skin. I caught a spurting artery with my forceps and made a temporary bandage. Next a man with both his arms horribly mangled.

The sight of the poor horses moved me as it always does, I was so thankful to hear someone shooting them.

We took our wounded to the CCS and then as the ambulances were being sent to pick up wounded I cleared away but some more crashes told their own tale.

I had also to take cover this afternoon from some shells which burst not 50 yards away whilst Sergeant Gardner and I were going up to render aid to some casualties near the trenches.

185

I feel a bit jumpy this evening. I am not moved at the sight of men being cut up, but it is distressing to see women, little children and dumb animals being knocked about.

Give me trench warfare or even crater warfare but spare me this whole-sale massacre of civilians in a town.[60,61]

Tuesday 8th.

I have just heard that some of the shells described above were 12 and 15-inch!! In the afternoon a shell fell right in the yard of the CCS at Bethune killing a lot of ambulance drivers, setting it on fire and completely destroying no less than five cars! Luckily none of the patients were hit.

Wednesday 9th.

We have now been relieved by 97th Field Ambulance[62] who have come back from the Somme. Captain Shaw and Lieutenant Thompson are here with their men. The latter exactly like Gill Hartley and I cannot help smiling at the resemblance. Shaw is one of the most splendid specimens

60. *134th Field Ambulance Diary.*
Bethune shelled. 133rd and 91st Field Ambulance evacuated cases here. The former 62 the latter 74 which were moved by the ambulance at 7:30pm to Allouagne. The adjoining school was acquisitioned, and its ground floor purposed for lying down cases. The hut in the billet behind the ambulance was similarly dealt with. ADMS visited at 5pm three French civilian wounded were treated by the ambulance of which one died, these cases were transferred later to the civil and military hospital. One British soldier arrived dead.
Cases arrived between 3pm and 6pm. Total number of wounded in shelling (CCS) eight and one killed, these were the only cases incurred in the ambulance besides the three civilians.

61. *The Military Medal was introduced in March 1916 as a gallantry award to match the Military Cross awarded to officers only. It was extended to women as well. Some of the first Military Medals for nurses were awarded to five members of the QAIMNS (Queen Alexandra imperial Military Nursing Service) after a fifteen-pound shell (7 August 1916) went into 33 CCS (Bethune) near the operating theatre. Mabel Tunley (sister in charge), Beatrice Allsop, Norah Easeby, Ethel Hutchinson, Jean Whyte. (London Gazette 1 September 1916. Issue 29731, page 8653) The CCS was again hit on 7 December 1917, this resulted in a further two nurses being awarded the Military Medal. Mary Fowley and Mabel Jennings.*

62. *134th Field Ambulance Diary*
Private Cullen RAMC acquitted manslaughter of Private Cunningham.
142805. Pte Cullen, J. Age 40. RAMC. Died 20/07/1920. Grangegorman military cemetery, Dublin

of man that I have seen for a long time. Well over six feet and proportionately broad with enormous muscles. He is a putting the shot man. Very cheerful.

They have undoubtedly gone through terrible times on the Somme. Shaw has told me a lot in a very nice humble way. I can see he has done some splendid and very dangerous work on the Somme.

Thursday 10th. Reimbert.

Said goodbye to the ADS at 8:30 and left in the car for Annequin where we found them busy packing. I am in charge of 13 Section.

Really quite an enjoyable march of about nine miles, a slight rain in morning had more or less laid the dust.

Major Hildreth made me act as CO as he was marching instead of riding and I had to give the words of command to get the field ambulance in motion – a thing I have not done in 18 months.

The field ambulance has quite a good drum and fife band with three buglers who were most surprisingly good, the fife too really played extraordinarily well considering the little time they have had to practice.

We passed through quiet country scenes away from the sound of guns, the sun was not shining and altogether it was most enjoyable, I walked nearly all the way. We passed an English aerodrome and saw one of the 'busses' alight.

Our little band assured us pretty large audiences as we passed through the various villages and small towns. It is a relief to be among broken country with hills and dales and twisting roads.

This place is uninteresting, a mining village, my billet is a miner's cottage, comfortable bed and a cup of coffee brought in the morning.

Friday 11th. Abbaye De Nouvelle Farm.

We had a long but delightful march of about 12 miles, the major and I walked all the way and I must say that I felt a bit fagged on arrival owing to the many miles we travelled over paving.

Our band played vigorously and drew large audiences at every village especially when it struck up Le Marseillaise.

We are now encamped in the grounds of a huge farm. Some of the officers and men in tents, others bivouacking in the wood which

187

immediately surrounds us. The weather is lovely and the whole life is healthy and delightful.

Saturday 12th.

Took a car round this morning to pick up sick from various units in surrounding villages. A pleasant round. This afternoon Huggins and I rode to St Pol to buy groceries, we rode through tremendous fields of yellow wheat and through beautiful woods where the horse flies bothered our horses excessively.

St Pol a small country town prettily situated. Here we were lucky to see the King drive through quite slowly and got our salute returned, he was making an unadvertised visit to this front. We rode home by another route and enjoyed a gallop over a recently cropped wheat field.

Russians took Stanislav.

Sunday 13th.

It is very pleasant sleeping under canvas while the weather is fine, we may be here for a week or a month. We have an hour's route marching twice a day – at 6:30am and at 6:30pm.

I took a section out for a march yesterday afternoon. They were extraordinarily rowdy – sort of a high spirited mob. I had the NCO up afterwards and talked to him on the subject. It is this kind of unmilitary discipline which makes the RAMC so often the laughing-stock of well-disciplined infantry battalions.

Monday 14th.

A good deal of rain today making camp life a most unhappy ordeal as I had anticipated. Things are running nice and smoothly from a social point of view.

I feel rather an intruder coming among them being placed second in command. I try not to disturb the harmony though indeed this has not called for much ingenuity as they are all such a nice lot of fellows (the officers) thus my position is made easy.

I had a long chat with the commanding officer, and he has told me that if I cared to take it on he would recommend me for CO of this field ambulance in the event of him being sent to a clearing station – a post he is anxious to get. I don't suppose they would give it to me, but one never can tell.

Tuesday 15th.

Major Hildreth is now promoted to the rank of temporary Lieutenant Colonel. We have now constructed a model camp. Hildreth is a regular genius at organising.

I think his success depends a good deal on the fact that he spends nearly the whole day pottering round the camp. He will fish out a bit of orange peel or bread from behind a bush.

And so, by continuously walking round, one idea after another suggests itself until everything is in most complete order. He is exceedingly even tempered and gets things done without being overbearing or strafing.

I don't feel I should make a very good CO of ambulance. I am inconsistent in my temper and inclined to have "humours." Even when enjoying the best of health, I am inclined to be peevish and irritable in the early part of morning.

During the rest of the day I keep a better mental balance veering on the soft side. Thus, in the morning I am always good for a 'strafe', while for the rest of the day I am too lenient and apt to overlook various minor offences.

Wednesday 16th.

Extraordinarily bad weather now. Thundery showers and the camp rapidly degenerating into quagmire.

Friday 18th.

Still heavy showers of rain – very miserable under canvas, cold too.

Colonel Parsons came to dinner. Huggins got an excellent bit of turbot for 15 francs. Our cook is very skillful. He was 35 years cook at Trinity College Cambridge and afterwards chef to the Duke of Norfolk at Arundel Castle.

We had a six-course meal, our band played four tunes during dinner and we gave them beer.

Saturday 19th.

Heavy rain at intervals but sun occasionally struggling out for a moment or two. We are now on nine hours' notice to quit and are therefore packing up our wagons etc ready to quit.

Sunday 20th.

No sun but fine and cold.

Had a nice walk with Simpson to the village of Troisvaux we trekked all the way by the fields. I found a wild mint which was new to me, its aroma reminded one closely of ordinary garden mint. The flower was a loose panicle of rosy red flowerets reminding one of the larger varieties of sedum.

Our CO jokingly 'told off' one of us today for using the word "We". He said only three men may use this word – the king, the ADMS, a portly person and the tapeworm!

I am extraordinarily energetic these days. I have a run around a field every morning before breakfast. It is a delightfully secluded field where I can perform these unusual antics without being observed. It promotes a good appetite and is most exhilarating.

Also, it is not a bad performance for an old man 38 next birthday. The balder I grow, the younger I feel.

Tuesday 22nd.

Rode out to scout the road preparatory to our march tomorrow. Also rode to brigade HQ with Huggins[63]. Huggins is one of the nicest fellows I have met for a long while. He practices dental surgery in Toulouse in partnership with his father and they run one of the biggest practices in the south of France.

He learnt his art in America and is devoted to it heart and soul. He showed me one of his molars and told me how he had a sinus owing to trouble at the root and how – in order to prove his case to some sceptical students – he extracted this tooth himself and then after excising the diseased portion of the root, replaced it. He kept his mouth tightly closed for two days. The result was immediate healing of the sinus and the tooth usefully consolidated in position. The camp practically all struck.

Wednesday 23rd. Mazieres.

Got up at 3:15am and set off at 5:00am and the day was just breaking as we marched away. Soon a rosy glow from the rising sun suffused the

---

63. George William Huggins. MID London Gazette 29/5/1917. Year of birth 1881 in Toulouse. His father Thomas was also a dentist (and British Consul). Educated HMS Conway School, Liverpool. Midshipman RNR 1899-1902. Played rugby for Toulouse. Post graduate course Philadelphia 1910. Injured in motorcycle accident 2/7/1917 and evacuated to No 10 hospital in St Omer. Died Paris 1963. (charlie962. Great War forum)

fields and the ripened barley looked like an altar cloth embroidered with old gold. It was a delightful march through sleepy villages and lonely roads. By making so early a start we found ourselves at our destination before 9am.

Huggins had procured our billets the night before. I have a very comfortable room in the house of the curate, I look out onto a rambling garden and a dear little church. The village is pretty and picturesque, but the houses are dirty and the people also.

The CO gave me the choice today of either remaining with the tent subdivision, or of taking charge of the bearers. For a moment I almost chose the easy and safe job of permanently joining the tent subdivision, but I am glad to say I chose the bearer post much to the discomfort of my body which all the time wants to avoid danger and enjoy ease and comfort.

Rode out with Huggins to find out our best route for tomorrow. We had coffee at a village and had a long talk with the old curate who showed us his garden with a magnificent collection of begonias and also a remarkable box hedge trained and cut to resemble a house.

Thursday 24th. Lichon.

Started this morning at 6:30am and marched behind the 234th Coy of Engineers. As I had yesterday partially ridden over the track I rode, or rather walked, at the head of the Engineers and their CO Captain Finch.

I feel rather tired after so much exercise on horseback the last few days.

We passed through lovely country with some very steep hills and finally marched through the centre of a delightful wood – Forest de Lichon – and we reached our destination about noon; the march was 10 miles.

This is a picturesque village with a very antique gateway, used in older times by the custom officers. I have a clean billet.

Have just counted 27 of our aeroplanes in the air at the same time at a great height and looking for all the world like a flock of rooks.

Friday 25th. Mesnil.

A poor night arose at 4:30am. At 6:30 we moved off, myself at the head of the column – the CO having gone on in advance to take over the field ambulance at Acheux from the 17th Field Ambulance.

We had a very wearying march of 13 or 14 miles. There was a lot of dust and we had to follow the transport and an engineering unit. I rode my horse this time a good deal of the way.

It was the most beautiful country – woods, hills and wheat everywhere, it was impossible to appreciate it. We ended our journey at about 1pm at Bus and after some lunch and a rest I got together with practically every man of my section and proceeded with Lieutenant Boyers to the above to take charge of the ADS.

Arrived, then I had to detail the NCOs and men to different relay posts etc. Officially take over these and sign up receipts.

Captain Lowden CO was soon packed up and by 8pm I was left with Boyers and in charge of the show.

Some heavy German stuff kept coming over, bursting among the batteries not far off and an intense artillery duel was proceeding on our immediate right.

Saturday 26th. Mesnil.

Boyers took on night duty and I went to bed dead beat in my dugout which seemed more than ever like a tomb after our breezy nights under canvas.

Harris[64], one of our Canadian RAMC officers came over, he had been sent here in advance from the Cookers and took me up to see RAP at Knightsbridge which received casualties from two batteries. We bring down cases from above by rail or by wheeled stretchers on the road.

Thiepval is immediately opposite us. We are probably going to have a push here within a few days, so we may prepare ourselves for a warm time.

---

64. *Temp/Lt Harris, Robert Inkerman. MC – Citation London Gazette – For conspicuous gallantry and devotion to duty in action. He commanded the stretcher bearers throughout the entire day under incessant fire and set a fine example of energy and pluck. T/Capt. Bar to MC – Citation London Gazette – For conspicuous gallantry and devotion to duty under exceptional circumstances. When his Corps main dressing station was shelled on three separate occasions, whilst crowded with patients, he supervised and directed the collection and evacuation of the wounded to a place of safety. This was quickly done owing to his coolness, promptitude and disregard of personal danger, which did away with all confusion and reduced casualties to a minimum. Wounded and evacuated 17/08/1917. (charlie962 Great War Forum)*

The whole place is bristling with our guns of every calibre including some French 75mm.

Sunday 27th.

Some shelling just behind and the top of the pretty little church steeple knocked off. Busy with my men filling in shell holes on the road in the immediate vicinity of the dressing station, some of which make it very risky for our cars, especially at night.

No papers for days and have not the foggiest idea what is going on. Heard that we made a successful advance near here yesterday.

Thiepval is now nearly surrounded by us. Have just heard that our new push on this sector will take place in 48 hours and that our field ambulance has to do all the evacuating as well as run the corps collecting station etc.

I shall look after the ADS and advance if necessary and Harris is running the Cookers and making it into an ADS on his side of the big wood which separates us. Went down to Acheux, our field ambulance to see CO.

Terrible weather, sheets of rain and roads flooded, very damp and wet.

Monday 28th - Tuesday 29th. Puchevillers No 3 CCS.

It is now decided that our field ambulance shall run two ADS. Harris to take charge of the right of Cookers with its RAP at Hamel and I to take charge of the ADS at Mesnil with my RAP at Knightsbridge.

I started away about 10am with Staff Sergeant Gardner in order to gain some useful information from CO in the trenches as to where I must form my new ADS in case an advance should occur.

I had planned to carry out any advance with Gardner, leaving Boyers in charge of dressings at the ADS and evacuation of wounded.

Unfortunately, a shrapnel burst over us as we were moving along the trench and a piece of it struck me on the back of the left hand, opening it up and severing four of the tendons.

There was no sensation of pain in the ordinary sense of the word as these wounds are inflicted too unexpectedly and too suddenly to give one time to coordinate one's feelings, and then the parts round about are so stunned by the blow as to be rendered numb.

There was nothing for it but to get back to the ADS where Boyers dressed my hand, then goodbye to all the boys and away by car to Acheux.

The ADMS saw me and asked me to stay if possible and give a hand in the office but Huggins who examined the wound advised me to go on to the CCS and have it properly attended. So, I said goodbye to everyone and took a car to Conray but found it closed.

Finally, I landed up at the above. Captain Hey, from Manchester operated on me and he found four tendons severed. I was told he took immense pains over the operation. I took chloroform very badly – went blue and refused to breathe etc.

Had a bad night and was horribly sick with a terrible headache. Sir Anthony Bowley[65] *(Bowlby)* the King's physician who happened to be there inspected my hand this morning after the operation and thought it looked favourable for healing by first intention.

Wednesday 30th. Train to Boulogne.

The whole of this 3-CCS is under canvas and very comfortable. A terrible thunderstorm, the clouds almost touching the earth and rain tropical. Tents however held out rain.

Two Bosch wounded officers were brought here this afternoon, into the beds opposite me, such an afternoon – one of the worst that I have ever remembered experiencing – the sky pea green and untidy slovenly looking men with dirty uniforms, nothing smart about them.

As Captain Hey was interested in my case I was destined to remain for some subsequent time and my spirits fell to see the other wounded preparing to go down to the base, however they received orders later in the day to clear out everyone able to be moved and so I found myself being ticketed after all for the base.

---

65. *Major General Bowlby, Sir Anthony Alfred. 1st Baronet. 1855-1929. During the second Boer War 1899-1900 he served as medical officer in South Africa at the Portland field hospital, Bloemfontein. He was Surgeon to King Edward VII household 1904-1910 and hon surgeon-in-ordinary to King George V.*
Served in France WW1 as consultant surgeon to the forces with the rank of Major General Army Medical Services, his main achievement being the development of casualty clearing stations into hospitals carrying out major surgery.
He died on holiday at Stoney Cross, Lyndhurst on 7 April 1929 and is buried at Brooklands cemetery. (Military Wiki)

Surgically, treatment was of the very best at this CCS but in other departments – e.g. the supervising of kit and ticketing of wounded – chaos reigned. No one was wholly responsible for any department and a perspiring orderly named Peach was attempting to run everything off his own bat.

My new cap was sent away with someone else's kit and inevitably lost and now today I find myself with an officer's Sam Brown belt and compass included among my things.

Thursday 31st. Boulogne-Southampton.

I was on the Red Cross train before 8pm yesterday – honourably wounded this time instead of merely sick.

We jogged along comfortably all night, my hand aching a good deal at times. About 5am we arrived at Boulogne and were taken to motor ambulances, then a slow journey to Wimereux some five miles outside Boulogne. Here I saw a hut hospital for Australians and myself was taken to the hotel – the officer's hospital. Very few officers seemed to be there.

Such delightful sisters and nurses are among them. Sister Nicholls whose husband is Major General of 5th Army Medical Services.

I have been down the line now twice, first as a medical case and secondly as a wounded case and I feel the greatest admiration for sisters and nurses of the CCS and general hospitals at which I came under their care, also for the hospital orderlies. Some of whom I found as gentle and sympathetic as the most successful of female nurses. The orderlies on board the train were the exception; they treated me like baggage. This could be prevented by moving personnel of ambulance trains up the line occasionally to the trenches:

SEPTEMBER 1916.

Friday 1st.

They are evidently expecting a big push (British) as I had the pleasure of finding myself booked and ticketed for Blighty early on Thursday afternoon. My hand looks well though very swollen around the wrist but no nearer signs of pus.

It was a long business getting on to the boat and we were gradually moved up the quay in a long line of motor cars taking our turn. Finally, I found myself on board the St Denis[66] which was bound for Southampton.

Everything is most comfortable, little beds and cribs. Altogether the on board accommodation for 900 wounded. Quite a good dinner on board. Frightfully hot in spite of portholes being open. Arrived Southampton about 10am after 10 hours sailing.

The journey to town was very pleasant, with kind, elegant girls bringing us cigarettes etc. At Waterloo we were allocated to our respective hospitals and placed on cars by very smart men of the London Red Cross.

Saturday 2nd. Second London General St Mark's College, Chelsea.

We officers occupy some huts, the sisters and nurses look after us very well and the Boy Scouts are always in and out ready to go all over the town for one on any imaginable errand. Joan and Alice visit me.

So glad to find Lieutenant Golds here. He was with the 7th East Surreys and got wounded after I had left. High explosive side of head, troubling middle ear.

Zeppelin raid on London and east coast at 2am. Thank God, brought down by our airmen.

Sunday 3rd.

Dressed this morning in slacks and started out for a walk but turned back because I found people too curious and it became obvious that one was simply a sideshow. However, I found very nice grounds behind the college and slept there in the sun for an hour.

Monday 4th.

The Zeppelin was brought down by Robinson* who is or was rather 'gone on Isa', Curious!

---

66. *HMHS St Denis was built in 1908 for Great Eastern Railway and originally named Munich. She served on the Harwich-Hook of Holland crossing before being requisitioned by the Admiralty in 1914, renamed St Denis and converted into a hospital ship with 231 sick berths. She returned to GER in October 1919 and resumed service keeping the name St Denis. She was acquired by LNER in 1923. In 1940 she was used in the evacuation of Holland, was trapped by advancing Germans and scuttled at Rotterdam to avoid being captured. She was raised by the Germans and was returned to service for their own use. She was eventually scrapped in 1950. (Worthpoint)*

134th Field Ambulance Diary. 3rd September.

Attack near the Ancre River

Operations commenced at 5:10am casualties arrived here about 8:30am. Evacuation proceeded smoothly from both advanced dressing stations, no congestion, things were delayed temporarily at Mesnil due to shelling.

The convoy worked well without any casualties. Lieutenant Mitchell was wounded. CCS and LDS during the 24 hours approached 1,500 of which 414 passed through the main dressing station, these were all attended to, fed and evacuated by 5am the following morning.

Evacuation was mainly by train as well as by convoy for stretcher cases. No congestion resulted either at headquarters or anywhere along the line. Headquarters was frequently visited by ADMS and during the afternoon by DMS General McPherson.

Admitted five officers, 71 OR, evacuated three officers, 42 OR. 75 of admissions were battle casualties.

Monday 4th.

Cases ceased coming in steadily about 2am. Admitted 25 officers, 324 OR; evacuated 27 officers, 356 OR – died two. Lieutenant Navarre re-joined his unit. Personnel resting both at ADS and headquarters, only necessary personnel on duty. 349 of admissions battle casualties.

Tuesday 5th.

Admitted two officers, 216 OR; evacuated 179, died 10. General cleaning up of camp and evacuations continued. 209 of admissions were battle casualties.

---

*Notes

Lieut Robinson, William Leefe. VC 14/07/1895 – 31/12/1918. Was the first British pilot to shoot down an airship over Britain during WW1. The first VC awarded for action in the UK. In the three months after, five more airships were shot down using the techniques he had proved to work. In his combat report he wrote:

Sir,

I have the honour to make the following report on night patrol made by me on the night 2nd - 3rd. I with instruction went up about 11:08pm on the night of the second with instructions to patrol between Sutton's Farm and Joyce Green.

I climbed to 10,000 feet in fifty-three minutes. I counted what I thought were ten sets of flares – there were a few clouds below me, but on the whole it was a beautifully clear night. I saw nothing until 1:10am when two searchlights picked up a Zeppelin south east of Woolwich. The clouds had collected in this quarter and the search-lights had some difficulty in keeping on the airship.

By this time, I had managed to climb to 12,000 feet and I made in the direction of the Zeppelin which was being fired on by a few anti-aircraft guns hoping to cut it off on its way eastward. I slowly gained on it for about ten minutes. I judged it to be about 800 feet below me and sacrificed some speed in order to keep the height. It went behind some clouds, avoiding the searchlight and I lost sight of it. After fifteen minutes of fruitless search I went back to my patrol.

I managed to pick up and distinguish my flares again at about 1:50am. I noticed a red glow over the north east of London. Taking it to be an outbreak of fire, I went in that direction. At 2:05 a Zeppelin was picked up by searchlights over London (as far as I could judge). Remembering my last failure, I sacrificed height (I was at about 12,900 feet) for speed and nosed down in the direction of the Zeppe-lin. I saw shells bursting and night tracers flying around it.

When I drew closer I noticed that the anti-aircraft aim was too high or too low, also a good many shells burst about 800 feet – a few tracers went right over. I could hear the bursts when about 3,000 feet from the Zeppelin. I flew about 800 feet below it from bow to stern and distributed one drum among it, alternate New Brock and Pomeroy, it seemed to have no effect. I therefore moved to one side and gave them another drum along the side – also without effect. I then got behind it and by this time I was very close – 500 feet or less below and concentrated one drum on one part underneath rear. I was then at a height of 11,500 feet when attacking the Zeppelin.

I had hardly finished the drum before I saw the part fired at glow, in a few seconds the whole rear part was blazing. When the third drum was fired there was no searchlight on the Zeppelin and no anti-aircraft was firing.

I quickly got out of the way of the falling Zeppelin and, being very excited, fired off a few red Very lights (flares) and dropped a parachute flare.

Having little or no oil or petrol left I returned to Sutton's Farm, landing at 2:45am. On landing I found the Zeppelin gunners had shot away the machine gun wire guard, the rear part of my centre section and had pierced the main spar several times.

I have the honour to be Sir, Your obedient servant,

W. Leefe Robinson. Lieutenant. No 39 Squadron R.F.C

::::

* The airship was in fact a Schutte-Lanz SL 11. Commanded by Hauptmann Wilhelm Schramm with 15 crew members. All were killed.

After bombing St Albans, it crashed at Cuffley and the crew were buried at Cheshunt cemetery, being re-interred at Cannock Chase German military cemetery in 1962. It was one of 16 airships that night, the biggest airship raid of the war over England.

It was the third attempt by Wilhelm Schramm to raid over the UK, the first two attempts being aborted.

SL.11 Naval crew members: Willhelm Schramm, aged 30; Jakob Baumann, 29; Hans Geitel, 24; Rudolf Goltz, 35; Karl Paul Hassenmüller, 28; Bernhard Jeziorski, 24; Fritz Jourdan, 24; Karl Kächele, 22; Fritz Kopischke, 25; Friedrich Mödinger, 30; Reinhold Porath, 23; Rudolf Sendzick, 25; Heinrich Schlichting, 25; Anton Tristram, 27; Wilhelm Vohdin, 24; Hans Winkler, 24.

There was huge public protest and indignation when it was reported that the crew members would be given a full military funeral. (The Globe) A full military funeral was carried out with gun carriages and firing party at Cheshunt cemetery, Waltham Cross on the 06/09/1916.

::::

Robinson woke up to find he had become an overnight celebrity; he was splashed across all major newspapers.

Just two days later he was awarded the Victoria Cross, receiving the medal on 9 September at Windsor Castle. He was also awarded £3,500 in prize money and a silver cup.

He was grounded after crashing his plane on 16 September because he was too valuable a national figure with a long list of official engagements to run such risks. In April 1917 Robinson was posted to France as a flight commander with No 48 Squadron. On his first patrol over the lines on 5 April in a formation of six aircraft he encountered enemy aircraft led by Manfred Von Richthofen and was shot down, wounded and captured.

During his imprisonment he made several attempts to escape. He was kept in solitary confinement because of the escape attempts which is thought to have badly affected his health.

Having been repatriated in December 1918 he was able to spend Christmas with his friends and family before falling victim to the flu pandemic. He died on 31 December and is buried at All Saints churchyard extension in Harrow Weald. (Wikipedia)

::::

72207 Sgt Gardner, James. Age 21. Acheux British cemetery. 134th Field Ambulance. Wounded 4th September died the same day.

::::

James Gardner enlisted 18 October 1915, aged 20. He was promoted to sergeant 28 February 1916. Disembarked 7 March 1916 at Havre; 14 August admitted to the unit with trench fever and transferred to hospital St Pol returning to his unit on 24th. On 3 September the 39th Division was involved in fighting at Ancre.

The ADMS wrote: "The position occupied by our troops was one from which it was most difficult to evacuate owing to the ground being exposed and the line of evacuation a lengthy one. The trenches were dominated on three sides, the aid posts small and inadequate and exposed to shell and machine gun fire. Added to this I am informed by officers commanding bearers and others that enemy snipers were most active, picking off our bearers when collecting, and wounding again

> the patients being carried on stretchers. Super-added to which were weather conditions which turned the frontal surroundings, roads and pathways into a boggy state."
>
> The RAMC casualties were: OR killed seven – Officers five – OR wounded 76. (RAMC in the Great War)

Tuesday 5th.

Had my stitches taken out today, healed completely by first intention[67]. Movement of the fingers present though slight, especially ring finger. Some numbness at base of the ring finger and some swelling over the back of hand and fingers.

Went up to London by bus, met Joan and Alice at Buzzards. Tea and then to the zoo and then to the Somme film. Went up to town and called on John and had tea in his office.

Thursday 7th.

Ran up to Flower House arriving at 11:07am. Alice, Joan and Lassie on the platform. Lassie was delighted to see me. Spent a happy day at Flower House and arrived back soon after 9pm.

Friday 8th.

Went before the Medical Board consisting of some dear old sympathetic people and they gave me 10 weeks sick leave!!

Went up to town and met John at Automobile Club, Pall Mall. Had dinner with him. He is tired and looks worn compared with when I saw him three months ago. I also notice that he is still very 'nervous'. (*John had previously suffered a breakdown.*)

Saturday 9th.

Have got my clearance arranged for tomorrow and my ticket to the Isle of Man booked for Thursday. I write this in Kew Gardens, how delightfully quiet and so few people about. Indeed, I have been sitting for a long while in one of the further corners and have scarcely seen a soul. Flowers however are nearly over, and the rock garden can offer but little to admire. I have just eaten nearly a pound of Victoria plums and now feel very sleepy. Have taken splint off hand but it feels very painful and is certainly more swollen.

---

67. *First intention is the healing of a clean laceration such as a surgical incision closed by sutures.*

Sunday 10th.

Got my papers signed up yesterday, I am so glad to get away today from the hospital. It is natural that one should feel very keenly the restraint of hospital life when one is in perfect health. Arrived Flower House about 11am, met by Alice and Joan.

Monday 11th.

Went up to town this afternoon with Joan and Alice and bought various odds and ends at Selfridges, then on to Harrods where we had tea, but they had run out of cakes. Home for dinner. Alice helped me pack. Very delightful.

Tuesday 12th. Dalton House.

Left London 10:10am. After a very long but enjoyable journey, arrived Dalton about 7:30pm. I was met by Cross, Miss Cond and Bab at home. Quite delightful to be all together again and to find everything in general so much the same. Went up to the club in the evening and found the same old crowd up there. It was very pleasant to chat with old faces amid such familiar surroundings.

Wednesday 13th.

I made a number of calls on old patients and received such a welcome from among the poorer people of the town as to be quite embarrassing at times. After all, there are few sensations in life more beautiful than to feel oneself to be appreciated even though it be only by the humble dwellers of the town. How I long to be back among them again so as to resume my work.

Mrs Cross, Bab and I made a lovely tour in the car this afternoon, to Kirby and then right over the moor and down to Coniston Lake. The mountains never looked so lovely and never so purple.

Thursday 14th. NWR Hotel,Liverpool.

Another lot of visits and a lot of beautifully fat babies to be admired. Mrs Barnes with a thumping great baby. Left Dalton at 9:10pm by train which should arrive Liverpool at midnight, but it was nearly 2am before the weary journey came to an end. A very comfortable but expensive room is seven shillings.

Friday 15th. Castletown.

Had a light breakfast of coffee and toast. Nasty drizzling rain. Taxied down to boat, the Tynwald,* and was on board 45 minutes before sailing.

Got a length of couch and lay down. A terrible crossing! We pitched and rolled all over the place and for the best part of four hours I did nothing but vomit. Felt like nothing on earth upon arrival. Angy and Captain Burne met me and the three of us drove back to Castletown in Angy's car 'Susie'.

*Note.

SS Tynwald was launched on 11 May 1891 by the Isle Of Man Steam Packet Company. Fast for her size she held her own with Queen Victoria. Tynwald did not serve as a military vessel during the First World War, but in 1914 she carried the first German prisoners of war to the island for internment at Knockaloe.

She had a number of close encounters with enemy mines and on 9 April 1917 a German submarine managed to get within a few miles of Liverpool and torpedoed SS City of New York. Tynwald inward bound was quickly on the scene, the weather was poor with a strong wind blowing with snow. The passengers were carried by the liner's lifeboats to the Tynwald, all were safely taken on board including Admiral Sims of the US Navy.

When the Easter Rising began in Dublin Tynwald was ordered to take troops to Ireland landing them in Kingston after evading enemy submarines in the Irish Sea.

On another occasion she was ordered to embark divers and other workmen at the Mersey docks along with equipment and make passage to the Isle of Man.

RMS Celtic had been torpedoed with the loss of many lives and was anchored off Peel guarded by destroyers. Tynwald went alongside and disembarked the men and equipment; Celtic was patched up and taken to Belfast for repairs.

In 1934 she was sold and turned into a private yacht and renamed Western Isles. She was requisitioned as an auxiliary in April 1940. In October 1941 was renamed Eastern Isles and used as an accommodation ship at HMS Eaglet Birkenhead until 1946 and returned to her owner in 1947. She was taken for breaking on 13 May 1951.

Saturday 16th.

How delightful to be here again but how sad without uncle. Angy drove me to Douglas and we had lunch with Henry Ainley[68] the actor at the hotel and afterwards a concert in the town where Ainley recited several things. Then tea with Lord and Lady Raglan etc.

Ainley and crowd are acting in The Manxman[69] and are being filmed. This evening Angy and I went up to Colonel Moore's where Ainley and Mrs Fearon were also at the party. We played a mild game of roulette.

Had a letter from Huggins containing bad news. It seems that the 'show' for which I was preparing when I was wounded, came off and out of 50 men at the ADS 29 were knocked out, six being killed and among the latter poor Staff Sergeant Gardner who by the bye was standing by me when I was wounded. Poor boy – only 21 and just married!

Lieutenant Mitchell was hit through the knee.

Sunday 17th.

Poured with rain all day until about 4pm. Burne spent the day here and went with us for tea to W Stephenson where we received the usual welcome. Smoked afterwards in Willie's smoking den.

Afterwards Angy, Burne and I walked to Scarlet and standing on the smooth rocks watched some magnificent waves breaking against the stack. Busy writing letters.

Read today for the first time of the new armoured motor cars – tanks – recently used on the Somme.

Tuesday 19th.

A lovely ride to Stock in Angy's car, the captain with us and in great form. A delightful way of reaching Stock as compared with the terrific struggle we used to enjoy with bicycle laden with all the paraphernalia for making tea.

There was still sufficient heather and gorse in bloom to give a glorious colouring to the hills. We made our tea in one of the prehistoric 'beehives' on the hillside here, sheltered from the wind and surrounded by

---

68. *Ainley, Henry Hinchcliffe. 1879 - 1945. English Shakespearean and screen actor.*

69. *The Manxman, 1916 silent film based on the novel by Hall Caine and one of the few British films to be a hit in the US. A second silent adaptation by Alfred Hitchcock was released in 1929.*

purple heather, we enjoyed our repast. The captain related his experiences at Virginia Waters. It was a delightful outing.

Wednesday 20th.

Angy and I put our tea in the car and drove to a lovely place quite new to me and only recently discovered by Angy. It is a bit of a cliff to the side of Spanish Head. I tried the car and managed all right.

We had a terrific climb from Port Mary as far as Craigneish and then strolled quietly down on foot. Grand rocks and caves are all around and the mixture of gorse and heather still delights the eye.

We ascended the steep hill and through the large telescope at the signalling station watched the patrol boat on which it was easy to see the gun ready mounted in the forecastle, while over the stern could be seen the mine ready to be lowered upon any hostile submarine that is caught in the nets. Behind the P boat could be seen a line of small steamers which were dragging along the steel net.

It was dull and cloudy after a glorious morning when Angy bathed at Scarlet and I sat on the rocks and watched her mermaiden antics in the little creek below.

Weight ten stone four and a half pounds in tennis shoes, slacks and puttees which is two pounds heavier since the 15th.

Thursday 21st.

Walked up to the college with Angy and took up the brass plate which Angy has had made and which will be placed in the chapel in uncle's memory below the memorial plate to the Manx poet Brown[70].

Went up to General Stephenson's at 5pm and played snooker. Willie S, Mellor and Colburn also played. We played for 'love' and to my mind the objectless game fell very flat and indeed I was bored stiff. We also engaged some very nice rooms for Alice and Joan who are coming over on the 30th.

Friday 22nd.

Very dull and cold wind. Went to tea at Proctor-Gregg's in order to

---

70. *Thomas Edward Brown (1830-1897), as T E Brown, he is celebrated as the Isle of Man's most eminent poet who captured the lives and ways of the Manx people in their own dialect.*

hear their son Humphrey[71] play. I thought his playing was quite extraordinarily good. I had expected him to play with feeling, but I did not look for such wonderful technique. He confined himself entirely to Chopin and delighted us for quite an hour.

Saturday 23rd.

Again, we took our tea in the car to the 'sound'. Mrs Proctor-Gregg in the car and Humphrey sat on his bicycle holding on to the side of the car.

It was a glorious day and we enjoyed our tea on Spanish Head sheltered by a piece of rising ground and with great deep tufts of bell heather to lie amongst.

Monday 25th Dalby.

Stuffing 'Susie' with groceries Angy and I set out for Dalby climbing on the low gear to the top of the mountains by a beautiful road with heather and gorse stretching away on all sides.

Halfway down the other side of the watershed we halted and after finding a sheltered nook made a most excellent luncheon. We could not resist the blackberries and picked a large basketful of some of the finest berries I have ever seen.

Arriving at Dalby at about 3pm we put our car up in a shed belonging to the Padre and took our basket of tea down to the shore. Here we found a delightful little cove sheltered from the wind and after tea walked a long way along the coast arriving at our lodgings in time for supper.

Wonderful air! How ridiculously young it makes one feel.

Tuesday 26th.

Blackberries and clotted cream served on fresh scones.

We started about 11am with eatables and worked our way on foot along the rocks towards the Sloc. There was beautiful sun and strong east wind from which we were sheltered by the steep hills rising abruptly from the beach. It was a good scramble, Angy extremely agile.

The tide was just beginning to fall; our progress was slow as we had to wait now and then for the necessary rocks to become uncovered before it was possible to move forward.

---

71. *Humphrey Procter-Gregg (1895-1980), British composer who studied with Charles Villiers Stanford, Charles Wood and Julius Harrison at the Royal College of Music, was head of the Opera Department at the RCM in the 1920s and at the University of Manchester taught the likes of Harrison Birtwistle, Peter Maxwell Davies and John Ogdon. (Wikipedia)*

On a beautiful bit of beach, we made a fire and had our lunch. Repeated visits to fascinating caves in search of the maiden hair fern but we found none.

We read, basked in the sun, had tea and got home about 6pm. The local parson shares our sitting room. He has resisted all attempts to evidence the slightest interest in any subject whatsoever. He cannot even comment on things in general and he cannot even pronounce his H's!

Wednesday 27th. Castletown.

In return for having used the Parson's coach house for our car, we invited him as far as Peel. The three of us set off at first against a very stiff wind. Peel, Ramsay, Douglas and home. A glorious round of 51 miles along perfect roads, through beautiful scenery. Lunch by the roadside and tea ditto, home by 6pm.

Have not seen a paper since Saturday, another English advance. Combles fell and two Zeppelins were brought down in Essex.

Friday 29th.

Angy, captain and self in 'Susie' to Dalby, a lovely day with sun. We drove over the beautiful hills and the little car climbed very well.

At Dalby we were joined by Mrs Proctor-Greggs and her son, who had driven over from Douglas in their car. We took both cars down a lane and this brought us close to the sea beach which we reached easily. Lunch and tea on the shore, then a delightful drive home.

Dined with Mellors. Mrs Mellors played two pieces of Chopin very beautifully and then chose to sing for the rest of the evening much to my disappointment.

Saturday 30th.

Angy, Capt and self drove to Douglas where we had tea and after dined at Pevril. Dinner was tedious owing to lack of waiters and before we got our coffee the 'hoot' of a steamer warned us that the Phenella (Fenella[72]) was arriving and we fled to the pier. It was almost dark. Joan and Alice arrived in great style. Angy and Capt returned by train, and I drove Alice

---

72. SS Fenella, built in Barrow for the Isle of Man Steam Packet Company and launched on 9 June 1881. Sister ship to Tynwald, she had an eventful life and served the island for 48 years, leaving her home port of Douglas for the final time on 9 September 1929. (Wikipedia)

and Joan home; roads frightfully dark. Put back watches one hour in readiness for tomorrow.

OCTOBER 1916.

Sunday 1st.

Weekend out to Scarlet rocks with Alice[73] and sat down near the lime kilns, 3:30pm.

There we mutually agreed to see the rest of our life together provided I came through the war unscathed. Upon this latter promise I insisted it would be foolish to agree to marriage since one cannot live alone on love only. Again, I consider it unfair to marry a girl while there is still a chance of becoming permanently disabled as a result of the war.

(Over this entry the doctor has heavily scrawled 'Not Alice'.)

Monday 2nd.

Heavy rain all morning, cleared in the afternoon when Joan, Alice and self, walked to Scarlet and enjoyed a good blow in a high wind.

Tuesday 3rd.

Foghorn going all morning. A walk with Alice up Silverburn. Afternoon, Joan, Alice and myself, walked to Fort island rocks and picked mushrooms, glorious sunshine on the way home.

Joan and Alice are very comfortable with Mrs Schofield's lodging.

Saturday 14th.

Angy, Alice, Joan and I by train to Port Erin with tea baskets. We walked up to Braddan Head and had the greatest difficulty in keeping our feet owing to a regular gale which was blowing. Our skirts were in danger of being blown over our heads.

However, we climbed to the top of the tower and watched the waves breaking on the calf. Then we struggled down and took refuge in a disused and asphalted reservoir some distance up the hill where we could get some protection from the wind. We had hardly begun to prepare tea when a deluge of rain swept over us, the shower lasting for 20 minutes.

Wet and bedraggled, we returned to the station where we made some hot tea. It was very enjoyable all the same, the strong air was magnificent.

---

73. *Alice Anne Whyte 1879 - 1938. The Doctor and Alice married at the parish church, St-Martins-in-the-Field on 17 April 1917.*

Spent the evening with Alice – Joan supping with Angy.

Monday 16th.

Drove Alice and Joan in Angy's car and lunched in a sheltered and disused quarry. Blackberried afterwards and then continued journey to Dalby and passed German prisoners' camp at St John's where we saw the Bosch contentedly at work.

Rain spoiled the run from St John's to Douglas where we had tea and shopped. Then home via Richmond Hill. A lovely spin along perfectly dry roads with glorious views of dark purple hills on our right seen especially well from the road near Santon Station. Arrived home just before lighting up time.

Monday 23rd.

Drove Alice to Douglas, where we arrived in good time and procured sheltered seats for ourselves and Joan and Burne who arrived by train, a good passage and no vomiting.

NOVEMBER 1916

Saturday 4th. Dalton-in-Furness.

Went over to Bank House with Bullock. The place is in rather poor condition with damp and water coming through the kitchen and other rooms. Rather inviting garden is quite delightful. He offers it at £530 or a lease at £35 per annum free of rates and taxes. He will alter the present arrangement by dividing off his own house from this one so to throw over to us the drawing room.

::::

END

:::

Here the diary ends. The Doctor relinquished his commission on 21 January 1917, two years after becoming acting lieutenant.

He had found 'honour'.

He purchased Bank House and carried on his practice in Dalton. He attended the birth of my father, Edward Towers Dunn, 1932-1995.

In 1945 he married his housekeeper, Henrietta Dunn, later retiring to Mudeford, Hampshire (now Dorset) where he tended his beautiful gardens (Ranunculi perhaps) and the grapevine in his much loved greenhouse until his death.

:::

From the Ping Suey journal 1906. Ships Doctor.

On completion of his degree, MB ChB at Edinburgh University in 1906 Regie's first position was as ship's doctor on board SS Ping Suey, a six month trip to the Far East, setting sail on Saturday 27 October 1906. He kept a daily journal of his adventure.

In one particular entry, on Friday 1 February 1907, when the Doctor was thoroughly unwell and feeling his own mortality, he wrote:

"Here I am in bed with my neck swollen up to bovine proportions - and I can't fix the disease! I noticed my left submandibular gland swollen the night before last. Yesterday it was excessively enlarged and painful. This morning it is large and its fellow on the opposite side is swelling. My temp is 100, I have had no sore throat - Mumps? - we have stinking hides onboard: what price Anthrax? However, we reach port by nightfall and tomorrow I can get a medical opinion I hope.

In case anything should go wrong with me, I would like to see that I am quite conscious of the fact that the literature contained in these pages is illiterate and extremely bad and I trust that this book will be torn up. To me of course, these pages are full of interest and have enabled me to pass by many an hour of weariness and frustration.

Please also note this. At the bottom of the portmanteau which contains my clothes in the box room at Allan Bank there lies a small box (wrapped in paper) containing letters etc and I am anxious for this box to be handed over unopened to John."

As well as the daily entries in the journal there are three compositions at the back of the notebook that show his deep passion for nature and his home, (Allan Bank) and just maybe a coded show of his affection for Jack in 'Know Ye The Joys Of Early Spring'. In 'A Quiet Summers Day' he considers the search to understand true happiness, casting back to his University days trying to understand the loose life of just looking for pleasure, both physically and mentally. But first, in 'A Scarlet Milestone' he writes a beautiful description of early summer and happier days at Allan Bank, as his mind wanders from his subject to "malicious talk and evil and leaden thoughts".

::::

A Scarlet Milestone

Happiness cannot be enjoyed unless the mind is tranquil and the body full of health. My mind was certainly tranquil that day (June 27th 06) for I had just arrived home after having successfully passed my final exam. I could therefore rest on my laurels for a time and enjoy the sweet fruits of success. It was such a morning as smiles but seldom during a summer in the Lake District, and least of all at Grasmere. How well I remember every detail of that and many other days that followed! Not that they were days full of busy doings or adventures; but they were filling sunny days and I was full of health. I remember how I awoke about seven am and leaned through the wide opened window gazing over the valley beneath. Not a breath of wind stirred the leaves on the great green Beech; the tennis lawn was silvered with a canopy of dew; the lake was scarcely visible being hid beneath a mantle of mist which was clearly rising from its calm surface betokening a hot summer's day to follow. I slipped into a wonderfully refreshing bath of cold water which had run straight from the mountains and was as clear as crystal; and while drying myself I drank in yet another view through the bathroom window which was festooned with green tendrils of Virginia creepers and roses. Ah! how familiar that outlook is! And how utterly dear to me - full of a thousand reminiscences of younger days. I gazed with delight upon the copper beech, the uncut hay bright with countless wild flowers sloping up to the batch of heather which crowned Sundial hillock, while beyond the beech tree lay another heavenly sweep of unmown hay intersected by the garden path and stretching up to finally merge with the undergrowth of the woods beyond. And then the woods themselves! What a refreshing barrier of green! Breathing forth the perfume sacred to their silent depths. By pressing back the creepers I could see the gravel leading to the billiard room; the rhododendrons now somewhat 'over' but even yet a haze of colours inflicted on the soil beneath them with petals they had shed. Even as I gazed, my eyes brimming over with tears - the sun which had by now flung off the streaming mist, flooded all around with balmy sunshine, the view became at once a thousand times more entrancing. I am a nature worshipper - I see in the joy of growing life and in these flowers: in the lush grass and trickling mountain brook - I see in them a manifestation of the divine being who rules the universe. I believe the almighty is present and moves lovingly among these simple and silent creatures of the soil. Nature as I find her in the fragrant woods and lonely mountain tops in the medium... when I can come closest to God in thought and my shrine of shrines is sheltered by the woods around Allan Bank. Yes these flowers that grow in lonely places. These bashful fronds of wild fern hidden away behind the moss grown boulder: these, and a thousand other emblems of silence, peace and solitude that together make a picture so dear to me - these are my Gods, and in my idolatry I differ from the heathen only that I worship them not for themselves but for what I see in and through them - the divine presence. Oh! what would I not give to be able to tear myself away from my present surroundings and flee from malicious talk and leaden thoughts, find my way to my native heaths; wander again over Silver How, visiting dear old folks brim-full of memories near twenty years gone by. Who can wander among the mountains and be harassed by evil thoughts? Who can push his way through the waving bracken; follow the windings of a mountain walk fresh with soft mosses and fragrant with scented ferns - who I say can enjoy these surroundings and not find himself filled with most sound and soul inspiring thoughts?

But I have wandered from my subject.

::::

Know ye the joys of early spring

Know ye the joys of early spring,

when nature wakes again.

And shakes the snowflakes from her hair,

They fall in gentle rain.

From yonder sheltered bank,

my love, will pluck

the leaves so sore.

To see the young shoots sprouting green:

they whisper 'spring is here'

Tis the first genuine spring day, an east wind blows, but the air is clear and the sun sheds rays which strike almost hot when one can enjoy them sheltered from the wild east wind.

Come with me to yonder grassy slope: it is protected from the north by a well wooded hill, and from the east by a dense barricade of laurels, rhododendrons and other evergreens: below, it is intersected by a foot-path. Reclining on this bank we see the old house shining white through the dark branches of the great copper tree. 'No sign of spring is here' you might say but let us only brush away some of these brown rustling leaves which dropped silently last autumn from the oak trees above, and we shall understand how nature makes use of them as a covering to protect from ice and snow the growing plants that she so loves. As we pluck away the dead leaves a delicious fragrance rises to our nostrils - a smell of growing things, strong with the promise of life and happy summer days: and then we see stretching up among the soft mosses, the delicate shoots and growing leaves of the wild strawberry anemone, while yonder are fresh violet leaves pricking towards the light. Beetles too, and a hundred and one insects have melted into life and are soon hanging in all directions among delicate growth.

And what of ourselves this welcome day of spring. 'Ah' we also take part in the rejuvenation of the earth. We feel our blood bounding through our frost bound veins, and we know that even as we have merely existed throughout the dreary winter, so we are now ready once more living things. Come, dear friend, let us embrace and swear eternal friendship this day of days. For in each other's eyes, we mark sincerity, and in the grasp of our hands we feel that sympathy seals the contact with its strongest passion.

:::

A Quiet Summers Day.

Some say that 'the state of happiness' is only attained when the mind is brought into temporary unconsciousness of pain. Whether happiness be this a delusion and illusion matters little to us of this life: but what does concern is the fact that happiness when once ours, even though it be only a few brief hours, brings colour into our lives and fills us with thoughts and feelings that we possess at no other time. So it is that we are forever pursuing happiness and often like fools, we think we are basking in her smiles when we are furthest from them. The reason for this is because people fail to understand there exists two forms of happiness, the true and the false, the natural and the artificial. The latter is easily gained and the definition of happiness in the opening sentence holds good in its case. The presence is felt in the gratification of some temporary sensation which is so keen as to exclude for a time all sensibility to the harder facts of life. It is but a nervous boxed up affair, and in the consciousness of it our mind is only focused on the bright evanescent spot of light from which we gain our pleasure, and we are otherwise dead to humanity and the world. We do homage to this shrine of artificial happiness when weighed down with cares, we rush to the theatre, a dance, then we dull the senses with opium and other morbid drugs. Now what of true and natural happiness? It is not often that we live in the warmth of her smiles; she has to be won before she can be enjoyed, and she is indeed fleet footed. Yes, she is seldom enjoyed because the path that leads to her is a rough one and full of side-tracks - smooth and easy. This rugged path is the way to self-denial and mental exertion and the shrine of true happiness has 'SUCCESS' emblazoned on its pillars in scarlet letters. You give yourself some task to perform: it may be in the nature of an examination to be conquered, or the strengthening of their character in some particular

214

direction, but delivers the 'stumbling block', self-denial is always taxed and self-endurance; while the amount of happiness extended to us relative to the amount of self denial exerted in the good cause whatever it be. Our state of happiness thus gained is a far wider consciousness than that enjoyed under the description of artificial happiness, and while, as we have seen, the latter focuses our senses: the state of happiness is ours wherever we look and whatever we are about, nor does selfishness play a part in its enjoyment and we are rather involved with a desire to impart our feelings to show them with our companions: and thus, we spread among men a host of sympathetic feelings and take pleasure in raising them from the mud of despond. Life too feels wonderfully bright, and we are filled with a great enthusiasm and desire to thank the almighty that we have life and can enjoy it for a time to its full. This true happiness has to end even as has the artificial; but while the latter ends suddenly, and the illusion is broken with an abruptness that imparts a very shock to the system, quite otherwise is it in the ending of true happiness; it may scarcely be said to end; perhaps it grows less in intensity. But in fading away it has shed around such sympathetic vibrations that these ever persist in reacting upon the donor and so leave him scarcely conscious of his loss until pressed upon with further endeavours and self-denials he looks up to find the goddess of happiness already welcoming him with outstretched hands.

THE FALLEN

June 1915

Monday 7th
2nd Lt Lascelles. John Frederick MC. Age 19. RFC. Beauval Communal Cemetery.

August 1915

Thursday 5th
Captain. Fraser, Hugh Crawford. Age 38. Royal Scots Fusiliers. Le Touret Military Cemetery.

Captain. Mills, Teulon Lewis. Age 23. Middlesex Regiment. Cite Bonjean military cemetery.

333. Pte Aldridge. J. Age 33. Cite Bonjean military cemetery, Armentieres. 7th E.S.R. (East Surrey Regiment}

Tuesday 17th
17376 L.Cpl. G DE Beger. Age 30. 5th Bn Northamptonshire Regt. Cite Bonjean military cemetery Armentieres.

Wednesday 18th
256. Pte Davis. J H. Bailleul communal cemetery. 7th E.S.R.

Friday 20th
8651. Pte. Kingsman, George Richard. Age 40. Pont-de-Nieppe communal cemetery. 7th E.S.R

September 2015

Thursday 2nd
80 Pte Kelsey, A. Colchester cemetery. 7th E.S.R.
Sunday 5th

298 Pte Froome, Arthur Charles. Age 36. Bailleul communal cemetery extension Nord. 7th E.S.R.

Monday 13th
Josef Suwelack. Pilot. Oscar Teichmann. Photographer. Erquinghem-Lys churchyard extension.

Friday 17th
G/827. Pte. Tullett, W A. Age 19. Pont-De-Nieppe communal cemetery.

Tuesday 28th

G/598 Pte Elliot, Arthur. Age 20. Netley Mill cemetery. 7th E.S.R.

October 2015

Saturday 2nd

1/10/1915. 39273 Sgt Butcher, Henry. Age 25. 36th FA. Vermelles British cemetery

46643 Pte Cooke, Noel Hannant. Age 22. 36th FA. Vermelles British cemetery

2/10/15. 416 Pte Goldsmith, Charles. Age 20. 36th FA. Vermelles British cemetery

Capt Bell, Thomas Henry Stanley. Age 23. 36th FA Vermelles British cemetery

1/10/1915. M2/078518 Dvr Jones, William. Age 56. ASC attd 36th FA

M2/079218 L.Cpl. Loring, William. Age 27. ASC attd 36th FA.

2093 Pte Bendall, William Thomas. Age 30. Bailleul communal cemetery extension nord. 7th E.S.R.

Sunday 3rd

177 L.Cpl Rose, Arthur. Age 30. Loos memorial. 7th E.S.R.

Monday 4th

715 Sgt Sturt, James. Age 35. Loos memorial.

1318 Pte Bussey, William Albert. Age 21. Loos memorial. 7th E.S.R.

Tuesday 5th

9010 Pte Wills, Frank Noel. Age 18. Loos memorial

2nd Lieut. Hastings, Aubrey J. Fouquieres cemetery

688 Pte Hilton, W G. Age 21. Chocques military cemetery. 7th E.S.R.

Friday 8th

31 Pte Watson, William. Age 19. Vermelles British cemetery

71 Pte Botting, George. Age 29. Loos memorial

Lieut. Gibson, Malcom Reginald. Age 23. Vermelles British cemetery

1643 Pte Green. John. Loos memorial. 7th E.S.R.

Sunday 10th

822 Pte Windebank, Francis Richard. Age 17. Vermelles British cemetery

643 Pte Byerly, J A W. Vermelles British cemetery

24 Sgt Smith, Henry James. Age 37. Vermelles British cemetery 7th E.S.R

Wednesday 13th

8965 Sgt Crooks, Alfred

306 L.Cpl Gorman, Thomas

8657 Pte Coppard, Thomas H. Age 28

8850 Sgt Groombridge, John Thomas

834 Pte Florey, Henry. Age 29

664 Cpl Dryden, Alfred Charles. Age 43

10065 Pte Dundon, Thomas

5960 L.Cpl Whatrup, William Thomas. Age 52

139 Pte Carter, Reginald

7088 Pte Chapman, William Henry

132 Pte Cotterell, Frederick. Age 20

8736 Watkins, Thomas

6197 Pte Williams, William George. Age 19

7027 Pte Wright, Harry

26 L.Cpl Creasey, William. Age 19

232 L.Cpl Culver, Frederick Thomas

1654 Pte Hicks. Albert,

508 Pte Hill, George

5812 Pte Roland, Frank

8793 Pte Humphrey, William

1947 Pte Humphrey, William Edward. Age 19

996 Pte Hutton. Percy

305 Cpl Joyner. Louis

265 L.Cpl Judd, Cyril Robert. Age 22

5927 Pte King, Henry Arthur

7054 Pte Lock, Alfred James. Age 32

76 Pte Lynch, James

779 L.Cpl Bates, Herbert Charles. Age 35

2nd Lieut Brasnett, Thomas John Grose (Jack) Age 21

7041 Pte Brocklehurst, John William Clarke. Age 25

9558 Pte Bashford, Walter

8965 Pte Battelley, Edward

9995 Pte Marks, William John

10144 Pte Martin, Leonard

462 Sgt Martin, Albert. Age 21

5958 Pte May, Frank Huxtable

9007 Pte Mills, Albert. Age 21

8754 Pte Ward, James Bromley. Age 28

10233 Pte Washer, George Trayton. Age 25

185 Pte Akerman, Walter. Age 20

861 Pte Antony, Ernest William. Age 24

273 Cpl Ayres, Charles William. Age 31

295 Pte Baker, William. Age 20

8721 Pte Barrett, Robert Frederick. Age 44

1559 Pte Murton, Herbert Alfred William. Age 19

6120 Pte Haddock, Christopher

5931 Pte Oram, William George

6092 Pte Parker, Charles. Age 45

163 Pte Patten, Archibald

4233 Pte Prior, William George. Age 19

558 Pte Rawlins, Frank Henry

173 Pte Richardson, Percy Edgar. Age 20

5831 Pte Staines, Arthur Henry

5899 Pte Stevens, James Age 28

6195 Pte Stevenson, James

51 L.Cpl Stilwell, Walter Frederick. Age 19

5937 Pte Stimson, Thomas Russell

805 Pte Strachan, Frank. Age 22

Capt Tomkins, Vigor

08 Pte Timpson, George James. Age 19

7037 Pte Goodyear, John. Age 19

6190 Pte Ritchie, Herbert Charles. Age 21

577 Pte Roberts, Arthur Cyril Thomas. Age 18

5814 Pte Rollins, Frederick John. Age 186192 Pte Rook, Victor. Age 18

5824 Pte Rout, Walter

6154 Pte Sadler, George

(Brothers) 2191 Pte Sandford, Ernest Alfred. Age 21 and 6 Sgt Sandford, Walter James. Age 25

307 Pte Seaby, Edgar Charles Herbert. Age 26

7032 Pte Selby, Hubert William

64 Pte Sheppard, Cecil Henry. Age 19

10203 L.Cpl Shore, William Edwin

8493 Sgt Shuttleworth, Frederick Thomas. Age 28

8662 Pte Smallbridge, Edward. Age 342159 Turner, Joseph George. Age 35. Loos memorial panels 65-67

1952 Pte Wyeth, Allen Fred. Age 19. Canadian cemetery No2 Neuville St-Vaast

8661 Pte Bream, Ernest William. Age 38. Arras Road cemetery Roclincourt

1043 Pte Tompkins, F. Rue- Petillon military cemetery Fleurbaix

4219 L.Cpl Wood, W H. Age 24. Rue-Petillon military cemetery, Fleurbaix

740 Pte Green, H J. Sailly Labourse communal cemetery

138 Pte Johnson, A. Bully-Grenay communal cemetery, British extension. 7th E.S.R.

Thursday 14th

159 Cpl Wellings, T. Age 23. Chocques military cemetery

864 Pte Parsons, John. Age 19. Sailly Labourse communal cemetery

8797 Pte Palmer, Thomas. Age 43. Loos memorial

10209 Pte Smith, Robert. Loos memorial

560 Pte Roe, Percy George. Age 23. Loos memorial. 7th E.S.R.

Friday 15th.

466 Cpl Grant, William Henry. Age 26. D.o.w. Lillers communal cemetery

582 Pte Williams, A. Age 21. D.o.w. Noeux-Les.Mines communal cemetery. 7th E.S.R.

Sunday 17th
489 L.Cpl, Powell. H L. Age 24. D.o.w. Chocques military cemetery

821 Pte Sparrow, H. Age 35. D.o.w. Bethune town cemetery. 7th E.S.R.

Tuesday 19th
6797 Pte Spires, H. Calais southern cemetery. 7th E.S.R.

Saturday 23rd
801 Pte Drummond, W G. Age 23. Longuenesse St Omer souvenir cemetery. 7th E.S.R.

Monday 25th
1815 Pte Douch, William Alfred. Loos memorial 7th E.S.R.

Tuesday 26th
831 Pte Clark, F S. Age 20. Le Treport military cemetery

711 Pte Fenn, C W. Calais southern cemetery. 7th E.S.R.

Wednesday 27th
3/707 Pte Samme, George Thomas. Age 19. St Sever cemetery Rouen. 7th E.S.R.

Saturday 30th
403 Pte Harman, Edward James. Age 24. Vermelles British cemetery

422 Pte Gee, Thomas. Loos memorial

5898 Pte Rowe, Arthur Sidney. Loos memorial. 7th E.S.R.

Sunday 31st
10507 Pte Taylor, T. Age 22. Bethune town cemetery

115 Pte Cannon, J. Quarry cemetery Vermelles. 7th E.S.R.

November 1915

Friday 5th
L/10931 Pte Heather, H. Guildford (Stoke) cemetery. 7th E.S.R.

Tuesday 9th
8650 Cpl Repton, Arthur Gerald. Age 20. Loos memorial. 7th E.S.R.

Wednesday 10th

5901 L.Cpl Sapsford, Edward Thomas. Loos memorial. 7th E.S.R.

Thursday 11th

6127 Pte Collar, Ernest Edward. Age 24. Hanwell. Kensington and Chelsea. 7th E.S.R.

December 1915

Saturday 11th

810 Pte Voller, T. Guards cemetery Windy corner Cuinchy. 7th E.S.R.

Tuesday 21st

538 Pte Miles, John Robert. Age 24. Pont-Du-Hem military cemetery La Gorque. 7th E.S.R.

Wednesday 22nd

8157 Pte Dipple, Alfred. Loos memorial

441 Cpl Reed, Harry. Age 27. Pont-Du-Hem military cemetery La Gorgue. 7th E.S.R.

January 1916

Thursday 6th

293 L.Cpl Major, Charles Robert. Age 30. Windy Corner cemetery, Cuinchy. 7th E.S.R .

Sunday 9th

250. Pte. Hanks, E. Chocques military cemetery. 7th E.S.R

Monday 10th

47218 Pte Shave, S.

53104 Pte Daniels, J E.

49226 Cpl Long, William Thomas. Age 28. d.o.w 09/01/1916

54082 Pte Heaven, G. d.o.w 11/01/1916 – Bethune town cemetery. 38th F.A.

Friday 14th

506 Pte Bradford, J C. Calais southern cemetery. 7th E.S.R.

Friday 21st

Pte L10532 Maclaren, J M. Age 21. Tancrez farm cemetery. 7th E.S.R. Saturday 22nd. Perrier.

February 1916

Thursday 10th
240 Pte Gross, Edward Beaumont. Age 33. Kensal Green cemetery. 7th E.S.R.

Tuesday 22nd
1111 Cpl Jones, David Thomas. Age 37. Bethune town cemetery

8671 Pte Bagshaw, Robert L. Age 30. Quarry cemetery Vermelles

584 Pte Howell, W. Quarry cemetery Vermelles. 7th E.S.R.

Wednesday 23rd
10481 Pte Randall. W F. Bethune town cemetery. 7th E.S.R.

Sunday 27th
Lieut Cliff-McCulloch, Walter Alexander. Age 29. Royal Irish Rifles. Vermelles British cemetery.

March 1916

Sunday 5th
922 Pte Copeman, William Albert. Age 19. Loos memorial.7th E.S.R.

6707 Acting Corporal Cotter, William Richard. Age 33. VC. The Buffs East Kent Regiment. Lillers communal cemetery.

Monday 6th
5916 Pte Doe, Stephen. Age 34

9085 Pte Sinnock, Walter Henry. Age 20.

955 Pte Cobb, William

9505 Pte Hope, Leonard

6108 Pte Hunt, Charles Ernest. Age 21

7075 Pte Mulady, John James. Age 20

10506 Pte Taylor, George

901 Pte Gadd, John. Age 21

6112 Pte Gray, Arthur George

858 Pte Robinson, Wallace

11034 Pte Saltmarsh, Harry. Age 20. Loos memorial.7th E.S.R.

Tuesday 7th
79 Pte Black, John Alexander. Age 23. Lapugnoy military cemetery

10499 Pte Smith, Sidney. Loos memorial.7th E.S.R.

Northants Pioneer (possibly) Pte Foster, Thomas. Age 19. Loos Memorial. 5th Battalion

Northamptonshire Regiment. (Stevie 9173 Great war forum)

Wednesday 8th

1799 Pte Betts, E W. Age 25. Vermelles British cemetery

5961 Pte Howe, C. Bethune town cemetery

402 Pte Cattell, George Clement. Age 21

7049 Pte Coles, Richard. Loos memorial. 7th E.S.R.

Thursday 9th

6792 Pte Barnesdale, Alfred. Loos memorial.7th E.S.R.

Friday 10th

3276 Pte Webb, Douglas Bertie. Loos memorial

6155 Pte Trimby, John Charles. Age 26. Loos memorial.7th E.S.R.

Sunday 12th

536 Sgt Dunham, Henry George. Loos memorial

8727 Pte Mathew, A T. Bethune town cemetery

9509 Pte Tester, C. Age 39. Quarry cemetery Vermelles

10400 Pte Dines, Thomas. Age 20. Vermelles British cemetery

10226 Pte Burton, B A. Loos memorial

737 Pte Millom Charles Robert. Age 20. Quarry cemetery Vermelles

G/10226 Pte Turton, Benjamin Arthur. Age 25. Loos memorial.7th E.S.R.

Monday 13th

672 L.Sgt Barton, R E. Age 26. Phalempin communal cemetery. 7th E.S.R.

Thursday 16th

1558 Pte Jones, Stephen Harry. Age 20. Longuenesse (St Omer) Souvenir Cemetery

2/2747 Pte Bateman, Alfred. Age 23. Vermelles British cemetery. 7th E.S.R.

Friday 17th

10299 Pte Ellwood, Thomas. Loos memorial

8995 Sgt Dye, W. Age 27. Sailly Labourse communal cemetery

10337 Pte Hughes, A E. Sailly Labourse communal cemetery

Lieut Robinson, Leonard Herbert Frank. Age 24. Sailly Labourse communal cemetery. 7th E.S.R.

Saturday 18th

Capt Jones, Llewelyn James. Age 34. 16/03/16. West India Regiment (att 7th Battalion East Surrey)Regiment) - Bethune town cemetery

8680 Pte Donnaby, Tom. Loos memorial

9542 Pte Eaton, James. Age 36. Loos memorial

9354 Pte Shults, J C. Quarry cemetery Vermelles

6388 Pte Head, J. Age 24. Bethune town cemetery

968 Pte Mildenhall, William. Age 24. Arras Road cemetery Roclincourt

1066 Pte Dundon, Alfred Childs. Age 20. Vermelles British cemetery

871 Pte Wright, David Robert. Loos memorial

187 Cpl Marshal, Harry. Age 27. Loos memorial

14734 Pte Ingham, Edward William. Age 28. Loos memorial

14598 Pte Bragg, Charles. Age 19. Loos memorial

5835 Pte Coombes, Frederick. Age 34. Loos memorial

193 Pte Gilmour, Cecil. Age 22. Loos memorial

249 Pte Plumbridge, William. Loos memorial.7th E.S.R.

Sunday 19th

438 Pte Thomas, J J. Chocques military cemetery

8409 Cpl Marcham, J. Sailly Labourse communal cemetery

7065 Pte Topcott, A J. Chocques military cemetery

9776 Pte Elmer, Percy William. Age 31. Bethune town cemetery

9383 Pte Webster, J. Chocques military cemetery

6821 Pte Philips, T W. Bethune town cemetery. 7th E.S.R.

Monday 20th

9383 Pte Webster, J. Chocques military cemetery. 7th E.S.R.

Tuesday 21st

20/3/1916. G/1799 Pte Beverstein, Abraham. Age 19. (alias Harris, A) 11th Middlesex Regiment. Desertion.

21161 Pte Martin, Harry. 9th Battalion, Essex Regiment. Desertion. Labourse communal cemetery.

There were two executions carried out on 19 March:

15/13211 Pte McCracken, J F. Age 19

15/890 Pte Templeton, J. Age 19. 15th Royal Irish Rifles. Mailly Maillet communal cemetery extension. (25/30 miles from KEH billets)

Wednesday 22nd

5739 Pte Brookes, Arthur. Age 22. Calais southern cemetery .7th E.S.R.

Thursday 23rd

9899 Pte Gibbings, B A. Abbeville communal cemetery. 7th E.S.R.

Friday 24th

2/9508 Pte Frost, H. Calais southern cemetery. 7th E.S.R.

BV - #0052 - 090924 - C0 - 228/152/14 - PB - 9781913675424 - Matt Lamination